50 *Hikes*

In Louisiana

Walks, Hikes, and Backpacks
in the Bayou State

First Edition

JANINA BAXLEY

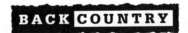

Backcountry Guides

Woodstock, Vermont

AN INVITATION TO THE READER

Over time trails can be rerouted and signs and landmarks altered. If you find that changes have occurred on the routes described in this book, please let us know so that corrections may be made in future editions. The author and publisher also welcome other comments and suggestions. Address all correspondence to:

Editor, 50 Hikes™ Series
Backcountry Guides
P.O. Box 748
Woodstock, VT 05091

Explorer's Guide 50 Hikes in Louisiana
ISBN 978-0-88150-598-6

Copyright © 2003 by Janina Baxley

First Edition

Cover and interior design by Glenn Suokko
Cover photograph © Alex Demyan
Interior photographs by the author unless otherwise noted

Maps by Mapping Specialists Ltd., Madison, WI,
© The Countryman Press

Composition by Blue Mammoth Design

Published by The Countryman Press, P.O. Box 748, Woodstock, Vermont 05091

Distributed by W.W. Norton & Company, Inc., 500 Fifth Avenue, New York, NY 10110

Printed in the United States of America

10 9 8 7 6 5 4 3

DEDICATION

For the agencies, employees, and volunteers in Louisiana who have worked to build, maintain, and preserve hiker-friendly trails for public use and enjoyment. In many ways, the odds have been stacked against you. Your efforts are appreciated and have not gone unnoticed.

50 Hikes in Louisiana at a Glance

Hike	Location
1. Walter B. Jacobs Memorial Nature Park	Blanchard
2. Cypress Nature Study Center and Trails	Benton
3. Bodcau Hiking	Haughton
4. Lake Bistineau State Park	Doyline
5. Sugar Cane Trail	Minden
6. White Tail Trail	Homer
7. Driskill Mountain	Bryceland
8. Lake D'Arbonne State Park	Farmerville
9. Kiroli Park Outer Loop	West Monroe
10. Black Bayou Lake Nature Trail	West Monroe
11. Poverty Point State Historic Site	Epps
12. Rainey Lake Trail	Tallulah
13. Saline Bayou Trail	Goldonna
14. Briarwood–Caroline Dormon Preserve	Saline
15. Dogwood Trail Nature Walk	Zwolle
16. Caroline Dormon Trail	Gorum
17. Backbone Trail	Gorum
18. Longleaf Vista Nature Trail	Gorum
19. Fullerton Mill Trail	Fullerton
20. Wild Azalea Trail	Woodworth
21. Valentine Lake Loop	Gardner
22. Kincaid Lakeshore Trail	Gardner
23. Indian Creek Trail	Woodworth
24. Glenn Emery Trail	Pollock
25. Water Hickory Trail	Rhinehart

	H	history
	G	geology
	W	wildlife
	F	flora
	B	backcountry
	D	developed

Distance (miles)	Features	Good for Kids	Camping	Notes
2	F	Y		Century-old shortleaf pine and stands of sugar maple
3	W	Y		Bluebird, owl, and wood duck nesting boxes
5	G		D	Hilly terrain formed by ironstone deposits and eroded ravines
4	H		D	Trail skirts lake originally formed by the 'Great Raft'
2	W		D	Wealth of migrant wood warblers in spring and fall
3	W		D	Winter bird population occasionally includes snowy owls
6	G	Y		Red ironstone-capped mountain is Louisiana's highest point
9	W	Y	D	Trail leads past antler-rubbed trees and a small waterfall
2	F			Beautiful variety of wildflowers and planted species
1	F	Y		Bottomland hardwood habitat rich with spiny water locusts
6	H	Y		Archaelogical site; giant bird effigy built over 3,000 years ago
8	W			Sizable population of Louisiana black bears
2	W		D	Upland and small stream habitats support rich variety of wildlife
6	F	Y		Forest features cultivated native plants, including Louisiana irises
5	W	Y	D	Mix of lake and woods host wide variety of migratory birds
.5	G		D, B	Sandstone buttes and a trickling waterfall
5	F		B	Stands of longleaf pine throughout Kisatchie Hills Wilderness
5	G	Y		Expansive vistas from sandstone outcrops
2	H	Y	D	Site of the once-bustling Fullerton Mill features pre-WWII ruins
6.2	F		D, B	Abundant spring wildflowers along Louisiana's longest footpath
.7	F	Y	D	Yellow irises bloom along lakeshore in March and April
9	W		D	Active beaver population
.3	W	Y	D	Herons and egrets plentiful along lakeshore
3	W	Y	D	Migratory wood warblers and wintering sparrows frequent visitors
.1	W			Duck Lake sees up to 75,000 wintering waterfowl annually

50 Hikes in Louisiana at a Glance

Hike	Location
26. Big Creek Nature Trail	Sicily Island
27. Sam Houston Jones State Park	Lake Charles
28. Peveto Woods Sanctuary	Johnson Bayou
29. Sabine National Wildlife Refuge	Hackberry
30. Lacassine National Wildlife Refuge	Lake Arthur
31. Cameron Prairie Levee Walk	Bell City
32. Louisiana State Arboretum	Ville Platte
33. Lake Chicot Trail	Ville Platte
34. Acadiana Park Nature Station and Trails	Lafayette
35. Lake Martin Loop	Breaux Bridge
36. Lake Fausse Pointe State Park	St. Martinville
37. Sherburne/Atchafalaya Trails	Krotz Springs
38. Tunica Hills Wildlife Management Area	St. Francisville
39. Blackfork Trail	St. Francisville
40. Mary Ann Brown Nature Preserve	St. Francisville
41. Port Hudson State Historic Site	Zachary
42. Baton Rouge-Area Trails	Baton Rouge
43. Tickfaw State Park	Springfield
44. Bonnet Carré Spillway	Norco
45. Horse Branch Trail	Covington
46. Fontainebleau State Park	Mandeville
47. Big Branch Marsh National Wildlife Refuge	Lacombe
48. Bayou Sauvage National Wildlife Refuge	Slidell
49. Barataria Preserve Trails	Marrero
50. Lafitte Woods Preserve	Grand Isle

DISTANCE (MILES)	FEATURES	GOOD FOR KIDS	CAMPING	Notes
4	G		D	Eroded foot of Macon Ridge features small waterfalls
3	F	Y	D	Trail winds through pocket of longleaf pine forest
3	W			Thousands of migratory songbirds visit chenier annually
5	W	Y		Healthy population of alligators and other marsh wildlife
1	W			Thousands of wintering waterfowl descend on freshwater marsh
2	F			Remnants and reforestation of wet prairie habitat
2	F	Y		Arboretum contains nearly every habitat native to Louisiana
2	F		D, B	Long boardwalks through cypress-tupelo swamp habitat
	W	Y		Rich wildlife population in bottomland hardwood habitat
1	W			Heron rookery sees thousands of breeding birds annually
7	W	Y	D, B	Bottomland hardwood habitat includes alligator and armadillo
7	W		D	Isolated trails at head of Atchafalaya Basin
+	G			Loess-formed hills of striking beauty
.3	F	Y		Ancient cypress trees line Blackfork Bayou
2	W	Y		Hills near St. Francisville home to the eastern chipmunk
.4	H	Y		Trails are site of longest siege in American history
8	W	Y		Baton Rouge area trails feature rich mixture of natural habitats
.3	W	Y	D	Visitors experience wide variety of native Louisiana habitats
5	W		D	Spillway sees huge varieties of migratory and wintering birds
.2	F	Y		Longleaf pine savanna is home to population of pitcher plants
.7	H	Y	D	Site of old sugar plantation owned by the founder of Mandeville
5	W			Increasing population of endangered red-cockaded woodpeckers
7	W	Y		Largest urban wildlife refuge in the U.S.
.8	H	Y		Trail through cypress swamp leads past Indian shell middens
2	W			Barrier island is legendary for its wealth of migratory birds each year

Legend:

H	history
G	geology
W	wildlife
F	flora
B	backcountry
D	developed

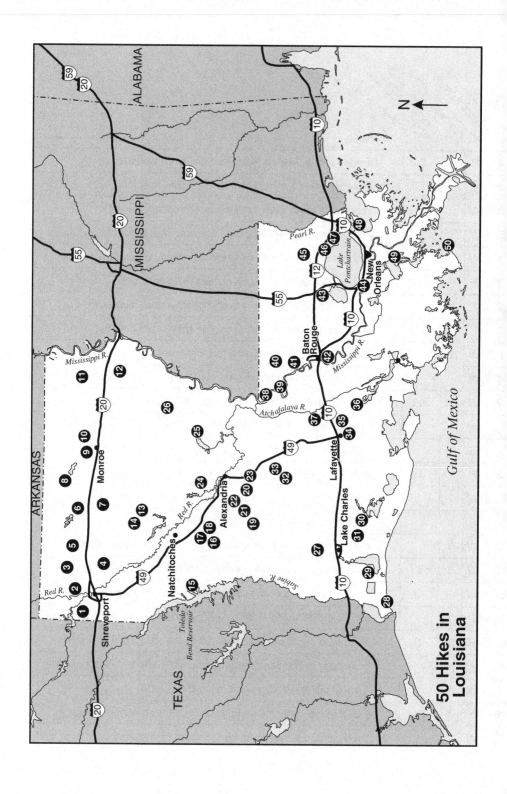

50 Hikes in Louisiana

CONTENTS

Acknowledgments

This book was definitely more than an individual effort, and I am indebted to dozens of people for its completion. My sincere appreciation goes to each of you for your help:

The rangers, staff, and volunteers of Alexander State Forest, Baton Rouge Audubon Society, Black Bayou Lake National Wildlife Refuge (NWR), Bodcau Bayou, Bonnet Carré Spillway, Baton Rouge Recreation and Park Commission, Cameron Prairie NWR, Cat Island NWR, Catahoula NWR, Chicot State Park, Cypress Nature Study Center, Kiroli Park, Kisatchie National Forest, Lacassine NWR, Lake Bistineau State Park, Lake Claiborne State Park, Lake Fausse Pointe State Park, Louisiana Office of State Parks, Louisiana State Arboretum, North Toledo Bend State Park, Port Hudson State Historic Site, Poverty Point State Historic Site, Sabine NWR, Sherburne Wildlife Management Area (WMA), Sicily Island Hills WMA, the Southeast Louisiana and Northeast Louisiana Refuges offices, Tensas River NWR, The Nature Conservancy, Tickfaw State Park, and Walter B. Jacobs Memorial Nature Park.

John M. Crochet of the Louisiana Hiking Club, Jim Huggins of the Ark-La-Tex Orienteering Society, and Don Hunter and Brian Cockrell for use of their map data; Bill Fontenot and Stacey Scarce for sharing their expertise of Louisiana habitats and wildlife; Joe Madere for his assistance with the southeast Louisiana refuge hikes; Richard and Jessie Johnson for so kindly sharing Briarwood with me and everyone else; and to IEM for·welcoming me back and allowing me to keep a maddeningly unpredictable schedule while working on the book.

Karen Berger for opening windows of opportunity; Sandra Friend for her helpful advice and kind support; and Kermit Hummel for believing this book to be a worthwhile effort.

The family and friends who took time to hike with me as I researched the book: Ghent Baxley, Cat, Becky Cavanaugh, Tali Engoltz, Kathleen Guinnane, Bev Koerner, Larry Langlois, Joe Self, Dave Snyder, Don Thibodeaux, and Cheryl Turrentine.

Finally, my endless appreciation goes to my parents, Hugh and Gwen Baxley, for their love and unquestioning support. To Megan, thanks for your friendship. And to Dan, thank you for bringing me so much joy.

Introduction

"Louisiana." For many people, this word conjures up images of New Orleans–the wild costumes and masked faces of Mardi Gras, the spooky aboveground cemeteries, jazz in the streets of the French Quarter, or perhaps voodoo and vampires. Others might picture Louisiana's Cajun Country: murky swamps teeming with alligators, looming bald cypresses laden with Spanish moss, and the lively fiddle and accordion music of the Cajuns. No doubt many associate Louisiana with its renowned chefs and world-famous cuisine. Whatever images, activities, and attractions people tend to associate with Louisiana, however, it's pretty safe to say that hiking and hiking trails are not among them.

This is unfortunate. For years, Louisiana has called itself the "Sportsman's Paradise," and for good reason. Our 49 wildlife management areas and 22 national wildlife refuges comprise more than 1.3 million acres throughout the state and include a broad range of wildlife habitats. Kisatchie National Forest, site of the Wild Azalea National Recreation Trail, covers 600,000 acres in the hilly central and northern portions of Louisiana. In addition, nearly forty-thousand acres of the state are home to Louisiana's 14 state historic sites and 17 state parks. Fortunately for hiking enthusiasts, many of these areas feature hiking trails of varying lengths. In fact, you might be surprised at the hiking opportunities offered by our watery little region at the mouth of the Mississippi River. From the rolling topography of the north to the rugged sandstone rocks of Kisatchie, from the marshes and cheniers (wooded ridges or sandy hummocks in a swampy region) of the southwestern coast to the hills of Tunica and the swamps south of New Orleans, Louisiana's trails have treasures in store for hikers of all stripes.

The short trails of **North Louisiana** (Part I of this book) explore a variety of habitats and terrains, from the rolling hills in the west to the forested wetlands along the Mississippi River floodplain. The trails of this region north of Sabine, Natchitoches, Winn, La Salle, Catahoula, and Concordia Parishes include Driskill Mountain–Louisiana's highest point–and Poverty Point, one of the most intriguing archaeological sites in North America.

With its small mesas, miniature waterfalls, rugged hills, and scenic vistas, **Central Louisiana** (Part II) is not what you might expect from a state known for its swamps and marshes. This region, which stretches south to Vernon, Rapides, and Avoyelles Parishes, includes five of the six ranger districts of the 600,000-acre Kisatchie National Forest. Central Louisiana offers scenic lakes, a hike through the ruins of an old mill town, and a rugged trek across an "island" of sandstone rocks that rises above the surrounding Mississippi River floodplain. Most of these trails are an easy drive from Alexandria.

Southwest Louisiana (Part III), a land of fragile marsh habitat and coastal cheniers, offers a different kind of hiking: levee walks across the marshes, strolls along a coastal chenier, and a dirt trail through a longleaf pine forest. The region of Calcasieu and Cameron Parishes is popular with birders, as it lies smack-dab in the overlap of the Central and Mississippi Flyways and is a haven for millions of migratory and wintering birds.

South-Central Louisiana (Part IV), much of which lies within or near the Atchafalaya Basin, comprises the region known as Cajun Country. Its trails offer the scenes many people associate with Louisiana: muddy remnants of bottomland hardwood forest, giant bald cypresses rising out of sluggish bayous, or a lone great egret wading along the shallow shores of a swampy lake while a pair of ibises nest overhead. Although a boat is required to see all that the Atchafalaya Basin has to offer, the trails in Evangeline, Lafayette, St. Martin, St. Landry, Iberville, and Pointe Coupee Parishes provide a valuable opportunity to explore this unforgettable region by foot.

Southeast Louisiana (Part V) defies easy description. From the rugged upland forests and pine-dominated woods of the Florida Parishes to the salt marshes and sea-sprayed oak and hackberry pockets of Grand Isle, the parishes south and east of the Mississippi River offer a plethora of opportunities for hikers in the Baton Rouge and New Orleans vicinities. Hikers of all levels will enjoy the variety of trails in this region, which range from the rugged Tunica Hills to the gentle trails and boardwalks of the Barataria Preserve.

Indeed, Louisiana's hiking opportunities are more varied than one might think. Trail types and conditions vary widely, as well. Because some of the state's most scenic regions—the swamps, marshes, and floodplain forests—hardly lend themselves to trail-building, a number of hikes incorporate old roads, reinforced all-terrain vehicle (ATV) trails, and levees. Boardwalks are not uncommon in the swamps, and some trails in the state are reinforced with limestone or gravel. While not traditional hiking trails, these types of paths are sometimes necessary to prevent erosion and provide foot-travelers with a comfortable yet authentic experience of Louisiana's fragile wetlands. Of course, Louisiana has its share of traditional hiking trails—regularly maintained, clearly blazed dirt paths through the woods. In writing this sampler of Louisiana's hiking opportunities, I have attempted to include a little bit of everything, though I've avoided urban walks and have kept paved trails to a minimum.

With its low elevation and subtropical climate, Louisiana has a hiking season that generally begins in late September and lasts through midsummer, when the heat and humidity become too oppressive for most people. In addition to offering fine weather and the opportunity to view any number of wildflowers, aquatic plants, and foraging forest creatures, these months are ideal for birding. Spring and fall summon thousands of migratory birds throughout the state, and winter sees the arrival of thousands more ducks, geese, and other waterfowl from the northern United States and Canada. Because the seasonal changes can be so striking, particularly in the marshes, I encourage hikers to visit the same trails at different times of the year.

ORGANIZATION OF THIS BOOK

The trails in this guide are organized geographically into five regions: North, Central, Southwest, South-Central, and Southeast Louisiana. Hikes range from short interpretive walks to weekend backpacking trips. Some of the short hikes, such as the loop trail at Lacassine National Wildlife Refuge (NWR), are presented as mere starting points for further exploration of an extensive trail system, and I encourage hikers to choose their own adventures after familiarizing themselves with an area.

Features, listed in the grid at the beginning of this book, indicate the feature of primary interest for each trail, whether it be flora, history, geology, or wildlife. In the "Sportsman's Paradise" that is Louisiana, one could argue that wildlife is a key feature for every trail—indeed, it is difficult to assign a single, one-word label to any hiking trail. Longleaf pine forests could easily be assigned the key feature of flora. However, these forests are often home to the endangered red-cockaded woodpecker, arguing for wildlife as the key feature. Similarly, the trails of the historically relevant Port Hudson State Historic Site traverse hills of loess (windblown silt from the Pleistocene Era bed of the Mississippi River) and are clearly interesting from a geological standpoint. I have assigned key features based on what I found most interesting and have tried to elaborate on other items of interest in the individual trail write-ups.

The total distance of each trail was calculated with a surveyor's measuring wheel and refers to the route described. In several instances, as with multiple-loop systems, I have picked a route that would allow the hiker to cover most of the system without too much backtracking or repeating of segments. Most alternative routes are provided in the trail maps that accompany each hike.

Hiking time refers to the time it would take for a group of relatively fit hikers to walk a trail at an average pace, with occasional breaks for snacks or nature obser-vation. Solo hikers and avid backpackers who are in excellent athletic shape can expect to hike the trails more quickly, while families with small children may take longer.

Maps listed include the United States Geological Survey (USGS) maps on which the trail region is found. This guide includes portions of each map, but you may want to obtain the entire USGS map from your local outfitter or survey supply store to get a better idea of the area in which you plan to hike. I've also listed other sources of maps for each hike, whether they are official, Global Positioning System-generated park maps or unofficial hand-drawn maps. In north Louisiana, the Ark-La-Tex Orienteering Society (ALTOS) has devised orienteering maps of some of the trails. These maps may be obtained through the ALTOS web site at www.softdisk.com/customer/jimh.

Habitats are the different natural habitats you will encounter on a particular hike. Shaped by a combination of the Mississippi River, the Gulf of Mexico, minor geological uplifts, and the hand of man, Louisiana is a marbled patchwork of habitats. Few pure stands of anything remain, and some—such as the coastal prairie—are only remnants or are the result of human efforts at habitat restoration.

All habitat descriptions, plant identification, and wildlife descriptions are my own, though I received valuable input from several Louisiana naturalists, particularly those at the Acadiana Nature Station in Lafayette. I use the accepted common names for flora and fauna and provide Latin scientific names whenever I discuss a species in some detail. Many species have several regional names in addition to their common names—an ambiguity that can cause some confusion. When this is the case, I provide the most common name of the species and discuss the sometimes-interesting source of its regional names. The summary below provides a general overview of the types of habitats you'll encounter when hiking Louisiana's trails.

FORESTED HABITATS

Among the more scenic of Louisiana's forest types are the *upland hardwood forests*, located primarily in the blufflands of Tunica and Chicot and in isolated parts of Maçon Ridge in northeast Louisiana. More than any other, these forests, with their large numbers of broad-leaved, deciduous trees, are likely to have the most color change in the fall. These wildflower-rich woods include scenic *beech-magnolia stands*, which thrive alongside the streams and seeps that have cut through the highly erodible loess soil.

Longleaf pine forests, once plentiful throughout the Gulf Coastal Plain, now exist only in small pockets, including isolated regions of Louisiana. Other piney woods include the *pine flatwoods* of the Florida Parishes. More common in the state are the *mixed pine-hardwood forests*, a broad term that can describe much of the state's northern and central regions. The prevalent pine of these mixed forests is loblolly, although you'll also find shortleaf and some longleaf.

Louisiana's Mississippi River floodplain was once home to a vast *bottomland hardwood* forest that remained flooded for half the year and gave rise to special flood-adapted trees, such as overcup oak, Nuttall oak, swamp red maple, water hickory, and bald cypress. Only remnants of that fertile, wildlife-rich land remain, the large portion of it having been used for agriculture. Islands of bottomland hardwood remain elsewhere, too, as former courses of the Mississippi left traces of these poorly drained soils in their wake. Similar to bottomland hardwood forests are the *small-stream forests*, which grow along small, low streams, particularly in southern Louisiana. Dryer than bottomland hardwood forests, this habitat may allow the growth of loblolly pine. Other common trees include swamp chestnut oak, water oak, cherrybark oak, ironwood, and sweet gum.

Cypress swamps are perhaps what Louisiana is best known for, in terms of scenery. These immensely beautiful habitats are constantly flooded and give rise to cypress and tupelo. Their edges are often populated with dwarf palmetto, black willow, and buttonbush. Some of these understory plants may also be found in the *oak-hackberry forests* that grow on the slightly raised areas of the state's cheniers and barrier islands. Resting on marsh, and just a few feet above sea level, these ridges provide just enough depth for oaks and sugarberries, also known as southern hackberries, to root.

NONFORESTED HABITATS

Prairie was once a major habitat in southwest Louisiana and existed in small pockets elsewhere in the state. These habitat remnants are host to a staggering number of wildflowers and grasses, including eastern gama grass and little bluestem. Another rare habitat in the state consists of the bogs and seeps, where you'll find carnivorous plants like the yellow pitcher plant.

Defined as unforested wetlands, *marshes* are ecologically vital habitats that provide food and shelter to countless species of birds, mammals, amphibians, and reptiles throughout the year. Tiny variations in salt content affect which plants will thrive and which will not in a marsh–as well as which creatures will feed on those plants, and which predators will feed on the smaller animals.

Fresh marshes are all rain-fed marshes whose salinity levels are not subject to tidal influences. These habitats frequently occur along poorly drained streams and in the shallow water along the boundaries of ditches, canals, lakes, ponds, and rivers. Here, you may find alligators, swamp rabbits, nutria, red-eared sliders, and various birds. Because water levels tend to vary from a few inches to a few feet, fresh marshes can dry out during a drought. Unfortunately, fresh marshes have become an endangered habitat. Theories vary on the reasons for the loss of Louisiana's fresh marshes, as do the efforts being made to research and mitigate this problem.

Salt, *brackish*, and *intermediate marshes* are classified as marshes that hold some degree of salinity. Their salt content can vary, depending on local conditions and the Gulf tides. Intermediate marshes often support the same species as fresh marshes, while the higher-salinity brackish marshes support salt marsh species, such as smooth cordgrass and saltwort. Like the nontidal marshes, Louisiana's tidal marshes serve several important environmental roles. As buffers between the sea and the coastline, they impede shoreline erosion, mitigate the damage of offshore storms to the mainland, and absorb oxygen-depleting nutrients before they reach the Gulf. Like the nontidal marshes, tidal marshes provide food and shelter to a great number of migratory and wintering waterfowl. Tidal marshes are also an endangered habitat, threatened by both coastal development and pollution.

DISTURBED AREAS AND FOREST EDGES

While tornadoes, hurricanes, and fires are the bane of trail maintainers, their aftermath can teach hikers important lessons about forest succession. In 2002, Tropical Storm Isadore and Hurricane Lili tore across the southern part of the state, causing extensive damage to a number of hiking trails. At the time of this writing, the scars left by these storms were still fresh, and future years will see small-scale patterns of succession in the many forest gaps caused by downed and twisted trees. Because the stages of succession are constantly changing and future storms will cause new disturbances, I avoid references to *specific disturbed* areas that I encountered when researching this book. Instead, I state whether a trail has been crippled by a major storm in recent years and try to provide hints of forest changes that you might notice as you hike.

The small-scale deforestation caused by canals, power lines, and water lines creates the miniature habitats called *forest edges*. The composition of forest edges—that line between forest and clear-cut—changes from habitat to habitat. This book names some of the species you might see growing at specific crossings, and points out the potential for a brief change in species as you move sharply from a major habitat to a small, interruptive break of another.

ADVICE AND PRECAUTIONS

ALLIGATORS AND BEARS
A major rule for black bears, alligators, and other potentially harmful creatures is the

same as with all wild animals: Never give them food. Animals that receive handouts from humans learn to associate humans with food, and it isn't long before they begin to exhibit the feeding behavior that can make them both a nuisance and a danger. In many cases, animals that adopt this behavior to the point of becoming dangerous must be relocated or destroyed. Alligators are common on Louisiana's wetland trails. Those that are accustomed to humans (as at Sabine NWR), may bask on the trail itself and not react when you approach. If this occurs, do not approach the alligator closer. Step back, stamp your feet, and make lots of noise. Wait for the grinning reptile to move before you continue hiking. You're most likely to spot an endangered Louisiana black bear in the Tensas River region of northeast Louisiana. This shy creature is most likely to run in the other direction when it sees or hears you coming, so you'll be lucky if you get to see one at all.

CLOTHING AND EQUIPMENT

As with any outdoor activity, when hiking you must be prepared for weather fluctuations. Because thunderstorms can sneak up on you, always carry a water-resistant rain jacket in your pack. In cool weather, add an insulating synthetic layer to your load.

Unless you have ankle or foot problems, you should be able to hike most of Louisiana's trails in comfortable tennis, walking, or running shoes. Wear lightweight hiking boots or shoes for backpacking trips or hikes along the more rugged trails.

Consider wearing two pairs of socks when hiking. I wear a good hiking sock over a thin polypropylene liner sock. This combination forces the socks to rub against each other, instead of against your skin. Always avoid cotton socks, which will get damp, stay damp, and rub against your feet, potentially causing blisters. If you feel a "hotspot" coming on, stop hiking immediately to apply moleskin or another blister preventative (check with your drugstore or outdoor outfitter) to the area.

Whether you are dayhiking or backpacking, your pack should always include the following items: first-aid kit, flashlight, knife, compass, toilet paper, and waterproof matches. A hat will keep your head cool; I like to wear a lightweight "boonie hat," available at your outdoor outfitter or at your local military surplus store. Be sure to pack plenty of food and water for your trek, as well as a lightweight plastic bag to carry out any trash. For most Louisiana day hikes, a fanny pack with a water bottle holster is the perfect accoutrement for carrying these basic items.

To learn more about hiking and backpacking equipment and how to use it, take advantage of local outdoor outfitters, friends who hike or backpack, and outdoor clubs such as the Louisiana Hiking Club. Novice hikers should feel free to pick the brains of these folks, who can provide valuable information. Many outfitters will rent equipment to you. When you do decide to purchase hiking or backpacking equipment, I encourage you to support your local outfitter, who will help to fit and adjust your equipment, allowing you, to some degree, to try before you buy.

Numerous books are available for further information. Try *Hiking & Backpacking: A Complete Guide* by Karen Berger, or *Backpacking: One Step at a Time* by Harvey Manning. One of my favorite hiking books of all time is Colin Fletcher's *The Complete Walker IV*, an often humorous and always educational tome on walking, hiking, and backpacking.

CONTROLLED BURNS

The continued growth and survival of some trees—longleaf pines in particular—are dependent on periodic fires to clear out the underbrush and allow young seedlings to take root. Kisatchie National Forest periodically employs controlled burning to its sizable longleaf stands. Contact the appropriate ranger district while planning a hike in Kisatchie to ensure that no burns are scheduled for the time and place of your hike. When exploring these pine-dominated trails, hikers will potentially traverse a recently burned site. While the Forest Service is generally assiduous in marking the burnt trees on a trail with orange tape until new trees can be blazed, route-finding can be difficult. Look carefully for blazes or tape on the distant tree line.

HEAT AND DEHYDRATION

Heat can be a problem throughout most of the year, and dehydration is a constant threat. Louisiana's extreme humidity may make it difficult to tell when you're becoming dehydrated. Drink as much water as possible when hiking. Carry at least 2 liters of water for hikes of more than 4 miles, and more if the temperature is going to exceed 80 degrees Fahrenheit.

HUNTING

In Louisiana, hunting is extremely popular. Unfortunately for hikers, hunting season coincides with much of the hiking season. Be aware of the hunting rules and regulations on the state forest, wildlife management area, and national wildlife refuge lands. Seasonal dates vary from year to year, so you'll want to look up specific hunting schedules as well. The *Louisiana Hunting Seasons and Wildlife Management Area Regulations*, published annually by the Louisiana Department of Wildlife and Fisheries (LDWF), is free and available at most places where hunting and fishing licenses are sold. This information is also available on LDWF's web site (www.wlf.state.la.us). When sharing the woods with hunters, consider hiking with a group, and be sure to wear blaze orange or hunter orange on your clothes or backpack.

INSECTS AND SPIDERS

When it comes to insect repellent, "Don't leave home without it" is a good slogan for Louisiana hikers—any time of year. Although Louisiana's bug season is typically April through September, mosquitoes are a potential problem for most of the year. Recent outbreaks of West Nile virus make mosquito bite prevention even more important. The Office of Public Health in Louisiana reported that, as of 2002, most West Nile virus cases had occurred in late summer and early fall. Although most people who get infected with the virus will experience mild, if any, symptoms, serious and sometimes fatal illness can occur, particularly in the elderly.

Ticks and chiggers (also called redbugs) can be avoided by spraying your hiking clothing with Permethrin before you hit the trail. To avoid these pests during your breaks, carry a garbage bag or a piece of foam (a portion of an old closed-cell foam pad works well) to sit on. Check yourself regularly and carefully for ticks. I generally wear long, lightweight pants when hiking Louisiana trails (even in summer) and take great care, in particular, to spray the bottoms of my pants legs and my socks before hiking.

The red fire ant was first introduced into the United States from South America in 1940, and fire ants have struck fear in the hearts of yard owners and outdoor enthusiasts ever since. In the last six decades, these aggressive insects have spread from Texas to the Carolinas. Their nests are elevated mounds of earth. Stay away from these! When disturbed, fire ants will swarm, stinging their victim repeatedly with a toxin that results in a burning effect and blisters.

Hikers who enjoy the early morning woods already know that spiders can build elaborate webs across the trail overnight. Watch for these as you hike. A good idea is to hold a stick in front of you as you walk in order to catch any human-height webs. Consider ducking beneath spider webs that you can see; not only is this their home, but they are ridding the forest of other insects. Also, spider webs are simply among the most awe-inspiring artworks in the forest gallery.

OVERNIGHT CAMPING

The best time for camping in Louisiana is between mid-October and mid-April, when the humidity is at its lowest. Backpacking sites at the state parks provide grills, and fire rings are available along the Kisatchie backpacking trails. If you must build a small campfire, always use the ready-made fire rings. Pack out all waste materials from your campsite. Use privies or public restrooms when available; otherwise, dig a hole at least 400 feet from any campsite or water source. Never wash yourself, your dishes, or your clothing in or near water sources. When using a primitive campsite, follow the principles of "Leave No Trace" (LNT) ethics. These include: Plan ahead and prepare; travel and camp on durable surfaces; dispose of waste properly; leave what you find; minimize campfire impacts; respect wildlife; and be considerate of other visitors. A good book on LNT is *Backwoods Ethics: A Guide to Low-*

Impact Camping and Hiking by Laura and Guy Waterman.

PERMITS

To enter and explore trails on Louisiana's Wildlife Management Areas (WMAs), hikers between the ages of 16 and 60 must possess a hunting license, fishing license, or Wild Louisiana Stamp. The Wild Louisiana Stamp is a permit specifically for "nonconsumptive users" of WMAs, such as hikers, mountain bikers, birders, and photographers. According to LDWF, you can get a Wild Louisiana Stamp anywhere that hunting and fishing licenses are sold. You can get a one-day stamp ($2) if you're planning to spend only a day hiking on a WMA. If you plan to hike on WMA lands throughout the year, you can get a seasonal stamp ($5.50).

PLANTS

Poison ivy is plentiful along Louisiana's trails. Long, lightweight pants or short hiking gaiters are a good investment for avoiding the three-leaved menace. Long pants are also good for preventing scratches on overgrown trails, which you may encounter in the late spring and summer months. Because the hiking season is generally fall, winter, and early spring, many trails are not maintained between late spring and early fall.

SEASONAL CONCERNS

Mention "Louisiana hiking" to most people, and their response will be something like, "but isn't it too hot to hike in Louisiana?" Of course it is—in summer. As mentioned previously, our hiking season begins in late September, when the thermometer finally dips below 90 degrees and the humidity lets up a bit. October and November are usually dry, with mild days and cool nights.

Late November and December see Louisiana's brief period of fall colors as our deciduous trees finally bed down for winter. January and February are generally mild, though the temperature occasionally dips below freezing at night. The first violets begin to peek out of the woods in January and are · joined by trillium, Carolina jessamine, and more violets in February. March and April, also nice months for hiking, see the blooming of wild azaleas in Kisatchie and Louisiana irises in Louisiana's bogs, borrow canals, and swamp edges. By the time May rolls around, Louisiana begins to see hot days again, but hiking is still a possibility and offers a chance to see the blooming of summer wildflowers.

Like the other Gulf Coast states, Louisiana is subject to sudden, heavy thunderstorms, particularly during the warmer months. While the average person will avoid hiking in such conditions, even the most cautious hikers may find themselves stuck in an unexpected deluge. Be aware that violent storms can spawn destructive tornadoes, particularly in the northern third of the state, where these twisters wreaked havoc on several hiking trails in 1999 and 2000. If you are caught in a storm, head for cover as quickly as possible.

True to their name, Louisiana's flat, poorly drained floodplains can become inundated with water during periods of heavy rain. During the particularly wet seasons, you may want to head for the higher, dryer trails of Kisatchie and avoid the lowland trails altogether. If you do decide to venture to these potentially flooded and most likely muddy trails, I encourage you to check with the trail maintainers to make sure the trails are hikable.

SNAKES

Louisiana's poisonous snake population consists of copperheads, cottonmouths (water moccasins), and coral snakes, along with three types of rattlesnakes—the eastern diamondback, the pygmy, and the canebrake or timber rattlesnake. The only one of these that does not occur throughout most of the state is the eastern diamondback rattlesnake, which you'll find only in the Florida parishes. Cottonmouths are highly defensive; should you encounter one on a trail, it may not get out of your way. The less aggressive copperhead can be a danger, as it may lie camouflaged among the leaves alongside a trail. Never handle a snake; most bites have occurred when the victim was attempting to handle it.

SUN

A high-strength sunblock is a must in Louisiana. A brimmed hat will protect your face and neck from the sun, and you might also find a pair of sunglasses useful. If hiking in a baseball cap, don't forget to apply sunscreen to your ears and neck.

MULTIPLE-USE TRAILS

Quite a few Louisiana hiking trails are also open to equestrians and mountain bikers. Always allow these trail users the right of way. All multiple-use trails are indicated in the text. Again, use the principles of "Leave No Trace" for the benefit of others.

VEHICLES

Unless you're having someone shuttle you to a starting point, you will have to leave your car at a trailhead. Although vandalism has not recently been a major problem for unattended vehicles at trailheads, be sure to put all items into the trunk and lock all doors. It's a good idea to let the trail authorities, such as the appropriate ranger district or the state park entrance station, know where you are leaving your car and when you plan to return to it. And don't forget your keys!

WATER

Most Louisiana trails have plenty of water, though not all of them provide easily accessible water sources. Dayhikers should provide their own water supply. I mention water sources for backpackers and state whether or not a backpacking trail even has accessible water sources. Filter, boil, or chemically treat all water obtained from trailside water sources. If you're in the market for a water filter, visit your local outfitter to learn about the water filters available. Two good–and popular–brands are Katadyn and Pur. Don't want to carry a water pump? To chemically treat water, hikers generally use some form of iodine, such as Polar Pure crystals or Potable Aqua tablets. These, too, should be available at your local outfitter.

LOUISIANA STATE PARKS, HISTORIC SITES, AND PRESERVATION AREA

A number of trails in this guide are owned and maintained by the Louisiana Office of State Parks (LOSP), which operates a total of 17 state parks, 16 state historic sites, and 1 state preservation area (the Louisiana State Arboretum). State parks are open 365 days a year, and the historic sites and preservation area, which are day-use only, are open from 9 AM to 5 PM every day, except Thanksgiving, Christmas, and New Year's Day. Gate hours vary for the state parks. Entrance fees are charged for all LOSP-owned facilities. For more information on the facilities maintained by LOSP, you can contact them at P.O. Box 44426, Baton Rouge, LA, 70804, or by phone at 225-342-8111 or 1-888-677-1400. You can also get information on the LOSP web site at www.lastateparks.com.

LOUISIANA HIKING CLUB

Based in Baton Rouge, the Louisiana Hiking Club was founded in 1999 and has been growing ever since. Club trips are free and range from nearby day hikes and birding forays to multiple-day backpacking trips in the Ozarks, the Appalachians, and the Rockies. Club volunteers have helped to build, maintain, and repair trails across the state. For more information on Louisiana hiking, visit the club's web site at www.hikelouisiana.org, write to president@lhc.org, or drop a note to Louisiana Hiking Club, 7436 Oak Meadow Drive, Baton Rouge, LA 70818.

SUGGESTED READING AND FIELD GUIDES

The list below focuses primarily on Louisiana-specific books and guides. Some of these books are no longer in print; if you can find them, they would make fine additions to the library of anyone with an interest in Louisiana. Books published by the LDWF are available from the LDWF Headquarters in Baton Rouge.

Alden, Peter, Ed. *National Audubon Society Field Guide to the Southeastern States: Alabama, Arkansas, Georgia, Kentucky, Louisiana, Mississippi, North Carolina, South Carolina and Tennessee.* New York: Alfred A. Knopf, 1999.
Baughman, Mel, Ed. *Field Guide to the Birds of North America* (Fourth Edition). Washington, DC: National Geographic Society, 2002.
Boundy, Jeff. *Snakes of Louisiana.* Baton

Rouge, Louisiana: Fur & Refuge Division, LDWF, 1997.

Cunningham, Edward: *The Port Hudson Campaign, 1862–1863*. Baton Rouge, Louisiana: Louisiana State University Press, 1994.

Dennett, Dan. *Louisiana's Wildlife Worth Watching*. Baton Rouge, Louisiana: Wildlife Division, LDWF, 1997.

Duncan, Wilbur H., and Marion B. Duncan. *Trees of the Southeastern United States*. Athens, Georgia: The University of Georgia Press, 1988.

Dundee, Harold A. *Amphibians and Reptiles of Louisiana*. Baton Rouge, Louisiana: Louisiana State University Press, 1996.

Fontenot, William R., and Brian K. Miller (photographer). *Birds of the Gulf Coast*. Baton Rouge, Louisiana: Louisiana State University Press, 2001.

Gibson, John L. *The Ancient Mounds of Poverty Point: Place of Rings*. Gainesville, Florida: University Press of Florida, 2000.

Gomez, Gay M. *A Wetland Biography: Seasons on Louisiana's Chenier Plain*. Austin, Texas: University of Texas Press, 1998.

Hatch, Stephan L., D. Lynn Drawe, and Joseph L. Schuster. *Grasses of the Texas Gulf Prairies and Marshes*. College Station, Texas: Texas A&M University Press, 1999.

Kniffen, Fred B., and Sam Bowers Hilliard. *Louisiana: Its Land and People* (Revised Edition). Baton Rouge, Louisiana: Louisiana State University Press, 1991.

Kniffen, Fred B., George A. Stokes, and Hiram F. Gregory. *Historic Indian Tribes of Louisiana: From 1542 to the Present*. Baton Rouge, Louisiana: Louisiana State University Press, 1994.

Lockwood, C. C., and Robert A. Thomas C.C. Lockwood's Louisiana Nature Guide for Kids. Baton Rouge: Louisiana State University Press, 1995.

_____. *Discovering Louisiana*. Baton Rouge, Louisiana: Louisiana State University Press, 1986.

Lowery, George H., Jr. *Louisiana Birds*. Baton Rouge, Louisiana: Louisiana State University Press, 1974.

Lowery, George H., Jr. *The Mammals of Louisiana and Its Adjacent Waters*. Baton Rouge: Louisiana State University Press, 1974.

Thieret, John W. *Louisiana Ferns and Fern Allies*. Lafayette, Louisiana: Lafayette Natural History Museum in conjunction with The University of Southwest Louisiana, 1980.

Petrides, George A. *A Field Guide to Eastern Trees*. New York: Houghton Mifflin, 1998.

ADDRESSES

Hike 1:
Walter B. Jacobs Memorial Nature Park
8012 Blanchard-Furrh Road
Shreveport, LA 71107
318-929-2806

Hike 2:
Cypress-Black Bayou Recreation Area
135 Cypress Park Drive
Benton, LA 71006
318-965-0007

Hike 3:
Bayou Bodcau Dam & Reservoir
171 Ben Durden Road
Haughton, LA 71037-7319
318-949-1804

Hike 4:
Lake Bistineau State Park
103 State Park Road
Doyline, LA 71023
318-745-3503
1-888-677-2478

Hike 5:
Kisatchie National Forest–
Caney Ranger District
P.O. Box 479
Homer, LA 71040
318-927-2061

Hike 6:
Lake Claiborne State Park
P.O. Box 246
Homer, LA 71040
318-927-2976
1-888-677-2524

Hike 7:
http://americasroof.com/la.shtml

Hike 8:
Lake D'Arbonne State Park
P.O. Box 236
Farmerville, LA 71241
318-368-2086
1-888-677-5200

Hike 9:
Kiroli Park
820 Kiroli Road
West Monroe, LA 71291-4945
318-396-4016

Hike 10:
Black Bayou Lake NWR
Rt. 2, Box 401-A
Farmerville, LA 71241
318-726-4400

Hike 11:
Poverty Point State Historic Site
P.O. Box 276
Epps, LA 71237
318-926-5492
1-888-926-5492

Hike 12:
Tensas River NWR
2312 Fred Morgan, Sr. Road
Tallulah, LA 71282
318-574-2664

Hike 13:
Kisatchie National Forest–
Winn Ranger District
9671 Highway 84 West
Winnfield, LA 71483-9501
318-628-4664

Hike 14:
Foundation for the Preservation of the
Caroline Dormon Nature Preserve, Inc.
216 Caroline Dormon Road
Saline, LA 71070
318-576-3379 (afternoons)

Hike 15:
North Toledo Bend State Park
P.O. Box 56
Zwolle, LA 71486
318-645-4715
1-888-677-6400

Hikes 16, 17, 18:
Kisatchie National Forest–
Kisatchie Ranger District
Highway 6-West
Natchitoches, LA 71457-2128
318-352-2568

Hikes 19, 20, 21, 22:
Kisatchie National Forest–
Calcasieu Ranger District
9912 Highway 28 West
Boyce, LA 71409
318-793-9427

Hike 23:
Indian Creek Recreation Area
P.O. Box 298
Woodworth, LA 71485
318-487-5058

Hike 24:
Kisatchie National Forest–
Catahoula Ranger District
5325 LA Highway 8
Bentley, LA 71407-9726
318-765-3554

Hike 25:
Catahoula NWR
P.O. Drawer Z
Rhinehart, LA 71363
318-992-5261

Hikes 3, 26, 37, 38
Louisiana Department of Wildlife and
Fisheries
2000 Quail Drive
Baton Rouge, LA 70808
225-765-2360

Hike 27:
Sam Houston Jones State Park
107 Sutherland Road
Lake Charles, LA 70611
337-855-2665
1-888-677-7264

Hike 28:
Baton Rouge Audubon Society
P.O. Box 82525
Baton Rouge, LA 70884-2525
www.braudubon.org

Hike 29:
Sabine NWR
3000 Holly Beach Highway
Hackberry, LA 70645
337-762-3816

Hike 30:
Lacassine NWR
209 Nature Road
Lake Arthur, LA 70549
337-774-5923

Hike 31:
Cameron Prairie NWR
1428 Highway 27
Bell City, LA 70630
337-598-2216

Hike 32:
Louisiana State Arboretum
4213 Chicot Park Road
Ville Platte, LA 70586
337-363-6289
1-888-677-6100

Hike 33:
Chicot State Park
3469 Chicot Park Road
Ville Platte, LA 70586
337-363-2043
1-888-677-2442

Hike 34:
Acadiana Park Nature Station
1205 East Alexander Street
Lafayette, LA 70501
337-291-8448
www.naturestation.org

Hikes 35, 40, 45, 50:
The Nature Conservancy of Louisiana
340 St. Joseph Street
Baton Rouge, LA 70802
225-338-1040

Hike 36:
Lake Fausse Pointe State Park
5400 Levee Road
St. Martinville, LA 70582
337-229-4764
1-888-677-7200

Hikes 37, 47, 48:
Southeast Louisiana Refuges
61389 Hwy. 434
Lacombe, LA 70458
985-882-2000

Hike 39:
Cat Island NWR
P.O. Box 1936
St. Francisville, LA 70775
225-635-4753

Hike 41:
Port Hudson State Historic Site
236 US Highway 61
Jackson, LA 70748
225-654-3775
1-888-677-3400

Hike 42:
Baton Rouge Recreation and
Park Commission
3140 North Sherwood Forest Drive
Baton Rouge, LA 70814
225-272-9200
www.brec.org

Waddill Outdoor Education Center
4142 North Flannery Road
Baton Rouge, LA 70814
225-765-2933

Hike 43:
Tickfaw State Park
27225 Patterson Road
Springfield, LA 70462-8906
225-294-5020
1-888-981-2020

Hike 44:
Bonnet Carré Spillway
U.S. Army Corps of Engineers
New Orleans District
P.O. Box 216
Norco, LA 70079
985-764-0216

Hike 46:
Fontainebleau State Park
P.O. Box 8925
Mandeville, LA 70470-8925
1-888-677-3668

Hike 49:
Jean Lafitte National Historical
Park–Barataria Preserve
6588 Barataria Blvd.
504-589-2330
www.nps.gov/jela

I. North Louisiana

1

Walter B. Jacobs Memorial Nature Park

Total distance (circuit): 2.2 miles

Hiking time: 1 hour

Habitats: Mixed pine and hardwood forest, cypress swamp, forest gaps and edges

Maps: USGS 7½' Blanchard, park map

Located on a 160-acre tract northwest of Shreveport, Walter B. Jacobs Memorial Nature Park offers over 5 miles of level trail through an ever-changing forest of pines and hardwoods. Springtime at the nature park sees a profusion of wildflowers that last through the first frost of winter, and late autumn witnesses a varied palate of leaf color, thanks to an abundance of deciduous trees—including southern sugar maples, which are uncommon in Louisiana. Bird migration periods are a great time to hike here; you're sure to see and hear various migratory birds, including northern parula as well as black-and-white, Tennessee, and hooded warblers.

The park was developed according to the wishes of the late Walter Jacobs, who was inspired by Briarwood (Hike 14) and wanted something similar for his legacy. His land proved an ideal spot for another, similar park—complete with a massive shortleaf "Grandpappy Pine," said to have sprouted in 1892. Trails are open between 8 AM and 5 PM on Wednesdays through Saturdays, and between 1 and 5 PM on Sundays. The park is free and open to the public.

To get there, take LA 173 north from Shreveport (Exit 5 on I-220). After 6.6 miles, turn left onto Blanchard-Furrh Road in Blanchard (a block south of the stoplight next to the post office). Approximately 3 miles down this road, turn right into the Walter B. Jacobs Memorial Nature Park. Park in front of the Interpretive Building. Trail guides and maps are available inside.

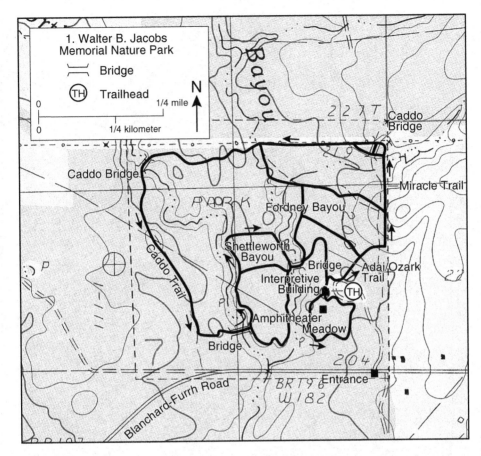

The system comprises several short segments, most of which are named for the Caddoans, a group of Native American tribes who ranged across northwest Louisiana and nearby areas of Arkansas, Texas, and Oklahoma from the first millennium A.D. Europeans discovered the Caddoans living along the Red River in the eighteenth century. Their friendship and the trading relationship that developed between these tribes and the French allowed the Caddoans to live peacefully and prosperously throughout the period of European exploration. In 1835, however, in the only Native American land cession treaty signed within Louisiana's boundaries, the Caddo lands were ceded to the U.S. Government. Louisiana's Caddoans—who included the Ouachita, Yatasi, Adai, Doustioni, Natchitoches, and Kadohadacho tribes—moved west to Texas, and ultimately ended up in the Indian Territory of present-day Oklahoma.

Begin hiking on the Ouachita Trail, which is to the right of the Interpretive Building and adjacent to the parking lot. Before 1700, the Ouachita, or "Cow River People," for whom the trail is named ranged as far east as the Ouachita River near present-day Monroe. On this short trail, you'll see southern sugar maples among the red buckeye, redbud,

The segment along Shettleworth Bayou is among the most scenic of the nature park's hikes.

yaupon, elm, and white oak. Abundant vines include muscadine and poison ivy.

The Ouachita Trail passes several numbered posts. The numbers correspond to the Ouachita Trail guide, available at the Interpretive Center. At post #3, you want to bear left. After crossing a small footbridge, the trail junctions at the Caddo Trail. Go straight ahead to pick up the Caddo. If you haven't noticed the southern sugar maples already, you'll see plenty in this spot, along with more common red maples. Red maples have red leafstalks, and their leaves generally have three shallow lobes, occasionally with two smaller lobes near the base. In contrast, the southern sugar maple has deeply cleft, five-lobed leaves. Although both trees are deciduous, southern sugar maple saplings will actually hold on to their leaves throughout the winter, much like American beeches. The long-dead leaves won't fall until the new bud pushes them out.

You'll reach an old road trace at 0.1 mile; turn left here to remain on the trail, which is quite straight and passes beneath towering oaks and pines. Spring-flowering trees on this part of the trail include parsley hawthorn, mayhaw, dogwood, red buckeye, and fringe tree.

The Caddo Trail junctions with the Miracle Trail at 0.2 mile. Go straight ahead to pick up the Miracle Trail—also called the Wildflower Trail. The path descends slightly, then veers right to enter a cleared highline. Because it receives so much sunlight, this cleared corridor is a great three-season environment for wildflowers. The diminutive Walter's violets, with their round, variegated leaves, pop out as early as January, to be joined by more violets as winter gives way to spring. Once spring has sprung (sometimes as early as February), look for bloodroot, trillium, red columbine, cardinal flower, phlox, and mayapples. As summer ad-

vances, you'll see blazing star, heal-all, and milkweed. Myriad summer wildflowers include asters, daisies, sunflowers, coneflowers, and thistles; these thrive throughout summer and die only with the first frost.

At 0.5 mile, you'll cross a bridge over a small ditch, then cross another soon afterward. In mid-April, look ahead to your left to see a stand of irises growing in the small sloughs. Before the irises bloom, the ground in much of this area may be covered with umbrella-like mayapples. The lower, swampier spots are home to lizardtail, an aquatic plant more common in south Louisiana's wetlands. Look for its distinctive heart-shaped leaves.

At 0.6 mile, the Miracle Trail crosses Fordney Bayou to rejoin the Caddo Trail. After crossing one more bridge, swing left to return to the woods. When you reach a junction with the Adai Trail, bear right to remain on the Caddo Trail. After crossing a tiny footbridge at 0.7 mile, the trail swings left to enter a low, swampy area, and one of the most scenic portions of your hike. You will cross five more small bridges as you work your way through this beautiful pocket of forest, filled with dwarf palmetto.

Cross Shettleworth Bayou at 0.9 mile. A side trail leads to the right, but you want to stay on the Caddo Trail. You'll see more southern sugar maples at the next bridge at 1 mile. After crossing another footbridge at 1.3 miles, the trail leads back alongside Shettleworth Bayou to the left. Cross the bayou once more at 1.4 miles, then bear left onto the Yatasi Trail. The Yatasi ("Those Other People") lived along the Red River northwest of Natchitoches before being expelled in the 1830s, with the rest of the Caddoans, to Texas and then to Indian Territory. This scenic segment follows a low, narrow ridge alongside Shettleworth Bayou to the left and a slough to the right.

When the trail forks at 1.5 miles, keep going straight to hop onto the Adai Trail. The Adai ("Place Along a Stream") settled southwest of Natchitoches, near the much-disputed border of Spanish Texas and French Louisiana. The trail swings left and leads through a hardwood-dominated area full of southern sugar maples. The path winds alongside Shettleworth Bayou and briefly heads uphill at 1.6 miles to reach a bench. Swing right to reach another junction—this one a shortcut to the Caddo Trail. Remain on the Adai Trail, veering to the right again before reaching the junction of four trails. Follow the signs to remain on the Adai. Just before you cross Fordney Bayou, a trail to the right leads to the Adai/Caddo trail junction. To finish your hike with a stroll down the scenic Audubon Trail, you want to stay on the Adai Trail.

At 1.8 miles, bear right onto the Ozark Trail, which will take you across another bridge to the Interpretive Building. Circle the front of the building to hook up with the paved Audubon Trail. An informative brochure is available for this self-guided, wheelchair-accessible route.

When the Audubon Trail forks at 2 miles, bear to the right. You'll soon reach the park's majestic Grandpappy Pine. Shortleaf pine, also called southern yellow pine, is widely distributed throughout the Southeast. Because shortleaf was extensively cut for timber in the last century, it is rare to find one this old. Like longleaf pines, shortleaf seedlings will sprout after a fire. If you're interested in seeing Louisiana's "Grand-pappy" longleaf, you'll need to go south to Briarwood (Hike 14). The Audubon Trail loops back to the Interpretive Building again after passing the Grandpappy Pine, for a total hike of 2.2 miles.

2

Cypress Nature Study Center and Trails

Total distance (circuit): 2.6 miles

Hiking time: 1 hour

Habitats: Mixed pine and hardwood

Maps: USGS 7½' Benton, nature center map

Nestled at the northern end of the Cypress–Black Bayou Recreation Area in Bossier Parish is the education-focused Cypress Nature Study Center. This fascinating place features live fishes, turtles, and frogs for observation. The Center also regularly takes in abandoned forest creatures found by local residents; as a result, you never know what kinds of animals you'll see when you visit. Kids–and grown-ups–can find wonder in seeing a baby squirrel, a litter of motherless 'possums, or even a migratory warbler recuperating from a broken wing. The Center's adjacent trails provide hikers of all ages with a chance to view wildlife in its more natural environment.

Adults, don't let the educational, good-for-kids aspect of Cypress Nature Study Center keep you from visiting this 100-acre facility north of Bossier City. Anyone who is interested in learning more about nature–or in just taking a simple stroll through the forest to see wildflowers and watch for birds–will gain from hiking the Center's trail system. Blooming dogwoods, red buckeyes, parsley hawthorn, and fringe tree bejewel the woods in spring. Closer to the ground, you'll see wild azalea, violets, shooting stars, toad trillium, bloodroot, wild ginger, wild geranium, phlox, and many other wildflowers. The circuitous, stacked loop system allows you to make your hike as long or as short as you wish. The hike is through mixed pine and hardwood forest, but you'll see several forest areas in early stages of regeneration–the result of a

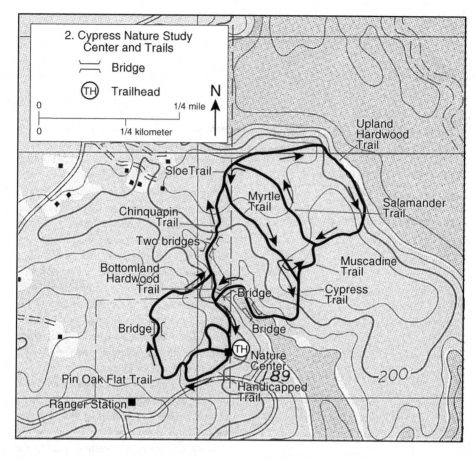

tornado that ripped through Louisiana's northeast corner on Easter Sunday 1999, felling dozens of canopy trees in its wake.

To get to the Cypress Nature Study Center, take LA 3105 (Airline Drive) north from Shreveport (Exit 22 from I-20; Exit 12 from I-220). Travel 5.5 miles north of I-220 and turn right onto Linton Road (at the Cypress–Black Bayou Recreation Area sign). From there, drive about 4.5 miles to the recreation area, where a $4-per-vehicle fee is charged. When the road splits at 4.7 miles, bear left and turn into the parking lot. The Center and trails are open to the public Monday through Friday from 8 AM to 3 PM and on Saturday and Sunday from 8 AM to 4 PM. No camping is allowed on the trails, though tent and RV sites are both available at the Cypress–Black Bayou Recreation Area for a fee.

The hike described here takes a circuitous route in order to provide a walk that covers at least part of all of the trails. To get to the trails, walk through the Center, exit at the back door, then turn left. You'll stroll the flat, winding, loops of the wheelchair-accessible trail before heading onto the primitive trail. As you descend the initial platform, look to the right to see a sectioned-off area. Here, many varieties of native Louisiana flora have been planted and are growing at all forest levels–from poison ivy and muscadine to shrubby French mulberries and towering shortleaf pines.

The trail forks almost immediately; bear right, passing a couple of benches before the trail forks again at 0.1 mile. Bear left this time. Although you're in a mixed pine and hardwood forest, you'll notice that the tornado-hit areas look different. These forest gaps, once shaded by large oaks and hickories, are now open to full sunlight, and allow many sun-loving, fast-growing "pioneer plants" a chance to thrive for a few years. Other plants take longer to grow but will eventually provide shade and replace the sun-loving species. Barring another major disturbance, these changing areas will eventually return to a mature state. This process—from the disturbance to the invasion of pioneer plants to their replacement by slower-growing plants over time—is called ecological succession. You're likely to see any number of vines, including muscadine and wild grape, along with quick-sprouting red maple, sweet gum, red cedar, and loblolly saplings. In spring, summer, and fall, the sunny forest gaps are a haven for wildflowers, particularly goldenrod and asters.

The primitive trail begins at 0.2 mile. Each small section of the trail system is named for a different plant, miniature habitat, or animal. Swing right to begin the Pin Oak Flat Trail, a segment that was hard hit by the 1999 tornado. The trail leads through a mosaic of forest gaps and tall, healthy trees. Cross a small footbridge at 0.3 mile; you might notice houses beyond the boundary fence. Because this area is part of the Bossier suburbs, you'll see a few more houses as you hike.

At 0.5 mile, the trail swings left, away from the fence and houses. In spring, the ground is covered with bright green, umbrella-like mayapples. Look for the white flowers drooping from beneath the double-stemmed plants.

Shooting stars in bloom.

The trail slopes downhill to reach the junction with the Chinquapin and Bottomland Hardwood Trails. For now, you want to bear left onto the Chinquapin Trail. Pass a bench, then cross a small footbridge. Not long after crossing a second footbridge, at 0.6 mile, you'll reach the junction of Chinquapin, Myrtle, and Sloe Trails. Swing right to hike the Myrtle Trail, named for wax myrtle, or southern bayberry, a shrublike tree that is widely distributed throughout Louisiana.

This segment begins a very mild uphill at 0.7 mile, passing wild azaleas and numerous low, thicketlike plants. The Myrtle Trail soon levels out, then splits once again at 0.8 mile. Here, you want to turn left onto the Muscadine Trail. A common pioneer plant, muscadine is plentiful throughout the state. In spring, you'll begin to see the sometimes rounded, sometimes heart-shaped, toothed leaves of these climbing vines, which flower in May and June and bear their sweet, flavorful fruits throughout late summer and fall.

The trail passes a couple of bluebird nesting boxes, placed here by the Cypress 4-H Nature Club. You may even spot an eastern bluebird, a blue-winged, orange-breasted thrush that roams in small groups and gleans its diet of insects and small fruits from the ground or from low shrubs. Listen for its soft whistles as you bear left onto the Salamander Trail at 0.9 mile. This segment includes a tiny loop—sort of a hiccup in the trail, actually. At 1 mile is another junction; this time, the trail seems to split three ways. Turn right onto the Upland Hardwood Trail. As you descend at 1.1 miles, look to the left in winter for a view of Cypress Bayou Reservoir through the trees. You might see the wood duck boxes and owl boxes, placed here as an Eagle Scout project by Adam Kruse and Boy Scout Troop #64 of Bossier City.

The trail descends rather steeply to reach the reservoir's banks. Throughout the year, but particularly in winter, you're likely to see various waterfowl here, including mallards, wood ducks, and pied-billed grebes. As you head back uphill, listen for downy woodpeckers, pine warblers, and wood thrushes if you're hiking in summer. Overhead, you may see red-shouldered hawks or broad-winged hawks. Northern cardinals are plentiful year-round in the surrounding trees. Listen for their calls—a series of descending slurred whistles followed by a repetitive chatter. The trail contours the ridge, then heads to the right, away from the lake, at 1.4 miles. The path seems to fork a couple of times when spur trails lead to the RV/camping area. Simply bear right until you've completed the Upland Hardwood Trail at 1.5 miles. Go to the right to repeat part of the Salamander Trail (including the "hiccup") before exploring the Sloe Trail.

Reach the Sloe Trail junction after another 0.1 mile. Also known as the flatwoods plum, sloe is a small, spreading tree found throughout much of the state. Turn left, passing sweet gum, red buckeye, and red maple. Soon you're back at the Myrtle Trail; bear left to repeat this short segment. At 1.9 miles, turn right onto the Cypress Trail, which will lead you past another bluebird nesting box and down a slight incline beneath tall pines, oaks, and hickories before swinging to the right at 2 miles. Several trails may seem to go off to either side, but just remain on the main trail. Soon, you'll be able to see a boardwalk straight ahead.

The Cypress Trail boardwalk leads along the bank of a small inlet of Cypress Bayou Reservoir before heading back into the woods at 2.2 miles. A boardwalk spur leads to the left; you want to keep going straight, back into the woods, to reach a footbridge soon afterwards. After crossing this footbridge, the Cypress Trail junctions with the Bottomland Hardwood Trail. Either way will take you back to the Center. If you take the shorter route to the left, you'll want to bear left when the trail meets the handicapped-accessible path. If you go to the right, you should bear left at the junction with the Pin Oak Flat Trail, then bear right when you get to the handicapped-accessible trail. This latter route will make for a total hike of about 2.6 miles.

3

Bodcau Hiking

Total distance (circuit): 4.5 miles

Hiking time: 3 hours

Habitats: Mixed pine and hardwood, bottomland hardwood

Maps: USGS 7½' Bodcau Lake, Bodcau WMA map, ALTOS map

Traversing the Louisiana-Arkansas border northeast of Shreveport, Bayou Bodcau snakes through the hilly mixed pine and hardwood forests that characterize this region. At the southern tip of the wide, winding bayou is the Bayou Bodcau Dam and Reservoir, built and maintained by the U.S. Army Corps of Engineers. The need for waterway management in this region of the Red River goes back to the days of the Great Raft, a massive logjam that Europeans first encountered during their early-18th-century explorations. Starting north of Natchitoches, a morass of logs, branches, silt, and other debris stubbornly impeded a 150-mile channel northward for hundreds of years. The Red's water levels were forced to rise and seek other outlets. The flooding from the main artery of the Red River sometimes resulted in "raft lakes," or outlets that became impounded by a combination of the logjam and the raised riverbed. The depth of the raft lakes constantly fluctuated with the river's whims.

Naturally, the Great Raft made navigation increasingly dangerous and sometimes impossible. Finally, the 1830s saw the steampowered removal of the Great Raft by Captain Henry Shreve, for whom Shreveport is named. Around this time, some of the raft lakes, Bodcau and Bistineau among them, were artificially dammed to maintain their levels. Interestingly, Bayou Bodcau served as an alternate route to the Red River when the logjam prevented safe travel down that main artery.

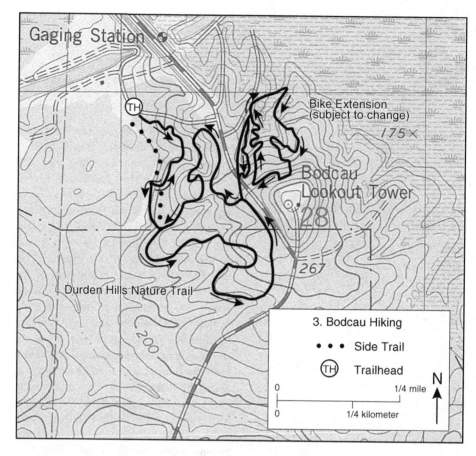

Today, this region offers dozens of miles for hiking. The Durden Hills Nature Trail began as a short walking trail, but area mountain bikers have extended it in recent years. The map provided here reflects the winding loop system as it existed at the time of this writing. Contact the Bayou Bodcau Project Office for updates on rerouted stretches and additions to this evolving system.

The Durden Hills Nature Trail begins at the Tom Merrill Recreation Area. To get there, take I-20 to Exit 33 at Fillmore and go north on LA 157. Drive 8.6 miles, then turn right at the Bayou Bodcau Recreation Area sign. Bear left after another mile and drive approximately 1.5 miles to the Tom Merrill Recreation Area. Turn left at the sign and drive an additional 0.1 mile to the Durden Hills trailhead and parking area on your left.

Two paths lead into the woods at the trailhead. Begin by taking the original Durden Hills Nature Trail (the "left" trail), which is marked by a sign. Hike through a low, sometimes muddy area to a footbridge at 0.1 mile, looking for red maple, white oak, and southern red oak, all of which can yield some color in late fall. When the trail forks at 0.3 mile, bear to the right. It forks again after 50 feet; this time, bear left. (The right fork will just take you back to the parking area and is the second of the two trails leading away from

Raccoons on the trail

the trailhead.) The trail soon leads beside a scenic little area to the right, characterized by red, claylike dirt and numerous ravines that snake steeply through it. The path itself rolls gently alongside the ravines. Also adding to this area's beauty are the blooming dogwoods in spring.

At your feet, look for smilax among the prevalent poison ivy. Commonly known as greenbrier, smilax is a perennial vine whose leathery, three-lobed or heart-shaped leaves are a golden bronze in early spring but are green for the rest of the spring and summer. Deer browse heavily on these, and cedar waxwings and other birds feed on the small, rounded clusters of berries that smilax produces in fall and winter.

At 0.5 mile, the trail will have ascended a wide ridge; on either side, you'll see dogwoods, parsley hawthorn, and fringe tree—all of which have beautiful white flowers in early spring. An understory tree and a member of the olive family (along with ashes and privets), fringe tree is also known as "old man's beard" for its slender, drooping clusters of lacy white flowers that appear in late March and April. Its genus name, *Chionanthus*, is particularly descriptive; it means "snowflower."

At 0.6 mile, swing to the right and downhill, off the ridge, to begin a scenic walk and to cross a footbridge at 0.7 mile. At 0.9 mile,

the trail crosses Bodcau Dam Road. Bear left as you return to the woods, where the trail splits, and begin another descent. You will parallel Bodcau Dam Road for a while through this dogwood-filled area. You'll reach another trail junction at 1 mile; keep going straight, crossing a dry ditch soon afterward. Like any good bike trail, this extension to the Durden Hills Nature Trail winds back and forth to take full advantage of the gently rolling terrain. You might start noticing the sometimes-flooded wetlands of Bayou Bodcau at 1.2 miles; the trail will eventually get closer to this wet area, though it never quite reaches it.

Cross a small bridge over a slough at 1.5 miles, then take a sharp right immediately afterward. Alert birders spot diminutive ruby-crowned kinglets in late fall, winter, or early spring. These nervous, excited little birds are a sandy olive color and tend to hover at the tips of branches as they seek to glean small insects for food. They inhabit a wide range across the United States, and many spend their summers as far north as Canada.

Reach another junction at 1.9 miles, this one with several arrows pointing in different directions. Bear left for now, following the downhill-pointing arrow, to begin a loop that will last approximately 1 mile. The descent ends at 2 miles and levels out briefly. After another mile of winding, ascending, descending, and even switchbacking through scenic mixed pine and hardwood forest, the trail crosses another small footbridge and completes the rolling, serpentine loop soon afterward. You may spot a white-tailed deer or a wild turkey, both of which are plentiful in these woods.

When you reach the arrows again, bear left to follow them. This time, you'll go uphill as you start another series of looping turns and twists. At 3.3 miles, the trail descends to cross a footbridge. Soon afterward, you'll head back uphill to approach Bodcau Dam Road and complete the loop you began when you first crossed it. You won't cross the road just yet, though; bear left when the trail forks, and head downhill again. The path winds and twists for a while, before exiting the woods at 3.7 miles. Cross Bodcau Dam Road to return to the original Durden Hills Nature Trail. Once you reenter the woods, bear right and downhill to a footbridge at 3.8 miles. The trail winds back and forth, crossing three more footbridges before ending at the trailhead and your car at 4.5 miles.

4

Lake Bistineau State Park

Total distance (circuit): 10.4 miles

Hiking time: 6 hours

Habitats: Mixed pine and hardwood, forest gaps and edges

Maps: USGS 7½' Koran, USGS 7½' Heflin, ALTOS map, park map

During the 15th and 16th centuries, when the Caddo people occupied present-day north Louisiana, and the first Europeans began to arrive, the Great Raft—a gargantuan logjam—formed to block the Red River. Massive amounts of driftwood, mud, sand, and other debris forced parts of the Red River to overflow and form backwaters and bayous—one of which ultimately became Lake Bistineau. Like Bayou Bodcau, Lake Bistineau nearly became part of the Red River system, as its frequently flooded waters were used as one of several alternate routes around the logjam. The Native Americans handled the problem by moving to higher ground; however, several hundred years after the formation of the Great Raft, European settlers finally cleared the massive logjam and made the Red River safe for navigation.

Since those days, a dam has been constructed, and this has stabilized Lake Bistineau's water levels. The dam also allowed Lake Bistineau (French for "Tub of Brown Water"), which the State of Louisiana purchased in 1939, to become a premier site for fishing and recreation. Located just a few miles south of Doyline in Webster Parish, Lake Bistineau State Park also features one of Louisiana's newest trail systems. Opened in 2000, the winding, hilly path for hikers and mountain bikers is 10.4 miles long, provides a view of the cypress-filled lake, and is a good full-day walk for hikers of all levels. In terms of habitats, most of what you'll see on this trail is the mixed pine and hardwood characteristic of northwestern Louisiana.

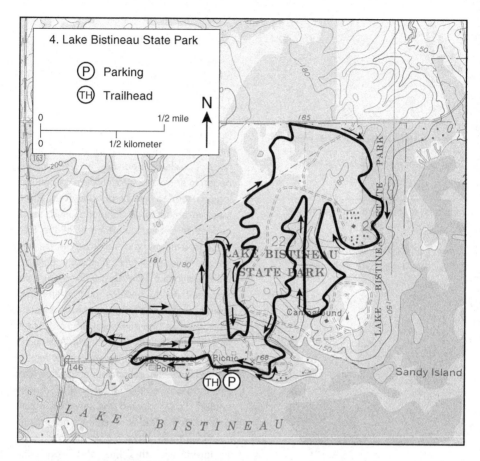

To get to Lake Bistineau State Park from I-20, take US 371 (Exit 47) south to Sibley, where you'll turn west (right) onto LA 164. Drive 4.5 miles west to Doyline, then turn left at the junction with LA 163 and drive the remaining 7 miles south to the park. Turn left into Lake Bistineau State Park Area I, where the trailhead is located. Pick up a brochure at the entrance station; while it does not include a map of the trail, it does provide an overview of the park. Drive straight ahead, following the signs for the boat launch, until you reach the picnic area on your left (which is before the boat launch). The trailhead will be on your right, across the road from the picnic area. Look for the bicycle sign that marks the beginning of the trail. The trail itself is marked occasionally with arrows. Numbered posts are placed at quarter-mile intervals along the entire trail, compliments of Boy Scout Troop 34 of Minden.

Don't let the bike picture deter you; hikers are equally welcome on this trail, though you may need to step aside for the occasional two-wheeled traveler. Typical of mountain bike trails, this one is very winding at first. You might even feel as if you're walking in circles, zigzagging the first 0.1 mile alongside the road. When the trail exits at a highline, bear right, following the trail signs. Cross a maintenance road at 0.2 mile, then swing left, back into the woods. You'll see a lot of pines in this area, as well as a many smaller trees and saplings—sweet gum, dogwood, oak, hickory, and elm among them.

When the trail exits the woods at 0.3 mile, you'll gain a view of scenic, cypress-edged Lake Bistineau. Swing to the right to walk alongside the grassy lakeshore. Look for great egrets and great blue herons in the lake, or watch for an anhinga roosting in one of the cypresses. This interesting, black-winged water bird, *Anhinga anhinga*, feeds by swimming with only its head above water, prepared to spear a fish with its pointed yellow bill. Because the wings of anhingas quickly become saturated with water, you'll often see them resting spread-winged on open perches to dry their feathers. Anhingas are summer visitors to north Louisiana. Similar in appearance to the anhinga, the double-crested cormorant is a year-round resident of this region.

At 0.4 mile, bear right to return to the woods. The reentry point is rather difficult to spot; you need to look for the clearing in the trees. The level trail continues to parallel the lakeshore until it swings to the right at 0.5 mile. Exit the woods again briefly, bearing to the right to hike through another small patch of woods. When you exit this stand, go left, back down the cleared highline. You won't be on this section long; look for the blazes directing you to swing to the right, back into the woods, at 0.6 mile. Look for the tracks of deer if the trail is at all muddy; you're sure to see a few.

You'll soon cross the cabin road and reenter the woods. Look for Carolina jessamine here in the early spring. In November, you might see some fall colors, compliments of the many deciduous trees here. Exit the woods briefly at 0.7 mile, where the trail forks. The path to the right leads to the park's nature center, so you want to bear left and reenter the woods after several hundred yards. You are still close to the lake; however, if you're hiking in summer, the leaves may block your view of it.

At 1 mile, swing right to walk down another highline. In early spring, you'll see lots of red buckeye and phlox blooming in this and other sun-exposed corridors. Head back into the woods soon afterward. The trail offers a pleasant, unbroken stroll through an island of mixed pine and hardwood forest for 0.3 mile before you reach another road. If you're getting tired of road crossings, you'll be glad to know that the northern segment of the trail is much more secluded.

The trail crosses this road, descends, and swings left at 1.5 miles to begin what seems like a large, wide loop. Many tall pines shade this area, which has a rich understory of red buckeye, elm, red maple, and southern red oak. Spring and summer see a profusion of vines at your feet: smilax, wild grape, and the ever-present poison ivy.

Walk briefly through a cleared area at 1.9 miles. You'll see a road off to your left, but the trail does not intersect with it. Swing right instead, weaving and winding through the mixed pine and hardwood habitat. When you reach the park's boundary line, marked by barbed wire fence at 2 miles, take a right. The path is very straight here, as it simply parallels the boundary line. It's also quite flat and may remain soggy and muddy after several days of rain. It's a nice walk, though; you'll see plenty of dogwoods, and wild grape grows all along the fence to your left. At 2.4 miles, the trail seems to split; just continue hiking straight ahead, along the boundary line.

You'll remain on a flat, potentially muddy trail for the length of the boundary line. Finally, at 2.9 miles, the trail parts from the line and swings to the right, back into the woods. Turn right again shortly thereafter, at

Ear fungus

a gas pipeline. When you reach a footbridge at 3.2 miles, the trail heads uphill. Just before it reaches a park road, it swings sharply left and begins a mild, brief descent. At 3.3 miles, you'll veer to the right; be sure to watch for the directional arrows. You might see some resurrection fern on some of the trees in this area; the deep-green fronds of this epiphyte become visible in wet weather.

The trail remains level and winding for the next mile, going through a few low, potentially muddy areas. When you exit the woods at 4.2 miles, turn right, following an arrow to walk along an old boundary line. Continue following the arrows, and at 4.4 miles you'll pass an old barn on your right. Park personnel aren't sure how long this barn has been standing; it was here when the state bought the property in 1939.

At 4.5 miles is a small pond to the left. Swimming is not recommended in this pond, which teems with snakes in spring and summer. Swing to the right at 4.6 miles as the trail begins to wind again. This flat, level area is full of large pines. At 4.9 miles, the trail meets Dement Road and joins it briefly. Swing to the right a short distance after this to return to the woods. When you swing right again at 5.1 miles, you'll see the boundary fence to your left. The trail continues to wind as it more or less follows the direction of Dement Road. It crosses a maintenance road at 5.2 miles and reenters the woods to continue winding gently over rolling hills for more than a mile.

At 6.6 miles the trail forks, and you'll see signs that bikers have indicated an "advanced trail" and an "easy trail." You can take either one—neither is difficult from a hiking standpoint. The two trails join up again soon afterward. At 6.7 miles, pass the back of the park's group campground to your right. Cross a low area at 6.9 miles and reenter the woods shortly afterward, then cross a footbridge at 7.2 miles. For a while, you'll hike between a ditch on your left and a dirt road (the highline) on your right. At 7.5 miles, the trail exits the woods to cross the highline.

The trail heads briefly down an old maintenance road but soon veers right to reenter the woods and wind through a low area of mostly hardwoods. At 7.9 miles, the trail begins to skirt Rally Field. If you're here at dawn or dusk, you're likely to see dozens of deer in this open, grassy spot. White-tailed deer are extremely common throughout Louisiana and most of the United States. The whitetail's genus name *Odocoileus* is from two Greek words: *odon,* meaning "tooth," and *koilos,* meaning "hollowed," probably referring to the cavelike hollows in the deer's unworn molars. The English word *deer* comes from the Anglo-Saxon *deor* or *dior,* which actually meant any kind of wild animal. The park's deer hardly look wild, however, as they gather peacefully in this area at what seems like an appointed time.

Follow the arrows to skirt the edge of Rally Field. At 7.3 miles, the trail passes to the right side of Rally Pavilion, where several trees wear Spanish moss on their gnarled branches. Once you pass the pavilion, you will walk down a cleared high line. At 8.1 miles, swing to the right to walk beneath the park's other power line. At 8.3 miles, the trail swings right, back into the woods, to avoid an often muddy spot on the highline. It returns to the high line shortly afterward. You will go underneath another power line and will approach a paved road before swinging to the left and back into the woods. At 8.7 miles, you'll reach a low, potentially wet area. A footbridge is provided, but you may still get your shoes muddy.

The trail crosses three more footbridges before intersecting the park's gravel-paved nature trail at 9.6 miles. There are lots of dogwoods in this area, and it's very beautiful in early spring. Cross one more footbridge at 10.1 miles, then exit the woods for the last time at 10.2 miles. Turn left onto the paved road, and follow this road until you reach the main road and the trailhead, for a total hike of 10.4 miles.

5

Sugar Cane Trail

Total distance (circuit): 6.2 miles

Hiking time: 4 hours

Habitats: Mixed pine and hardwood, forest gaps and edges

Maps: USGS 7½' Minden North, Caney Lakes Recreation Area map, Caney Ranger District Recreational Opportunities flyer

Located in Kisatchie's Caney Ranger District, the Sugar Cane National Recreation Trail is popular with hikers and mountain bikers alike. And it's no wonder: This loop traverses pleasantly rolling terrain and offers nearly continuous views of scenic Upper Caney Lake. Springtime brings the blooming of wild azaleas, red buckeye, dogwoods, and numerous other wildflowers, and both spring and fall see the fleeting arrivals and departures of migratory wood warblers. Parts of this trail have suffered tornado damage within the last decade; as a result, you will pass through several open, sunny areas that are quickly becoming thicketed with muscadine and poison ivy, along with various pine and hardwood saplings. Between the lake's scrubby shore edges, the pine and hardwood forest, and the disturbed areas, you stand a chance of spotting all kinds of wildlife, from green anoles to great blue herons, and from red-tailed hawks to white-tailed deer.

To get to the trail, take I-20 to LA 371 in Minden (Exit 47). When LA 371 junctions with LA 159 in the center of town, go north on LA 159 for about 4.7 miles. Turn left onto Webster Parish (WP) Road 111 and travel 2.3 miles, following the signs to Caney Lakes Recreation Area. Turn left at the information area to reach the trailhead, which will be just ahead on your left. You can park at the trailhead.

Begin hiking, following the trail's metal, diamond-shaped markers. It's clear that these markers have been here for a long time; many look as if they've been eaten by the trees as the bark grows around them. Often covered with sweet-smelling pine needles, the trail is quite level; you will meet a few rolling inclines a little farther on. Among the trees, you'll see sweet gum, pine, red maple, yaupon, dogwood, and sassafras. At the time of this writing, much of the first 0.3 mile of the trail was scrubby and exposed to sunlight. You won't feel as if you're fully in the woods until you cross a small footbridge, descend briefly, then cross a short boardwalk. After making a sharp left turn, the trail remains straight and level until it reaches the Turtle-Slide Loop Campground road at 0.4 mile. Follow the road across a drainage area, then bear right to reenter the woods. Following the blazes, you'll immediately turn left after stepping into the pine-dominated woods.

The loop segment begins at 0.5 mile. Bear to the right where the trail forks to hike it counterclockwise. The trail will fork a second time; bear left. (The spur to the right will just take you back to the campground.) The trail forks once more at 0.6 mile, with the trail to the left leading to the boat launch. Bear right, then exit the woods approximately 100 yards beyond the fork. Turn right here, heading toward a bridge, which you'll cross over the bottleneck between Upper Caney Lake to your left and Lower Caney Lake to your right. Before these lakes were dammed, the land was used for farming sugar cane—hence the name of the trail. Although no longer farmed in this spot, sugar cane is still an abundant crop in other parts of the state.

The path leads to a T intersection at Upper Caney Lake. Turn right to walk across the dam, a narrow levee between the two lakes. Small trees and shrubs grow on either side of the path, blocking the upcoming view of Upper Caney in late spring and summer. In winter, however, this walk is particularly scenic.

The levee segment ends at the junction with the Lost Woman Bike Trail, one of three connecting bike trails blazed by local mountain bikers. This trail literally got its name because a local woman became lost while hiking the trail before it was fully blazed. The woman got so disoriented that she ended up having to swim part of the lake to get back to an area that was familiar to her. If you choose to hike this rugged side trail, be assured that it is now well blazed, and that you're not likely to share the fate of the lost woman. Be aware that this trail does *not* loop back to the Sugar Cane Trail.

Bear left to remain on the Sugar Cane Trail. Regardless of the season, you'll gain expansive views of Upper Caney Lake here. The remainder of the trail circles Upper Caney, generally staying close to the sometimes marshy bank. In mid-March, this area is made more scenic by the blooming wild azaleas, red buckeyes, and dogwoods.

The trail crosses two footbridges in the next 0.2 mile and passes several interpretive signs. In early spring, you're likely to see violet wood sorrel blooming in the open areas of the hike. A common wildflower in Louisiana, violet wood sorrel has lobed, cloverlike leaflets, each of which may be streaked with a smudge of reddish brown. These wildflowers often grow in clumps and have five lavender petals. Wildflowers are particularly abundant in the forest gaps along the trail, where large trees have fallen and opened up the forest canopy. The resulting minimal shade and intense sunlight also allow scores of oak, pine, and red maple saplings to sprout. You'll also see huckleberry, muscadine, and poison ivy vines along the trail.

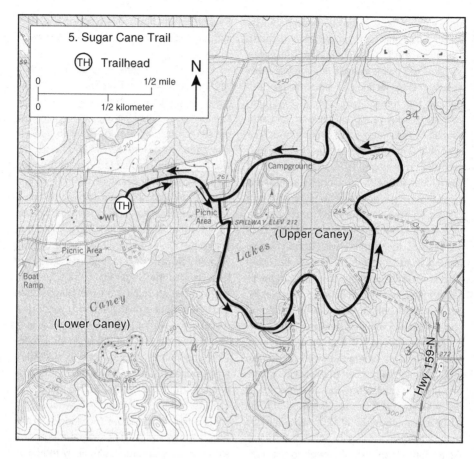

Occasionally, the Sugar Cane Trail meanders briefly away from the lake. Cross a small dirt road at 1.5 miles, and bear left to return to the scrubby bank, where wax myrtle is plentiful and wild azaleas bloom in March. The trail here is very sandy and heads uphill for a short distance before leveling out in a cleared area at 1.6 miles. In this sunny spot, look for shrub-size yaupon and sassafras saplings. The trail heads downhill at 1.7 miles, passing red buckeye and various oaks. You'll have another view of the lake to the left when the trail levels out again. In spring, look for the graceful flowers of the fringe tree.

You'll also see some witch hazel, the tiny yellow flowers of which bloom late in the year. You can identify this shrub by its wide, wavy-lobed leaves and the aromatic smell of its leaves when crushed. According to a myth of witchcraft, its forked branches could lead to groundwater. More fascinating to me is the witch hazel's fruit. These hard, light brown capsules mature in autumn and, upon drying out, will shoot their shiny black seeds up to 30 feet away!

After swinging to the right at 1.8 miles, you will reach an old road trace to the right. Here, the Sugar Cane Trail forks. The right fork is the Kona's Run Bike Trail, which will

Metal blaze being "eaten" by tree trunk

rejoin the Sugar Cane Trail later. Bear left to continue the Sugar Cane Trail, which enters a low, wet area at 1.9 miles. Look for blackberries among the shrubby wax myrtle and yaupon. When crossing a footbridge at 2 miles, you might notice the short, quick movements of a green anole as it skitters nearby. This chameleonic little lizard is common in Louisiana, though it's not always its characteristic bright green and can change to dark brown in a matter of seconds.

The trail soon swings right, away from the lake view to begin winding through the woods, making for a pleasant, level walk. You'll reach another low, potentially soggy spot at 2.2 miles. As you cross a 100-foot boardwalk, look for southern sugar maples—a somewhat common tree in the hilly regions of the Gulf coastal plain, but present in only a few isolated areas of inland Louisiana.

You're still in a low, hardwood-dominated area at 2.3 miles when the trail crosses another footbridge over a slow-moving creek. Although the path can be muddy here, the area itself is particularly scenic—not only is the creek a pleasing sight, but this low area is full of ferns, some lichens, and numerous dogwoods.

Swing to the left after crossing the footbridge. At 2.5 miles, you're back in pine country, hiking on flat, level trail. The sandy, beachlike path has approached the lake again by 2.7 miles, and it swings right to head uphill and level out at 2.8 miles. This is where the Kona's Run Trail rejoins the hiking trail. Continuing the Sugar Cane Trail, head back downhill, noticing the scenic views of the lake to your left.

You've moved away from the lake again by 2.9 miles, and will walk beneath large, fat pines and smaller hardwoods. When you reach a power line clearing at 3.4 miles, turn left to walk down the cleared corridor. The trail is not well marked here, and hikers may get confused about where the trail swings back into the woods. You actually want to stay on this straight path for a while. At 3.6 miles, it crosses a bridge, then passes through a not-so-scenic area that is often muddy and wet. Cross another bridge (still beneath the power line) at 3.7 miles; then, at 3.8 miles, you will veer left, back into the woods.

The Sugar Cane Trail widens and soon begins a long, flat, mostly straight segment that is nicely shaded in spring and summer. At 4.2 miles is an interpretive sign for American beech. You may not see any beeches next to the sign, but you will see plenty in the next half mile of the hike, many of them quite large. At 4.3 miles, the trail passes a little creek on the left. If you make too much noise, you might spook the turtles that can often be seen sunning on the logs in the creek. Cross a footbridge at 4.4 miles, then cross another soon afterward. You may start hearing cars soon, as you're nearing the road to the Beaver Dam Loop campground. After passing a 4.5-mile marker (look for more southern sugar maples here),

you'll cross yet another footbridge. While beeches are still dominant here, you'll also see the usual mix of pines, oaks, hickories, and dogwoods.

At 5 miles, the Sugar Cane Trail seems to split. The path to the left goes to the Beaver Dam Loop Campsites—and a couple of nice lunch spots, along with a restroom. Another trail goes to the left soon afterward. Both times, bear right to remain on the Sugar Cane Trail.

Cross a power line clearing at 5.2 miles and enter a beautiful area of mostly hardwoods before exiting again at the boat launch road. Bear right to follow the road, exercising extreme caution. Because the road has no shoulder and a curve lies just ahead, hikers may be vulnerable to oncoming cars.

Fortunately, this little road walk is only about 100 feet long, and you'll soon turn left to return to the woods, following the metal diamonds past eastern hophornbeam and ironwood. When you reach the main road, bear to the right, keeping an eye out for the trail sign that directs you back into the woods. Two trails are visible when you reenter the woods; take the right fork. Soon, cross the campground road, then pass the 5.5-mile marker. This is where the Sugar Cane Loop ends. You will need to rehike the spur trail back to the trailhead for a total hike of 6.2 miles.

6

White Tail Trail

Total distance (circuit): 3.3 miles

Hiking time: 2 hours

Habitats: Mixed pine and hardwood

Maps: USGS 7½' Marsalis,
State Park map

Hikers who treasure the challenge of hilly terrain, thrill at the sight of small waterfalls, and enjoy spring wildflowers would do well to trek Lake Claiborne State Park's White Tail Trail, a 3.3-mile hike through hilly, mixed pine and hardwood forest. To get to the park from I-20, take LA 9 (Exit 67) north for 7.8 miles to Athens, where the highway junctions with LA 518. Turn right onto LA 518 and travel 8.4 miles through Marsalis to LA 416. Following the signs to the park, turn left after another mile onto State Park Road, which leads to the entrance station. Here, you can obtain a map of the trail system.

Identifiable by an archway, the trailhead for the white-blazed White Tail Trail (as well as the red-blazed Whispering Pines Bike Trail) is to the right of the entrance road as you drive in. The bike trail immediately veers to the left, so you want to hike straight ahead, following the white blazes. As you descend slightly, look to the left for an old homesite, identifiable by smooth-trunked crepe myrtles growing among the oaks, hickories, maples, and pines. Although not native to Louisiana, crepe myrtles have been heavily planted and thrive in neighborhoods across the state.

The hiking trail and the bike trail braid back and forth, intersecting often, so you'll need to watch closely for the white blazes. You'll soon begin a downhill trek that includes a set of steps. The trail levels out before its junction with the yellow-blazed Dogwood Trail, a 0.2-mile spur that leads back to the entrance station. Bear left and resume the descent, some of which runs

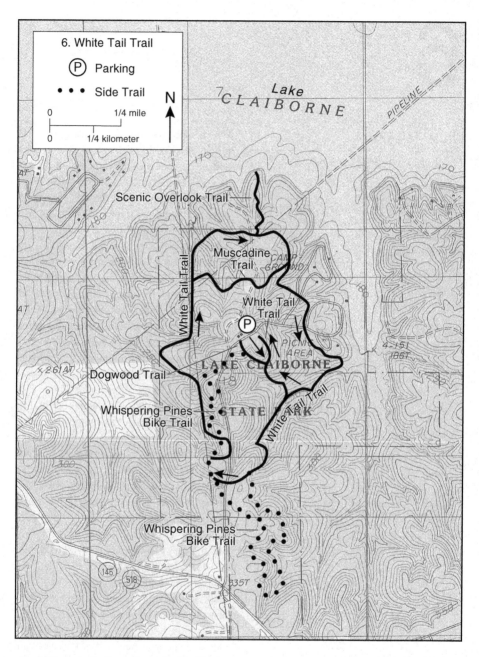

6. White Tail Trail

Ⓟ Parking

• • • Side Trail

N

alongside a dry gully to the right. You'll start to see more beech trees as the elevation decreases. Cross an unnamed creek over a footbridge at 0.3 mile. This creek, which empties into Lake Claiborne, features a small waterfall to the south. Waterfalls are rare in Louisiana, and the ones we do have are barely big enough to be worthy of the

Oak leaf hydrangeas bloom in spring throughout Louisiana.

name. You can, however, find them in a few places in the state, where sandstone and gravel have resisted erosion, unlike the surrounding landscape, thus resulting in small but significant elevation changes.

Swing to the right after crossing the bridge, passing several more large beeches. The White Tail loop begins at a T intersection just ahead. Bear right to hike the trail clockwise. The trail here is pretty level, and the terrain to the right slopes down to the creek. With numerous beeches and dogwoods, this section is both scenic and shady. At eye level, you might notice some cottony "balls" with brownish-pink spots growing on the leaves or stems of white oak saplings. Wool sower galls and the similar, brown oak apple galls are formed by the grub secretions of tiny pests called gall wasps. Although they can be harmful, the

spring-occurring galls usually do not occur in great enough abundance to cause lasting damage to a white oak.

The bike trail joins the hiking trail at 0.4 mile. After crossing another footbridge, you will enter an area that was disturbed by the pine beetle epidemic of the late 20th century. While the effect at Lake Claiborne was not as severe as at other areas in Louisiana, you'll see clear evidence of the damage here, as many pine saplings are now growing where the older, diseased trees had to be removed. In early summer, look for blackberries growing in this spot, which will continue to receive lots of sunlight until the saplings grow large enough to provide shade.

At 0.7 mile, atop a small hill, the bike trail parts from the hiking trail once again; bear right, following the white blazes. You'll soon cross the park's entrance road and a cleared highline. Shortly after reentering the woods, keep your eyes open for a prickly ash, also known as Hercules'-club or toothache tree. Rangers have found only one prickly ash in the entire park, and it's right here on the White Tail Trail.

The hiking trail descends and soon reaches a gas pipeline. This cleared corridor serves intermittently as the White Tail Trail—and, at times, the bike trail—for a good portion of the hike. Once you've turned right to reenter the woods at 0.9 mile (watch for the white blazes and sign), the trail follows gently rolling terrain beneath a wealth of blooming dogwoods as it crisscrosses with the bike trail.

Lake Claiborne State Park is home to any number of owls, those fascinating birds that haunt the night as they seek small mammals for their meals. Great horned owls, barn owls, barred owls, and eastern screech owls are all common here. But did you know that the winter migrations bring two less-common owls to this little region of Louisiana? The burrowing owl, with its distinctive long legs and habit of perching on the ground in broad daylight, has been spotted here, even though it is more common south and west of Louisiana. Strangely enough, this area has also been a site for winter-migrating snowy owls. These large white raptors generally winter in the marshes and open fields of the northern United States, but every now and then, one has been spotted as far south as Texas, in parts of Florida, and in the vicinity of Lake Claiborne in Louisiana.

Return to the gas pipeline at 1 mile, bearing right to hike the cleared corridor for about 0.2 mile before reentering the woods to the left at a large post. The White Tail Trail descends, and then levels out at 1.4 miles to begin a pleasant, gently rolling hike past

sweet gum, pines, muscadine, and a sizable white oak. You'll see more white oak as the trail descends in elevation, then reaches a low, wet area at 1.6 miles, where ironwoods, with their smooth, sinewy trunks, are abundant.

When the White Tail Trail rejoins the gas pipeline, swing left to hike the pipeline corridor for 0.1 mile, then reenter the woods to your right. The trail soon junctions with the Muscadine Trail, an alternate route—and a shortcut—that rejoins the White Tail Trail in 0.4 mile. Continuing along the white-blazed White Tail Trail, you'll cross a creek bed at 1.9 miles. Head uphill briefly, then back downhill to a footbridge and a very scenic area. You may be able to see the guest cabins off to the left of this moist, shady spot, which is dominated by numerous pines and beeches.

When you reach a T intersection at 2 miles, bear right. (The left is a spur trail back to the cabins.) The path briefly parallels a small, dry creek bed before exiting the woods to cross the cabin road at 2.2 miles. After passing through the overflow parking area, you'll find yourself at the junction with the red-blazed Scenic Overlook Trail, actually a spur to a platform affording a view of Lake Claiborne. By hiking this spur and back, you'll add approximately 0.5 mile to your total trek.

Bear right and back into the woods to continue the White Tail Trail, which soon swings left to parallel the gas pipeline. On this segment of the hike, you might notice some furrowing of the ground—a result of farming, which was the primary use of this land before the Louisiana Office of State Parks purchased it. This area is full of pines, and the ground is covered with fragrant pine needles.

Head downhill at 2.3 miles to cross a road leading to Camping Area 2. Following the white blazes, you'll continue downhill to a beech-lined, fern-filled creek. The footbridge that crosses it is a good spot for a break, with the steep creek walls below and the shady beeches overhead. Can you spot the tiny oxbow lake-in-the-making to your left? Bear right on the White Tail Trail after crossing the bridge (an unofficial trail goes straight ahead to the camp area), and head back uphill. The trail approaches Camping Area 1 at 2.5 miles, then crosses the park's entrance and exit roads shortly afterward. Follow the white blazes to reenter the woods, and begin a steep descent to a footbridge. In spring, this spot sees a profusion of blooming wild azaleas.

The winding White Tail Trail heads back uphill, straightening out to parallel a road to the left. Exit the woods at 2.7 miles, then walk straight ahead to cross the road near the entrance station, looking for the small post indicating where the trail returns to the woods. You'll hike past numerous red cedars before reaching a T intersection. To the left is a short path to the picnic area, which is clearly visible from the trail at this point. Bear right on the White Tail Trail, looking for more wild azaleas in bloom. Swing to the left after a short drop-off, following the small creek bed to the right.

The trail crosses the creek bed a couple of times before veering to the right, away from the creek bed, at 3 miles. You'll pass through a cleared area, then at 3.1 miles, after a short descent, you're heading back uphill and will soon reach an intersection and the completion of the loop. Bear right to return to the trailhead. You'll pass the Dogwood Trail junction at 3.2 miles and will reach the trailhead and entrance station shortly afterward.

7

Driskill Mountain

Total distance (round-trip): 1.6 miles

Hiking time: 1 hour

Habitats: Mixed pine and hardwood

Maps: USGS 7½' Bryceland

Driskill Mountain, the highest point in Louisiana, towers 535 feet above sea level—the lowest high point west of the Mississippi River and the third-lowest high point in the United States. "High-pointers" (people who aim to climb each state's high point) come from all over the country to climb this little mountain in north Louisiana—which, admittedly, is really more of a hill than a mountain. The Louisiana Hiking Club has a tradition of climbing Driskill each year on January 1. On a particularly cold New Year's Day in 2001, the enthusiastic climbing team was thrilled to find a snow-covered summit.

Although the mountain is not as visually impressive as the rugged, flat-topped hills of Kisatchie National Forest, Driskill has its own intriguing stories. It was near here that Bonnie and Clyde had their last stand; they were killed on May 23, 1934 approximately 16 miles north of the mountain. The outlaws were actually quite well known in this part of Louisiana. If you travel to nearby towns, you might find some old-timers whose families were known to the duo.

Geologically, Driskill Mountain lies in the Nagodoches Wold, a rim of high ground (relatively speaking) that encircles the Sabine Uplift, the series of domed rock beds comprising Louisiana's hilly northwestern corner. Driskill itself is capped with ironstone, which has allowed it to stand tall while the surrounding land eroded down. The short hike to the top will provide several views of the surrounding piney woods.

To get to Driskill Mountain from Shreveport, take I-20 to Arcadia, exiting on

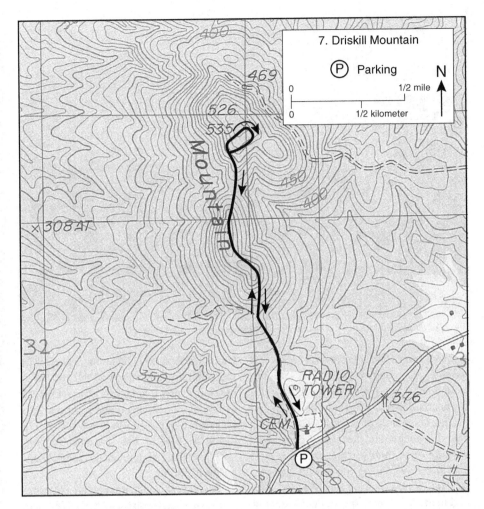

LA 147 (Exit 69) and driving south. Stay on LA 147 until it junctions with LA 797, then go south on LA 797 until it hits LA 507. Park at Mount Zion Presbyterian Church and Driskill Memorial Cemetery, which is on LA 507 and will be on approximately 2 miles down the road to your right.

If you are traveling from the south, your best bet is to get onto US 167 at Alexandria and travel north to Jonesboro. Just north of Jonesboro (at Hodge), get onto LA 147, driving north until it junctions with LA 507. Turn left onto LA 507 and proceed to the church and cemetery. Outhouses are available in the parking area.

The "trail" begins on the dirt road to left of the cemetery next to the church. A path skirts the closed gate, which is about 100 feet up the trail. Note that this is private property; however, no signs are posted, and the few hikers and high-pointers who frequent this area are welcome. Please respect the fact that private landowners allow us to visit this high point. Swing to the right after passing the gate, rejoining the road and heading uphill through this heavily

The hike up Driskill Mountain provides views of the surrounding piney woods.

timbered area. Pass a tower at 0.1 mile. You haven't really begun the "climb" up the mountain; in fact, the mostly level trail actually heads *downhill* every now and then.

The road forks at 0.2 mile. Go straight ahead, through the next gate. Bear right after the gate, and you'll soon see a sign with an arrow pointing you toward the summit. You're now in a pocket of mixed pine and hardwood forest and will see plenty of fringe tree, pine, loblolly pine, red maple, dogwood, hickory, redbud, red oak, red buckeye, and sweet gum. In spring and summer, vines of wild grape trail from the trees and carpet the ground.

The trail descends slightly into a Louisiana-style "saddle" at 0.3 mile, and at 0.4 mile you'll reach a piney area that also features lots of white oak and wax myrtle, as well as more red maple and redbud. The trail continues downhill shortly afterward, then heads uphill at 0.5 mile in the final climb to the 535-foot summit. When the trail levels out at 0.7 mile, it forks into a loop. Bear left to find an old campsite and an overlook of Louisiana's piney woods. There is also a lot of red buckeye on this "mountaintop" site; look for their characteristic red-flowered spikes in spring.

Swing to the right, through the old campsite. Just ahead, you'll see the official summit, marked by a cairn of red rocks. In sunny, warm weather, look for lizards sunning on this rock mountain; you may have to look closely, as their effective camouflage renders them nearly invisible against the terra cotta-colored rocks. Next to the cairn is a box with a register; don't forget to sign it!

To return to your car, you can retrace your steps past the overlook, or you can continue the loop. Either way, your hike will total approximately 1.6 miles.

8

Lake D'Arbonne State Park

Total distance (circuit): 3.9 miles

Hiking time: 2.5 hours

Habitats: Mixed pine and hardwood, nontidal marsh

Maps: USGS 7½' Farmerville, park map

Lake D'Arbonne State Park occupies a delightfully hilly region in north Louisiana. The park, along with its trail system, has undergone extensive expansion in recent years. A newly developed maze of trails includes a scenic walk on the shores of Lake D'Arbonne and a descent to a small, fern-choked waterfall on the route through mixed pine and hardwood forest.

Because the park's five trails often interconnect, it would be difficult to cover every foot of trail in a single hike. You can choose from an endless number of routes, though. The trail system offers loops and allows for shortcuts (and "longcuts") using the park's road system. At the time of this writing, the trails did not have specific names, so I will refer to them by the colors with which they are marked (for example, the arrows that mark the Yellow Trail are on a yellow background). The hike described here will take you through a little bit of everything, starting with the Yellow Trail at the entrance station, then shifting to the White Trail for a walk along the shores of Lake D'Arbonne. Next, you'll hop onto the scenic Orange Trail, which crosses a small bridge in the center of the park. You'll turn onto the Green Trail, which will rejoin the White Trail and lead back to the entrance station for a complete loop of 3.9 miles. The Green and Orange Trails are the most secluded in the park, while the others pass by more populated areas from time to time. All trails are open to mountain bikers as well as hikers.

To get to the park from I-20, take LA 33 (Exit 86) north from Ruston to Farmerville. In

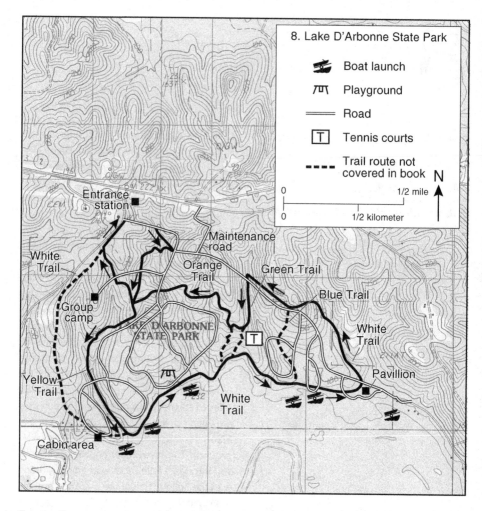

Entrance station

Maintenance road

White Trail

Orange Trail

Green Trail

Blue Trail

Group camp

LAKE D'ARBONNE STATE PARK

White Trail

Yellow Trail

T

Pavillion

White Trail

Cabin area

Farmerville, turn west onto LA 2, following the signs to the park. Drive the short distance to Evergreen Road, then turn left onto Evergreen and drive approximately 0.3 mile to the park entrance, where parking is available.

Begin hiking on the Yellow Trail, which begins just south of the park's entrance station (on the right as you drive in). Less than 100 yards into your hike, the trail forks; bear right to begin a winding descent. In spring, you'll see flowering dogwoods, wild azaleas, and mayapples all over this path, which lev-

els out after 0.1 mile. Cross the cleared group camp road after this, bearing slightly left. The trail reenters the woods; look for yellow and orange blazes. Although you're still on the Yellow Trail, the orange blazes indicate that this is one route to reach the Orange Trail. As the Yellow Trail contours a small ridge, look downhill to your left to see a small creek.

At 0.3 mile is the junction of the Yellow and Orange Trails with the group camp up the hill to your right. Hike straight ahead, remaining on the Yellow Trail. You will hike part

Resurrection ferns

of the Orange Trail later on. The trail here is straight, level, and rather rocky—particularly rocky, if you compare it to most of the state's other trails. The ironstone of this terrain is a red iron oxide formed from the rusted remnants a green mineral called *glauconite*. Because glauconite generally forms on shallow sea floors, the presence of ironstone here today is a reminder that this hilly region was once at the bottom of the sea, and that these rolling hills have been heavily carved by erosion since the last Ice Age.

As in much of the United States, white-tailed deer are common throughout Louisiana. When the male deer's antlers first begin to grow, they are covered with a soft layer of skin or "velvet" that has numerous blood vessels to transport vital nutrients, such as calcium and phosphorus, for building the antlers. That layer of skin remains plush until early fall, when the blood supply shuts off and the antlers begin to harden.

The skin on the antlers begins to dry and peel, and the buck furthers that process by rubbing its antlers against trees and other woody vegetation. You'll see evidence of deer rubbings on two red cedars after 0.4 miles, shortly after passing over a culvert. Notice how the bark has been worn away on their trunks.

The trail traverses a bridge through a low area at 0.5 mile, then winds a bit and begins a descent. You will reach a scenic view of the creek below at 0.7 mile. These woods are a great place to hike in winter, when the leaves are down and you can get a clear idea of how hilly this region's terrain really is. Wind down a little further until the creek is about 10 feet to your left. This moist bottom area is full of pine and beech, and the creek banks are rich with ferns.

Continue hiking to cross the cabin road, turning left to cross the creek as well. Following the arrows, swing right to return

---

Lake D'Arbonne State Park

to the woods. Back on the trail, you're still in a low area, only the creek is now to your right. Large American beeches make this spot particularly scenic. In late fall, the leaves of this smooth-trunked tree turn a blazing gold. Beech leaves will ultimately give way to a light brown color and will hang on throughout the winter, until the new, tightly rolled leaves begin to push their way through. Wildlife, particularly squirrels and raccoons, feed on the autumn-maturing beechnuts. Other trees in this low, moist spot include common sweetleaf, ironwood, eastern hophornbeam, and American holly.

The Yellow Trail leads south, approaching scenic Lake D'Arbonne, with its tall cypresses rising from the water. At 1 mile, the trail crosses a footbridge and turns into gravel as it nears the populated cabin area. It soon reaches a T intersection, where the Yellow Trail ends at the White Trail. Bear left onto the White Trail, staying on the gravel pathway. The flat trail runs alongside the lakeshore toward the camping area, crossing a footbridge and passing a boat dock at 1.1 miles. As you approach the camping area, you might notice several side trails leading to the left. Stay on the main trail—unless someone in your group needs to use the camping area's comfort station, or perhaps the kid with you—or the kid in you—wants to take a break to explore the park's nearby playground.

Continuing to provide excellent views of Lake D'Arbonne, the White Trail soon passes a sizable fishing pier and several small boat docks. These piers are a great vantage point for watching great egrets as they forage along the lake's shallow margins. The paved trail returns to dirt when it reaches another long pier. At 1.5 miles, the path temporarily departs from the lake. A spur trail to the left leads to the camping area; you want to bear right, following the white blazes. Soon afterward, this path meets the Orange Trail. If you turn left here, the Orange Trail will eventually take you back to where you crossed it earlier in your hike, near the group camp. For now, keep following the White Trail. You will hike a portion of the Orange Trail toward the end of your trek.

The rest of the White Trail is flat, level, and scenic as it continues to hug the shores of Lake D'Arbonne. You'll cross a footbridge, then at 1.7 miles you will reach the intersection with the Green Trail. Again, stick to the white blazes. You'll walk part of the Green Trail a little later in the hike. After passing the park's pavilion at 1.8 miles, the trail becomes paved again. You're now in an active, populated area of the park; in the next half-mile, you will walk by the visitor center, a comfort station, several boat docks and fishing piers, two pavilions, and a picnic area, in addition to crossing several park roads. You'll also leave the scenic lakeshore to begin a more secluded hike through mixed pine and hardwood forest. If you're ready for a mid-hike break, you might want to step into the visitor center, which will be on your left. Nature exhibits, bathrooms, and a water fountain can all be found in this building, which was just completed in 2002.

At 1.9 miles, the trail swings right to follow an old railroad tram, then crosses a footbridge. The path forks soon afterward; you can really go either way, as the spur to the right rejoins the railroad tram after about 100 yards, shortly before it meets the south end of the Blue Trail. The Blue Trail cuts through the populated day-use area, whereas the White Trail goes around it. Stay on the White Trail, which will lead you to the parking area for the boat dock. Walk down the road on the other side of the parking lot for a short distance; you will soon see an arrow next to the playground, pointing you back into the woods. The White Trail leads through the playground and past a picnic area and a comfort station. Cross a footbridge, then bypass two more pavilions. When you reach the next road at 2.2 miles, bear left as you cross. Here, you'll finally see the sign for the nature trail.

Reenter the woods at this point. The trail swings left and quickly becomes more secluded. When it forks at 2.5 miles, bear left rather than going straight ahead (the spur merely leads to a property line). The trail slopes downhill, swings left, and reaches the road again soon afterward. When you reach the road, you'll see the north end of the Blue Trail. You'll now hike a 0.3-mile road walk to the Green Trail. Turn right onto the road, passing the Blue Trail access point and heading uphill. As you walk, look to the left for evidence of an old homesite. You can recognize former homesites by the planted tree species, such as the sinewy crepe myrtles, growing among the oaks, hickories, and pines more typical of northern Louisiana forests.

At 2.9 miles, you will see a sign on your left for the Green, Orange, and White Trails. Turn left here, back into the woods; you are now on the Green Trail, which winds downhill for a short distance. Soon after it levels out, it meets the Orange Trail. Take a sharp right onto the Orange Trail, which continues the downhill trek for approximately 0.1 mile before reaching a bottom area that is rife with hardwoods and has very few pines. Blooming red buckeye and dogwood make this area even more scenic in spring. The trail arcs to the right and begins to descend again, very gently, toward a bridge. Cross the bridge at 3.1 miles, and look to your right to see a small waterfall. Unless there has been a severe drought, these "falls" are believed to flow all year long.

Reach a T intersection after crossing the bridge. The route to the left will take you back to the camping area, so you want to bear right to continue the Orange Trail. Begin a gentle ascent, winding past hardwoods and an increasing number of pines. The trail meanders over the rolling hills before exiting the woods again at 3.4 miles. Cross the road just ahead, bearing left until you see the arrow pointing you back into the woods on the right.

The Orange Trail heads back downhill, only to level out at a footbridge. You'll go back uphill after crossing the low area, and at 3.6 miles the trail intersects with the Yellow Trail again. Turn right to follow the Yellow Trail, walking another 0.3 mile to finish your hike at the entrance station, for a total trek of 3.9 miles.

9

Kiroli Park Outer Trail

Total distance (circuit): 2.2 miles

Hiking time: 1 hour

Habitats: Mixed pine and hardwood forest, cypress swamp

Maps: USGS 7½' West Monroe North, park map

Kiroli Park's 3-mile trail system is a popular walking trail for Monroe-area residents and is particularly scenic in spring, when the mayapples are out, the red buckeye spikes are visible, and the azaleas are in full bloom. If you're looking for a rugged wilderness adventure, Kiroli Park's paved trails probably won't meet your needs. But if you're seeking a pleasant, wildlife-rich walk through a mature mixed pine and hardwood pocket of forest, you might want to check out this trail system, which is just a few miles north of I-20 in West Monroe.

Kiroli Park has been an active part of the Monroe community for more than 75 years. In 1925, a group of 40 pioneers of Scouting purchased 126 acres of rolling hills west of Monroe, with plans to make it a Scouting camp. Because the Kiwanis, Rotary, and Lions Clubs each put up $100 for the purchase price of the land, the area was dubbed Camp Kiroli—"Ki" from *Kiwanis,* "ro" from *Rotary,* and "li" from *Lions.* Camp Kiroli was a successful Boy Scout camp for five decades and even served as a refugee camp during the infamous Mississippi River flood of 1927. In 1974, a new property was purchased for the Scouts, and the Ouachita Parish Police Jury bought the Kiroli property. In 1987, the City of West Monroe took over and made major improvements to it. Today, Kiroli Park has numerous amenities for area residents and visitors; one of its latest additions is the Wetlands Trail, a quarter-mile boardwalk that begins near the park's entrance.

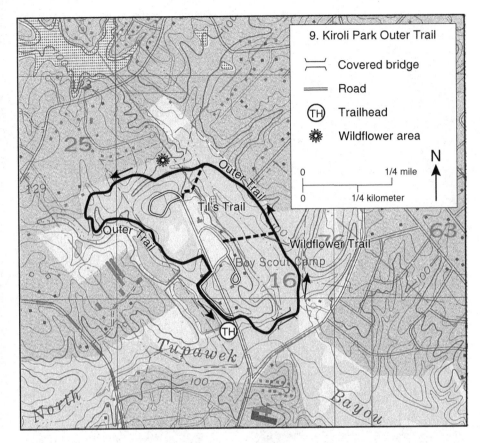

9. Kiroli Park Outer Trail

	Covered bridge
	Road
(TH)	Trailhead
✳	Wildflower area

N

0 _____ 1/4 mile

0 _____ 1/4 kilometer

To get to Kiroli Park, take I-20 to LA 617 (Thomas Road) in West Monroe. Follow LA 617 north; it will turn left to merge with US 80 and LA 15 (Cypress Street). A quarter of a mile down Cypress Street, turn right onto Warren Drive, continuing on LA 617. Less than a mile farther, turn left onto Arkansas Road. From there, follow the signs to Kiroli Park, located at 820 Kiroli Road. The park charges a fifty-cent fee to visitors.

A short distance past the entrance station is a parking area on the left. The trail, which is paved, starts on the right side of the road, directly across from the parking lot. In the spring, you'll notice tulips, camellias, and numerous other flowers planted in the gardens near the trail. The trail itself winds into the woods after about 200 feet, where you'll encounter loblolly pine, sweet gum, various oaks and hickories, and the invasive Chinese privet. Planted azaleas grace the trails in early spring, with the flowers beginning to bloom in mid-March.

Kiroli Park's trail system is a maze of interconnecting paths, but the hike described here primarily covers the system's Outer Trail. To remain on this outer loop, bear right whenever you reach a fork in the trail. You'll come to several such junctions within the first 0.1 mile. You'll eventually happen upon a covered bridge across a low, wet area at 0.3 mile. Shortly after this is another bridge

A trail bridge leads to a small observation tower.

through this same low area; after crossing it, head up an incline toward a small tower. Once the leaves are out, there isn't much to see, but winter affords a pleasant view of the surrounding area. Look for resurrection fern growing above your head after you've climbed the tower.

Back on the trail, swing to the left to reach the spot where the Outer Trail joins the Wildflower Trail at 0.5 mile. Bear to the right. Many mature pines and a minimum of undergrowth characterize this section of the hike. Soon, you'll reach a cleared area dubbed Wildflower Hill by the park. If you're here in April, you'll see southern blue flag, clasping leaf coneflower, mimosa, yellow-fringed orchid, pinewood lily, cardinal flower, Japanese honeysuckle, wild azalea, trumpet creeper, spiny thistle, and passion flower, among others.

Back on the Outer Trail, reenter the woods at 0.6 mile, and you'll find yourself among a stand of mature pines. At just under 0.7 mile is a bench. Soon afterward, as the land drops slightly in elevation, notice that more beeches are present. Cross a drainage area, where moisture-loving southern magnolias grow—not as common a tree here as in southern Louisiana. The prevalent trees in this section, other than loblolly pine, are oaks and hickories. You'll also see plenty of sweet gum and ironwood.

Cross a bridge at just after 0.8 mile, then go right when the trail forks. You'll cross two more bridges before the trail swings left, bordering a nearby neighborhood on the right. The trail swings left once again before reaching the junction with Til's Trail at 1.1 miles. Til's Trail is a loop nestled within the Outer Trail. As usual, bear to the right, winding past pines, oaks, hickories, and an over-growth of Chinese privet. Til's Trail parts from the Outer Trail at 1.3 miles; continue to the right on the Outer Trail, exiting the woods and nearing a picnic table overlooking a pond to your right. From here, you'll pass numerous trees, many of them labeled—sweet gum, American elm, winged elm, and others.

At 1.4 miles, you definitely get the sense that you've rejoined civilization, as your immediate surroundings quickly change from flowers and trees to picnic tables and tennis courts. At 1.5 miles, an old fire engine and caboose are to your right, adding a bit of historical interest to the hike. When you reach the road at 1.6 miles, you can continue to bear right, walking a quarter mile to return to the main gate and parking lot.

If you're not ready to stop hiking, you can extend the hike by rejoining the Wildflower Trail. Simply turn right at the open field as if you're heading to the parking area, but turn left when you reach the first road. Walk past the bathrooms, then turn left when you reach the adjacent playgrounds. Turn right onto the paved trail, back into the woods. The more obvious signs of civilization disappear soon enough, as you are suddenly surrounded by pines and heading downhill toward two bridges. If you take the connecting trail to your right, just before the bridges, you'll get to cross the park's only suspension bridge. Because this bridge crosses another low, wet area, watch for beech and magnolia once again.

Once you've crossed the suspension bridge, you can go straight to retrace your steps over the covered bridge and beyond. To return to the parking area, go to the right. You'll reach the parking area after another 0.2 mile.

10

Black Bayou Lake Nature Trail

Total distance (circuit): 1.1 miles

Hiking time: 30–45 minutes

Habitats: Bottomland hardwood forest, prairie, cypress swamp

Maps: USGS 7½' Monroe North, "Wetland Connections" brochure

Even though northeast Louisiana does not boast long hiking trails, Monroe-area hikers have plenty of opportunities to stroll through various natural habitats within a short driving distance—from piney hills to pockets of bottomland hardwood forest, and from islands of upland hardwood to murky cypress swamps. Yes, north Louisiana has swamps. While these infinitely fertile, inimitably scenic wetlands are more associated with our coastal regions and bayous farther south, northeast Louisiana, located at the edge of the Mississippi Alluvial Valley, has its share of low-lying swamps, brakes, sloughs, and bayous. In fact, the North Louisiana Refuges Complex, based in Farmerville, manages approximately 10,500 acres of wetland habitat in 20 north Louisiana parishes.

Hikers can explore some of these wetlands by visiting Black Bayou Lake National Wildlife Refuge (NWR), just a few miles north of Monroe. Established in 1997, the 4,400-acre refuge features a gravel/boardwalk trail that snakes through cypress swamp and bottomland hardwood habitats. A spur trail leads to a 400-foot observation pier stretching into Black Bayou Lake. The beginning of the trail features plots of prairie revegetation. This 1.1-mile trek is more of a nature walk than an actual hike—one that begs you to take your time, preferably as you carry a pair of binoculars and a camera, to spot the refuge's rich variety of wildlife.

To get to the refuge, take US 165 north out of Monroe (Exit 118 on I-20) for approximately 4 miles. Following the Black Bayou Lake NWR signs, turn right off US 165 and

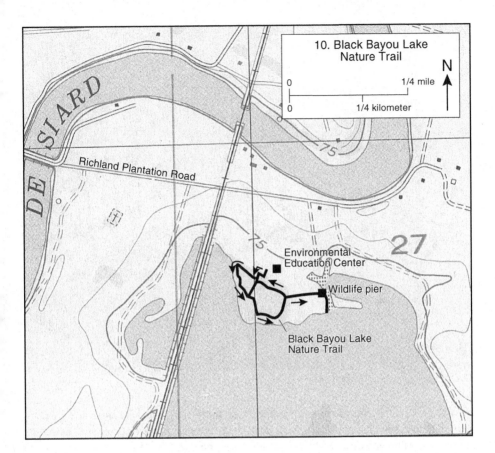

10. Black Bayou Lake Nature Trail

N

| 0 | 1/4 mile |
| 0 | 1/4 kilometer |

DESIARD

Richland Plantation Road

Environmental Education Center

Wildlife pier

27

Black Bayou Lake Nature Trail

drive to the parking area next to the Environmental Education Center. Be sure to step into the education center to pick up a copy of "Wetland Connections," the refuge's highly informative trail brochure.

The trailhead is located at the kiosk to the right of the education center. This spot also features an historic bell forged by the Buckeye Bell Foundry in 1892. Before you start hiking, notice the small, marshy pond next to the trailhead, full of irises and other showy flowers in spring.

The gravel trail leads you into a typical mixed bottomland hardwood habitat. "Typical" is a misleading description, however. Just a few feet in bottomland elevation will drastically change what kinds of trees will grow in a forest—a result that depends on differences in drainage and duration of flooding. The highest elevations tend to have willow and water oak, water locust, cedar elm, and persimmon. Just a few feet lower, you'll see Nuttall and overcup oak, water hickory, bitter pecan, box elder, American elm, sugarberry, sweet gum, and red maple. The lowest, most poorly drained areas of bottomland forests are the constantly flooded swamps, where you'll see bald cypress, often paired with water tupelo. The trail begins by passing beneath a mix of water locust, sugarberry, American elm, and willow oak—indicating that you are in a transition zone between the high and medium elevations of this forest. When the trail splits

Cypress trees in Black Bayou Lake

after approximately 100 yards, you want to bear right to begin the south loop. You'll see a low area with cypresses off to the left at 0.1 mile, then pass a bench shortly afterward. The trail swings left past another bench, then reaches the boardwalk at 0.2 mile.

Take a sharp left onto the boardwalk. Although you're not in the swamp just yet, you'll begin to see cypresses. You'll also see overcup oak, water locust, and bitter pecan, a hybrid of water hickory and pecan. Similar to the more common honey locust, the water locust has numerous clusters of heavy, sharp-pointed thorns along its trunk. Young water locusts are likely to have many spines, whereas the older, larger trees have fewer to none. The spines make this tree easy to identify. Honey locusts, which you won't see on this trail, have similar spines, but they gener-

ally thrive in slightly dryer areas and are common in other parts of Louisiana. On occasion, however, you'll see these two cousins growing in the same area.

As the boardwalk snakes through the swamp, look for all kinds of life in the murky water below. Red-eared sliders comb the muddy bottom, while a black racer slithers through the water beneath your feet. The trail becomes gravel again at 0.3 mile as you gain a bit of elevation. You'll reach the connecting trail shortly after that, but you want to keep going straight ahead to hike the northern loop. The trail passes another bench before turning to boardwalk again. Once it does, you'll find yourself in another swampy area.

At 0.5 mile, the trail forks. By bearing to the right, you can take the spur to the Wildlife Pier. The path includes an opportunity to see numerous wildflowers and butterflies in the open fields on either side of the paved walkway. At the end of the pier is a view of Black Bayou Lake. In fall and winter, look up to see a flock of greater white-fronted geese flying high in their characteristic V formation. On the surface of the lake, a large wintering flock of lesser scaups may be diving for small aquatic creatures, or a small group of gadwalls and American widgeon may be dabbling for aquatic plants nearby. You may spot a great blue heron or a great egret wading gracefully through the waters of this shallow lake.

Back on the main trail, you've worked your way out of the swamp and are on higher ground once again. Look for a flash of yellow in the persimmon understory as a prothonotary warbler, a common summer resident, flits among the branches in search of insects on the leaves and twigs. The boardwalk changes back to gravel trail, then you pass a bench soon afterward. Reach the cut-through trail again at 0.6 mile and bear right. You'll soon reach the end of the trail for a hike of just over 0.6 mile. If you walked to the end of the pier, you'll have walked a total of 1.1 miles.

11

Poverty Point
State Historic Site

Total distance (circuit): 2.6 miles

Hiking time: 1½ hours

Habitats: Upland hardwood

Maps: USGS 7½' Pioneer,
Poverty Point guidebook

Tucked away in Louisiana's northeastern corner, along the blufflike banks of Bayou Maçon, Poverty Point State Historic Site is a common side trip for visitors touring nearby Vicksburg, Mississippi. There is nothing common about this site, however, and it is worth a trip all its own. The 2.6-mile trail, built by Boy Scout Troop 8031 of Monroe in the mid-1980s, leads through scenic upland hardwood forest to some of the most intriguing archeological finds in all of North America.

It is a modest-looking little site. At first glance, you might find it hard to believe that this plot of land in Epps, Louisiana was once home to an advanced trading culture. After all, the artifacts are not so obvious. There are no huge pyramids to command your attention from a distance, no Stonehenge to impose on your sense of the present. Relatively little is known about the Poverty Point culture, though our knowledge constantly grows with the careful work of archeologists and historians.

We do know that the culture existed from about 1730 to 1350 b.c., and that it spanned parts of Louisiana, Mississippi, and Arkansas. Archaeologists posit that this was a trading culture, because many of the rocks found here, such as hematite and copper, are not local, and therefore must have been imported. The site, which includes a huge bird effigy, is characterized by a huge C-shaped arc formed by six concentric, manmade embankments that were once 6 to 10 feet tall. The exact purpose of

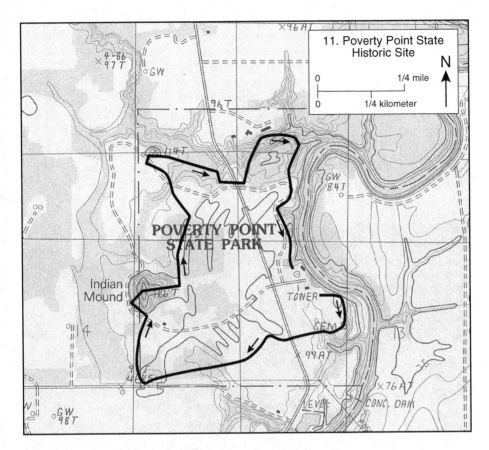

this massive series of earthworks—which stretches nearly three-quarters of a mile to end at the drop-off of Maçon Ridge—is unknown, but one thing is clear: No "primitive" culture built this strategically executed, highly organized mound system.

This tract of land, so shrouded in mystery, is maintained by the Louisiana Office of State Parks and is open to the public. To get there from I-20, take LA 17 at Delhi (Exit 153) and travel north to LA 134 in Epps. When LA 134 meets with LA 577 east of Epps, go north, following the signs to the site. Before starting your hike, be sure to visit the museum, which is manned by a staff knowledgeable in geology, history, and archaeology, and offers a fascinating display of artifacts. Consider watching the museum's 20-minute film to learn more about what you'll see on the hike. Don't forget to pick up a trail guide.

Wooden posts mark the 2.6-mile trail, though some of the trees in the forested areas are blazed with blue paint. Begin just behind the museum to the east, next to the archaeology laboratory. Yes, Poverty Point is an active archaeological site. Please be respectful of this and do not touch any artifacts that you might spot on your hike. As you begin hiking, notice a restricted area to the left. Beyond it is a 25-foot drop-off. If you have hiked at Port Hudson or Tunica

---

On Sarah's Mound is a small 19th-century cemetery situated on an Indian mound.

Hills, you'll recognize the vertically eroding terrain as loess, or windblown river silts from Pleistocene times. This is Maçon Ridge, a major bluff that reaches from southeastern Arkansas south to Sicily Island and marks the cutoff of the concentric Poverty Point embankments.

After passing the picnic area, you'll reach your first stop of interest: a "ghost hut" built by the park staff to give visitors an idea of what huts might have looked like during the time of the Poverty Point culture. Head downhill toward the next trail marker. When you reach it, look behind you to get a view of Maçon Ridge, noting its sharp contrast to the surrounding flatness.

The trail turns right and ascends toward a guidepost atop the mound just ahead. In spring, you'll see grape hyacinth blooming at your feet. These wildflowers look like tiny clusters of grapes shooting up from the ground. This open area also affords the opportunity to spot various raptors soaring overhead. Sharp-shinned, red-tailed, red-shouldered, and broad-winged hawks are regularly spotted at Poverty Point.

At the top of this mound, known as Sarah's Mound, is a much more recent artifact collection than those of the Poverty Point culture: a small 19th-century cemetery, burial ground of Sarah Guier and Amanda Malvina. It is from the Guier family that we get the name Poverty Point—which was what they called their plantation on this land. As the trail guide will tell you, it was not unusual for early Mississippi Valley settlers to bury their loved ones in Indian mounds, as the higher elevations rendered the mounds ideal for that purpose.

From here, the trail veers to the left, past a profusion of blooming redbuds in spring. Cross Highway 577 to reach Ridge 1, the innermost of the concentric ridges, at

Guidepost #5. This "ridge"—which is hardly noticeable, unless it's rained and water has collected in the dips between ridges—was originally between 6 and 10 feet tall. Archaeologists' discovery of tool-building implements here, as well as tools in different stages of preparation, suggests that this was the "industrial" area of the Poverty Point community.

Going straight ahead, you might notice animal tracks or disturbed earth at your feet. Wild hogs ravage parts of this site from time to time, and their evidence is obvious. At 0.5 mile, the trail enters the woods at another guidepost. Sweet gum and dwarf palmetto are common here, and the mayapples and violets put on quite a show in spring. The path briefly follows a "causeway" of the ancient Poverty Point civilization—a prehistoric, constructed berm that served as a raised path through this low, swampy area and possibly connected the outer communities to the inner hub of the site.

You will reach a cleared spot at just under 0.7 mile. When you get to the guidepost straight ahead, go to the right, walking alongside the road and up the slope of Mound E. From here, the trail leads across the flat, raised surface of the mound into the woods. Head back downhill at 0.9 mile, then walk through another small forest pocket toward the next guidepost.

After crossing an open field and passing a shelter at 1 mile, the trail heads to the left down the site's tram road. Straight ahead, the land rises up in a very different kind of mound; this is the tail of the giant bird effigy, which is clearly visible only from the air. Bearing to the right, walk toward the steps that lead up the bird's south wing. This is the toughest climb of the hike; while not a hard hike by most standards, it is amazing to think that this hill was built by human hands.

From the top of the effigy, look to the east. In wet seasons, you can see water in the swales between the Poverty Point ridges. The downward stairs also head to the east. Do you notice that the slope up the wing was much steeper than the slope down the tail? This suggests that the stairs you're now using were indeed the route that the ancient people used to travel up and down the effigy. As you descend, look to your left for the bright red spikes of blooming red buckeyes.

After descending from the effigy, the Poverty Point trail enters a brief wooded area. Listen for gray squirrels scurrying up the branches of the oaks. Occasionally a barred owl will create a rustling overhead as it swoops through the trees. At 1.4 miles, after you've exited and entered the woods again, notice a slightly raised area to your left. You're standing on the backside of Ridge 6—the outermost ridge of the Poverty Point earthworks. In only this section of the site, you can see evidence of a new ridge that the Poverty Point civilization had begun to construct—and a suggestion that the culture was making efforts to spread even further before its decline. As yet, no artifacts have been found on the unfinished Ridge 7.

As you continue hiking, be sure to stick to the mowed area that designates the trail. It will lead you back to the tram road at 1.5 miles, which you'll follow to a guidepost and through a drainage area that is low and usually wet. The trail heads to the right, leaving the road once again. You'll see a guidepost marker straight ahead and Mound B to your left. After reaching the guidepost, the trail veers to the right to reenter the woods. This section of the hike is particularly beautiful, as Spanish moss hangs from the trees, and resurrection fern on the bark comes to life in moist weather.

Cross a footbridge over tiny Holland Bayou at 1.7 miles, keeping an eye out for the next guidepost. The trail veers to the *left* to remain in the woods, even though it would seem to lead straight ahead. You'll recross the bayou and ascend the mild uphill slope of Ridge 5. Once you return to the tram road, veer to the left, looking to see another guidepost ahead. Looking back, notice the various wavy ridges behind you. The nearby ghost hut up ahead is on Ridge 3.

Depart from the road again at 1.9 miles, bearing left and keeping an eye out for blue blazes on the trees. The trail crosses beneath a power line before veering to the left into the woods. You'll notice a slight upward incline as you ascend Ridge 4. At 2 miles, look to your right to see Ridge 5. To your left, Ridge 6 is missing; this is the result of natural decline in this highly erodible area.

At this point in the hike, you'll definitely have a sense of being in the woods, particularly in spring, as the trail follows blue blazes beneath tall oaks and hickories. When you reach a gully at 2.1 miles, take a right to walk alongside the gully and up the slope of Ridge 3. The trail descends the ridge to exit the woods at 2.2 miles, then heads left to skirt the edge of an open, cane-lined area before swinging back to the right. If you're lucky enough to hike this trail in mid- to late March, you'll see a profusion of dogwoods from here on. Bayou Maçon is to your left, and you're back on Maçon Ridge, overlooking the Mississippi floodplain to the east. From here to Vicksburg, the soil is nothing but rich, low floodplain.

The trail soon reaches guidepost #21, after which it follows a gully and crosses a footbridge at 2.4 miles. You'll next head up Mound C, which affords a view of Bayou Maçon and, in spring, numerous flowering dogwoods in the distance. Behind you is a noticeable trench, the remains of the Maçon Trace, an old wagon road used for travel and trade in the 1800s.

Head out of the woods and back to the tram road at 2.5 miles. Once you pass the picnic tables, turn left to go back to the museum and the end of your hike.

12

Rainey Lake Trail

Total distance (circuit): 3.8 miles

Hiking time: 2 hours

*Habitats: Bottomland hardwood,
cypress swamp, forest gaps, and edges*

*Maps: USGS 7½' Waverly SE,
refuge map and brochure*

Late one autumn in 1902, an ambitious party of hunters journeyed to Louisiana's swampy delta country for a Louisiana black bear hunt. Led by former slave and legendary bear-hunting guide Holt Collier, the group was a distinguished lot that included future Louisiana Governor John M. Parker and Tabasco Sauce heir John McIlhenny. The party also boasted at least two ancestors of future fame: Huger L. Foote, grandfather of Civil War authority Shelby Foote, and future United States Senator LeRoy Percy, great-uncle of the novelist Walker Percy. Most distinguished among their crew was President Theodore Roosevelt, addressed simply as "Colonel" by his fellow hunters. An avid sportsman, Roosevelt had long desired to bag the elusive Louisiana black bear, and this was his chance. That first evening, the party camped in a virgin forest on the banks of the Little Sunflower River, several miles north of the present-day Tensas River National Wildlife Refuge (NWR).

Early the next morning, after the hounds had caught a scent and struck a trail, Collier instructed Roosevelt and Huger Foote to head for a cutoff farther up. The plan: Collier and his men would trail the bear to this cutoff and provide the president a clean shot at the beast. In the course of the chase, however, Collier's favorite hunting dog got in a scuffle with the bear. Unable to shoot the bear, the guide knocked it out with the stock of his gun, tied a rope around the animal, and dragged it out of the bayou. After tying the stupefied creature to a tree, he blew his hunting horn to reconvene the party.

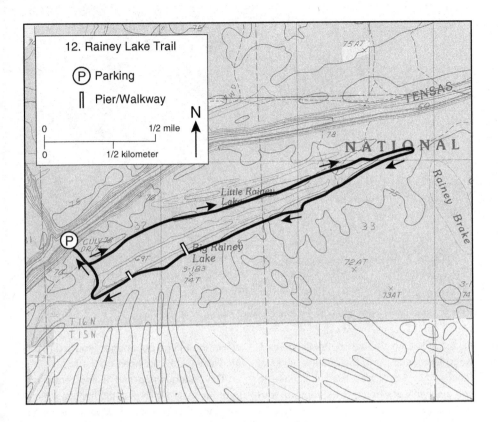

12. Rainey Lake Trail

P Parking

Pier/Walkway

N

| 0 | 1/2 mile |
| 0 | 1/2 kilometer |

President Roosevelt arrived at the scene amid urgings to shoot the helpless bruin. But, with three major news reporters in his camp, a history of public criticism for his hunting activities, and the much-diminished thrill of the hunt, Roosevelt declined—and became a hero, once again, in the public eye. As the media related the story in subsequent weeks, the old bear morphed into a cute, cuddly little cub. Meanwhile, toy store owner Morris Mitchtom was displaying his newly created toy bears for sale at his establishment. In a stroke of marketing genius, he wrote to the president and asked permission to call these new toys "Teddy's Bears." Permission was granted, and the rest is history. Teddy bears became a perennial favorite in the world of children's toys.

Today, Tensas River NWR, several miles west of Tallulah, is one of the few remaining havens for the threatened Louisiana black bear. With an estimated 120 bears on the refuge, this is one of the few places in the state where you stand a decent chance of spotting one. While they're not the cuddly little creatures of teddy bear fame, you should consider yourself fortunate if you do see one lumbering through the refuge's lush mixed bottomland hardwood forest. In all honesty, though, you're more likely to spot other, more common forest creatures, such as turkeys, white-tailed deer, raccoons, and squirrels.

By hiking the Rainey Lake Trail, a delight-

View from the observation tower on Hollow Cypress Trail.

ful 3.7-mile loop through bottomland hardwood forest and along the quaggy banks of Rainey Lake, you'll also have a chance to see a rich mix of wading birds, raptors, warblers, sparrows, and waterfowl. Pick your hiking season wisely, however. As it was in the early 20th century, this area is a haven for hunters. Hikers won't want to be here during the height of the hunting season, when the refuge, a paragon of Louisiana as "sportsman's paradise," is crawling with hunters on all terrain vehicles. Check hunting season dates or contact the refuge staff before making the trip to Tensas River.

To get to the refuge from I-20, go north on LA 17 at Delhi (Exit 153). Turn east onto US 80, which will take you to the small town of Quebec, where you want to turn right onto Fred Morgan, Sr. Road, following the sign to the refuge. Until it reaches the refuge boundary, most of this parish-owned, dirt-and-gravel road is poorly maintained. After about 8 miles of this road, which is paved

within the refuge boundaries, you will reach the Rainey Lake trailhead on the left.

The headquarters and visitor center are approximately 1 mile past the trailhead. Here you can obtain refuge brochures and maps, view life-size wildlife exhibits, and study an interesting collection of documents and pictures relating to the area's history. Behind the visitor center is the Hollow Cypress Trail, a short path that leads to an overlook where hikers can view wintering waterfowl such as mallards, green-winged teals, gadwalls, northern shovelers, and greater yellowlegs.

Begin your hike of the Rainey Lake Trail at the trailhead on Fred Morgan, Sr. Road. The trail immediately swings to the right after entering the woods. Hundreds of palmettos grace the start of the trail; in fact, they'll dominate the woods throughout your hike. After crossing a boardwalk, the trail forks to begin the loop around the lake. Bear left for a hike that takes you through mixed bottomland hardwood forest and culminates in a scenic view of Rainey Lake.

The refuge is characterized by ridge-and-swale topography—a series of subtle, barely noticeable undulations in the terrain. Born of the mighty Mississippi, these ridges are former point bars of the developing river's meanders. As the meanders grew and moved outward, the great river abandoned the former point bars, leaving a series of concave "ridges." What is so fascinating about this terrain in the bottomland hardwood forest of the refuge is that the species you'll encounter clearly change with only mild rises and falls in elevation.

As you begin the trail, notice sweet gum, black gum, American elm, sugarberry, and sweet pecan—typical of higher-elevation bottomland hardwood forest. Other tree species include water, willow, and cherrybark oaks. Later, as the land around you drops in elevation, look for bitter pecan, overcup oak, and Nuttall oak. A typical bottomland tree, the Nuttall oak has a relatively small range in the United States; it primarily follows the Mississippi River floodplain from the delta north to extreme southeastern Missouri. You can recognize this large tree by its swollen trunk and its strikingly oblong, darkly striped acorns at your feet. As you hike, note the decrease in dwarf palmettos, which prefer higher ground less prone to flooding. You'll see more bald cypress and tupelo as you approach the low areas that are constantly flooded.

After a mile of snaking through a scenic, palmetto-filled swath of forest, the trail approaches the edges of Rainey Lake to the right and crosses a small footbridge. Listen for the numerous songbirds that are common in the refuge, particularly in fall, spring, and winter: Carolina chickadee, tufted titmouse, brown thrasher, hermit thrush, swamp sparrow, Carolina wren, and winter wren.

At 1.7 miles, you may hear the occasional refuge truck pass by, as the trail parallels a nearby road. You might also hear the clear, rhythmic whistling of *old sam peabody, peabody, peabody,* otherwise known as the song of the white-throated sparrow, a common winter resident. You also stand a chance of seeing a Louisiana black bear at this point! Sadly, one creature you will not see or hear is the ivory-billed woodpecker, once common in these woods, but now presumed to be extinct. Theodore Roosevelt once referred to the ivory-billed wood as the area's "most characteristic" of birds. The last sighting of this creature was of a female in 1944, spotted in the area now occupied by the refuge headquarters. Loss of habitat due to timber industry demands was the primary cause of this "most characteristic" bird's extinction.

Cross a small footbridge at 2.2 miles. The trail soon leads alongside Rainey Lake to the right. Cypress and tupelo rise up from the lake's edges, mixed in with the ever-present sugarberries. You might also see devil's walking sticks—small, spiny-trunked trees that grow in clumps alongside the path.

At 2.8 miles, the trail reaches a walkway that leads to a view of the lake. This is perhaps the most scenic part of the hike; huge cypresses, with Spanish moss hanging from their branches, arch gracefully over the walkway. Watch as a green heron roosts in the overhead branches of a bald cypress. Back on the trail, you'll cross another footbridge and hike through a slightly higher area. Even though cypress and tupelo still thrive to your right, look for higher-elevation trees to your left, sweet gum, water oak, and willow oak among them.

The path continues to skirt Rainey Lake and reaches another walkway—this one a wheelchair-accessible pier—at 3.4 miles. Willow oak is especially plentiful along the shores of the lake here. This large tree has long, unlobed, lance-shaped leaves—similar to those of the willow—but produces acorns, a fact that unquestionably distinguishes it as an oak. Also plentiful in this area, particularly in summer, are a variety of aquatic plants that include duckweed, alligator weed, and pennywort.

At 3.5 miles, the trail forks. The spur trail straight ahead will take you 0.2 mile to Rainey Brake Observatory and a refuge road. Bear right to return to the trailhead. After crossing a footbridge, you will complete the loop after 3.7 miles. From here, retrace your steps the remaining 100 yards to the trailhead.

II. Central Louisiana

13

Saline Bayou Trail

Total distance (round trip): 6.2 miles

Hiking time: 2–3 hours

Habitats: Mixed pine and hardwood forest, small-stream forest, cypress swamp

Maps: USGS 7½' Goldonna, Winn Ranger District Recreation Opportunities flyer, Saline Bayou National Scenic River map

Cloud Crossing is a secluded, little-known campground in a northern pocket of Kisatchie's Winn Ranger District—and an ideal base camp for folks who want to experience the awe-inspiring beauty of the serpentine, cypress-studded Saline Bayou National Scenic River. Saline Bayou, referred to by Louisiana photographer C. C. Lockwood as "the Miss America of our scenic rivers," seems to be among Louisiana's best-kept secrets. Perhaps it is the remoteness of the area—it's a bit of a road trip from just about anywhere—that keeps the weekenders and vacationers away from this northernmost region of the Winn Ranger District. I know that I've rarely encountered other hikers along the Saline Bayou Trail, a peaceful hike alongside the bayou's dreamlike banks. Although the "best-kept-secret" aspect is part of what makes Cloud Crossing so attractive, outdoor enthusiasts who want to float the bayou, fish for bass, bream, and catfish, climb nearby Driskill Mountain, or hike the Saline Bayou Trail would do well to put Cloud Crossing on their list.

The Saline Bayou Trail begins across the narrow bayou from the Cloud Crossing Campground, winds alongside the Saline Bayou, and traverses mixed pine and hardwood habitat to end at the Pear Field launch site on FS Road 507. While it is easy enough to shuttle a car to the launch site, the Saline Bayou Trail makes for a great there-and-back day hike of 6.2 miles. Start in the morning, after a night at Cloud Crossing Campground, if you can. You just

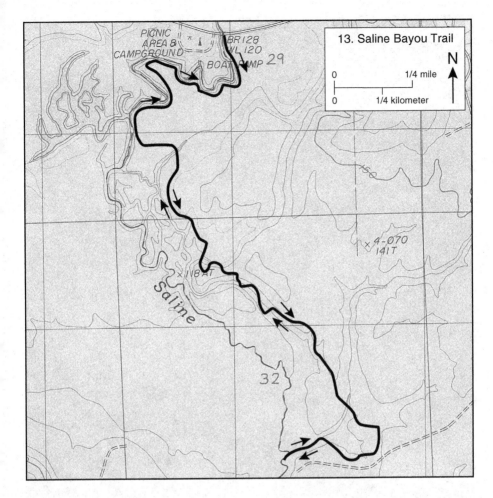

13. Saline Bayou Trail

might have the good fortune to see the fog as it rises off the water into the gnarled, mature, moss-laden cypresses—a truly enchanting experience.

The drive to Cloud Crossing will take you over backroads and through several small Louisiana towns. From I-49, take LA 6 (Exit 138) east to Natchitoches. This highway turns north in Natchitoches, then turns east to junction with US 71/84 in Clarence. Go north on US 71/84 to Campti. At Campti, take LA 9 north to Readheimer. Here you'll go east on LA 126 to LA 1233, where you'll see a sign for Cloud Crossing. Turn left onto

LA 1233 and drive 1.3 miles, following the signs and crossing a small bridge to the campground, parking area, restrooms, and pay station. Nominal fees are charged for both campground and day use.

The orange-blazed Saline Bayou Trail begins on the east side of the bayou—you might have seen it on your left, just before you crossed the bridge into the camping area. You will need to backtrack across the bridge to begin your hike. Look for the kiosk, along with a sign that reads *Welcome to the Winn Ranger District*. Once when I arrived at the Saline Bayou Trail after a rainy early

---

The Saline Bayou Trail winds along cypress-filled Saline Bayou.

spring, I found this same sign standing in several inches of water. Because the Saline Bayou drains a sizable land area, heavy rains can result in serious flooding. That afternoon, the Saline Bayou Trail—boardwalks and all—was 6 to 8 inches under water! If the Kisatchie region has seen a lot of precipitation in recent weeks, you'll want to call the Winn Ranger District Office to check on trail conditions before making the drive.

As you begin your hike, you'll agree that the Saline Bayou Trail is unbelievably scenic from the very start, as it runs atop a low, narrow ridge that separates the cypress-lined bayou to the east from a series of shallow sloughs to the west. Both the bayou and the sloughs of this small-stream habitat are excellent for water-loving trees; in addition to cypress, you'll also see sizable American holly and southern magnolia, mixed in with the smaller ironwood, yaupon, and eastern hophornbeam. Resurrection fern grows on many of the trees; this epiphyte opens its newly green fronds to make this scenic area even lovelier after a recent rain. If the low areas to your left happen to be merely muddy—or even dry—as you begin hiking the Saline Bayou Trail, notice the cypress knees rising from the ground. They are an indication that this area floods enough to provide a favorable environment for the cypresses. You will also see a number of the yellow pines that are so ubiquitous throughout Kisatchie National Forest—even in this initial swampy, wet area.

Cross a short boardwalk over a slough about 100 yards into the hike. Louisiana natives, myself included, can sometimes get dulled to the beauty of the state's characteristic bayous, cypresses, ferns, and lichens, but no one would argue that this section of the Saline Bayou Trail is a particularly awesome slice of Louisiana. Lichens

seem to have taken over in some places. For example, look at the cypress knees jutting out of Saline Bayou on your right. Gray-green reindeer lichens grow on their sides and tops, giving the gnarled knees an even more ancient and grizzled look.

The trail, which is marked with orange metal diamonds, crosses a small footbridge at 0.1 mile, then swings right to continue winding alongside the bayou. The woods to your left consist mostly of tall, fat pines and minimal understory, and the land is flat and somewhat sandy. Much of the trail itself is the typical Kisatchie mix of sand and pine needles. Cross another bridge over a low area at 0.2 mile, then bear slightly right to continue the meandering path along the bayou's banks. If you are staying at the nearby campground and are able to hike this trail early in the morning, you may spot the flash of a white-tailed deer as it bolts away from you, or catch a glimpse of a raccoon feeding along the quiet banks. On a night hike in spring or early fall, listen for the *wills-wi'dow, wills-wi'dow* of the chuck-will's-widow. Although it is a common summer resident of Louisiana's pine and hardwood forests, you're not likely to see this shy bird during the day.

This region is also home to a couple of interesting amphibians, both of which you should be able to hear on misty, rainy evenings: the eastern narrow-mouthed toad and the East Texas subspecies of Woodhouse's toad. The eastern narrow-mouthed toad is not a true toad; however, this diminutive, 1.5-inch-long amphibian has a triangle-shaped body and a pursed-looking mouth at the tip of its narrow head. Listen for its medium-pitched chirpy buzz. Woodhouse's toad is a true toad, growing up to 4 inches or longer. Although it primarily occurs on the Great Plains and farther west, the East Texas subspecies can be found throughout most of Louisiana—as far east, in fact, as New Orleans. You're most likely to see these sizable toads in the evenings as they forage for insects along Saline Bayou's banks.

Although the cypresses generally form an intermittent wall between the trail and the bayou, there are a few short "spur trails"—no more than a few feet long—where you can turn right to get a clear view of the cypress-lined corridor. The trail passes some impressively large magnolias a 0.7 mile, and then it crosses a footbridge and heads away from the bayou at 1 mile. Thus ends what seems to be the "beaten path" of the Saline Bayou Trail. However well blazed, the rest of the path is not as well worn as the first section; it seems that many hikers get to the end of the bayou walk, then turn back. Their loss. The next section leads through some-times-hilly, mostly deciduous woods that occasionally yield some good fall colors in late November. I love to hike this trail in the winter, when the leaves are off the trees and crunch beneath my feet as I walk. Because the trail is not as worn, you'll want to watch closely for the orange diamonds that mark it. The trail will follow the curves of Saline Bayou, but not as closely as previously, and you won't always be able to see the water.

Pass beneath several large southern magnolias before bearing right to cross a footbridge over a usually dry slough. At 1.2 miles is another bridge, and the trail begins to parallel another slough to the right. The Saline Bayou Trail winds back and forth, going away from the slough and coming back to it, and it soon climbs a bank that slopes downhill to the slough—which is starting to look more like a full-fledged cypress swamp. At 1.4 miles, the bayou walk has become a woods walk. The trail crosses a small footbridge at 1.5 miles and enters an

area of red buckeye, beech, oak, and hickory. As always, loblolly pines are scattered among the deciduous trees.

The Saline Bayou Trail changes slightly in elevation, going uphill to a spot overlooking a pocket of a cypress swamp to the right. At the top of this small climb, the trail swings left and leads alongside the swampy area, which is about 20 feet downhill to the right. This little ridge is full of pine and beech and makes for a nice, shaded walk in late fall. Descend off the ridge and swing left, making a U around it. The trail begins gently rolling as it continues to skirt the large slough to the right.

At 2 miles, the trail arcs to the right to line the edge of a flat, bowl-like area full of beech and pine, along with several large American hollies. In early spring, look for mayapples at your feet. The Saline Bayou Trail reaches an old road trace at 2.2 miles. Take a sharp right here, hiking until you reach a gravel road several hundred feet beyond. Take a left onto the gravel road, hiking for about 150 feet until the trail swings back into the woods to the right. It's easy to miss the orange diamonds here, so watch carefully for them.

Back on the wooded trail, you will see more impressively large American hollies. Look for cedar waxwings, one of many bird species that feed on the holly berries in winter. These beautiful, dark brown birds with black faces and yellow-tipped tails are possibly more plentiful in your backyard than in the national forest, but they're common throughout Louisiana and can often be seen in their characteristic noisy flocks wherever berries are available.

Cross a bridge over a dry slough at 2.3 miles, then swing right to walk through more beech- and holly-dominated woods. Cross another small bridge at 2.5 miles. Bear right, following the orange diamonds. You'll hike through rolling hardwood forest and cross several more footbridges before the trail ends at the Pear Field launch site. If you turn right to walk down gravel FS Road 507, you'll reach the boat launch—a pleasant spot to sit, take a lunch break, and marvel at the beauty of Saline Bayou. Hike back to Cloud Crossing for a round-trip trek of 6.2 miles.

14

Briarwood–Caroline Dormon Preserve

Total distance (circuit): 1.6 miles

Hiking time: As long as it takes

Habitats: Mixed pine and hardwood (pine, oak, and hickory); cypress swamp

Maps: USGS 7½' Saline

Anyone who has enjoyed the trails of Kisatchie, has recognized the need to conserve Louisiana's forests, or simply admires the state's inimitable natural treasures should make the pilgrimage to Briarwood. Yes, pilgrimage. This preserve and sanctuary in Natchitoches Parish was the home and hideaway of Caroline Dormon, the late artist, naturalist, botanist, conservationist, author, educator, and native-plant collector. This remarkable woman worked tirelessly with the United States Forest Service to establish Kisatchie National Forest and preserve Louisiana's natural heritage.

As the first woman in the United States to be employed in forestry—she went to work as Instructor of Forestry for the Louisiana Forestry Commission in 1921—"Miss Carrie" was a true pioneer, and her legacy is an inspiration to anyone who loves the outdoors. At Briarwood, she collected and replanted Louisiana native plants, propagated and hybridized native flowers, including the Louisiana iris, and shared her vast knowledge of Louisiana flora and fauna with visiting students of horticulture and forestry. When you visit Briarwood, remember that, with some hikes, the journey truly is the destination. The vistas along the way include an iris bog, a collection of pitcher plants, a reflection pond (dug by Caroline Dormon herself), and the ancient "Grandpappy" longleaf pine.

Although Caroline Dormon is no longer with us, Briarwood is, and Mr. Richard L. Johnson and his wife Jessie lovingly carry on her legacy. For first-time visitors, the

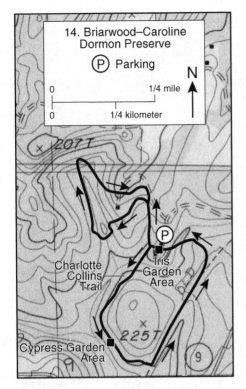

14. Briarwood–Caroline Dormon Preserve

(P) Parking

N

0   1/4 mile

0   1/4 kilometer

2077

Charlotte
Collins
Trail

Iris
Garden
Area

(P)

2257

Cypress Garden
Area

9

Johnsons require an initial, 1.5-hour guided tour of the trails. Experienced hikers may shy away from this, but they shouldn't. By walking the trails with Mr. Johnson, a lifelong resident of Briarwood, you will gain an appreciation of these woods—and of nature in general—that I could not even begin to provide in this book. The preserve is open to the public during the weekends of March, April, May, August, and November, from 9 AM to 5 PM. However, you can make an appointment to visit the preserve for almost any time, day, or month of the year. Members of the preserve's foundation can visit Briarwood anytime and are free to explore the trails on their own. The short hike described here will give you an idea of what you'll see at the preserve. Once you've had a tour of the trails, you'll want to choose your own path.

Briarwood is located 32 miles north of Natchitoches, near Saline, Louisiana. From I-49, take LA 6 (Exit 138) east through Natchitoches. After crossing the Red River, LA 6 junctions with US 71/US 84, where you'll head north to Campti. At Campti, go north on LA 9 for approximately 18 miles. After passing LA 126 at Readheimer, turn left onto Caroline Dormon Road and drive beneath the Briarwood gate ahead. You'll soon reach the parking area on the right.

The trail, intermittently marked by dark blue blazes, begins at an opening just behind the parking area, to the right of the headquarters building. The hike begins by crossing two other trails; just keep going straight ahead. The second trail leads to a showy iris garden on the right. You'll stroll through this beautiful spot later in your hike.

The trail swings right at just under 0.1 mile. In spring, you'll see hundreds of mayapples, also called "umbrella plants" for their umbrella-like leaves that unfurl in early spring. Long, creeping rhizomes can produce large colonies of mayapples, which can grow up to a foot tall and a foot across. With their bright, shiny leaves, carpets of mayapples are easy to see on the springtime forest floor. Their nodding white flowers, growing at the forks of the two-leafed plants, are a little less obvious. Before blooming, these flowers look like small, green fists hiding beneath the mayapples' leaves. Also trailing along the ground, you'll see maple leaf viburnum and Indian cherry. Above you are the trees typical of a mixed forest: American beech, flowering dogwood, winged elm, red maple, white oak, and shortleaf and loblolly pine.

At 0.2 mile, approach a boggy area to your right. You're at the edge of swamp habitat, where you'll see black gum, sweet gum, sylvatica, sweet bay, and black alder. Of course, you'll see more bald cypresses as you con-

Smell a wet dog? It might be wet dog flower, which grows along the trails at Briarwood.

tinue your hike. In the understory is button-bush, whose spring-blooming white flowers resemble pincushions. These twisty shrubs, which bear buttonlike brown fruits in autumn, are common in swampy areas. Their seeds are a favorite of ducks and water birds.

At 0.4 mile, a T intersection marks a tram for a railroad that ran from Veal, Arkansas to Natchitoches until it was abandoned in 1947. Plans are in the works at Briarwood to make this segment into a wheelchair-acces-sible path. To your right, the raised path leads to private property, so turn left to walk the tram for 0.3 mile. The path is nearly flat; in fact, you'll gain only a single foot in eleva-tion as you hike it! Look for jack-in-the-pulpit in the low area to your right, and notice the mountain laurel—rare in Louisiana—blooming in early summer. In the distance, you may catch sight of a pileated woodpecker before it disappears into the thick woods.

You might also spot yellow pitcher plants here and there. The northern extremity of this odd, beautiful flower's range is about 1.5 miles north of Briarwood. Also known as huntsman's horns, these exquisite carnivo-rous plants have long, trumpet-shaped leaves. They're more common in the pine sa-vannas south and east of here. To see more of these fascinating, insect-eating plants, check out the Horse Branch Trail (Hike 45).

Bear left at 0.7 mile, then cross an old service road. The trail turns right at a crepe myrtle and reaches another road at 0.8 mile. Cross the road, then bear right into the woods again. A walkway leads through an area rich in spring wildflowers: violets, phlox, jack-in-the-pulpit, trillium, and mayapples are just a few of the blooms you'll find here. Continue straight ahead to reach the park-ing area at 0.9 mile.

The second leg of your hike will take you through the iris garden and within sight of

Briarwood's Grandpappy Pine, one of the largest and oldest longleaf pines in Louisiana. Begin this hike as you did the last one. When you see the iris garden on your right, however, turn toward the garden, en-tering at a small gate. If you are interested in flowers at all—or just love gazing at them—you'll want to stay here for a while. In April, the large Louisiana irises make quite a show.

Once you exit the garden through its back gate, bear left. When you reach a nar-row dirt road soon afterward, turn left onto the road. Hike a short bit along the Buffalo Road, which, as Richard Johnson will tell you, is of intriguing historical significance. You'll bypass another road to your left. When a foot trail leads to the right, bear right onto it.

The trail reaches a pond at 0.2 mile. Turn left here, looking across the pond for the Grandpappy Pine, towering above the other trees. Measuring 112 feet tall, 39 inches in diameter, and over 10 feet in circumference, this magnificent tree is estimated to be more than 300 years old. As you circle the pond, you'll notice that a side trail leads directly to the tree.

At 0.3 mile, turn left toward a small log building—now a restored cabin, this is where Caroline Dormon would come to relax, write, paint, and meditate. After passing the cabin, bear right and decent an incline to cross a small bridge. Swing right at 0.4 mile toward Caroline Dormon's log house, which is now used as an interpretive center for educa-tional groups. At 0.5 mile, the trail suddenly breaks up, leading in four different direc-tions. For now, take the second trail from the right; you can come back later to take one of the trails less traveled. The path to the far left leads to a wildflower meadow that you'll want to visit in spring and summer.

You'll soon reach an open area to your

left. This is the site of the house where Caroline Dormon was born in 1888. Two large post oaks mark where the long front steps led up to the front porch of the house, which was occupied from 1872 to 1909. Soon, the trail forks. Bear left to return to the Buffalo Road. Go left onto the road, and you'll soon find yourself back at the parking area, at the end of your hike.

Interested in learning more about Caroline Dormon? Louisianans should be able to obtain books by and about Caroline Dormon from their local libraries. *Gift of Wild Things* by Fran H. Johnson is a biography of Caroline Dormon. You will also enjoy the following three books by Caroline Dormon: *Flowers Native to the Deep South* (1958); *Natives Preferred* (1965); and *Bird Talk* (1969).

15

Dogwood Trail Nature Walk

Total distance (circuit): 1.5 miles

Hiking time: 45 minutes–1 hour

*Habitats: Mixed pine-hardwood forest,
bottomland hardwood forest,
cypress swamp*

*Maps: USGS 7½' Beech Bayou,
park map*

In Louisiana, many folks identify Toledo Bend with water sports. Indeed, the 185,000-acre Toledo Bend Reservoir, with 1,200 miles of shoreline, provides endless opportunities for fishing, swimming, boating, and waterskiing. North Toledo Bend State Park, located on a small peninsula on the reservoir's eastern shore, is the perfect base camp for anyone wanting to explore this popular area. The Dogwood Trail Nature Walk, the park's 1.5-mile hiking trail, leads through a mix of pines, hardwoods, and swamp habitats along the shores of the scenic reservoir.

The Toledo Bend region has a long and interesting geological history, having been formed over millions of years. The Sabine Uplift, a huge, flat-topped, subsurface fold of northwest Louisiana, stands high above the surrounding flat land. Geologists believe that the Sabine Uplift—a true oddity, in geological terms—was pushed upward by molten magma during Triassic times, more than 200 million years ago. Westward movement of the North American plate—the same movement that gave rise to the Rocky Mountains—forced the Sabine Uplift even farther upward. The result was a "bend," or a series of bluffs along what would become the west-central border of Louisiana. Although its surface effect is much less jaw-dropping than that of the Rocky Mountains, the Sabine Uplift actually caused traps to be formed in the land, ultimately creating ideal conditions for oil and gas production along Louisiana's western border.

Early Spanish explorers originally named this area Toledo, as the bluffs reminded them of Toledo, Spain. Although it was almost renamed Lake Texanna—after the two states whose borders it shares—this huge "bend" kept its original name of Toledo. The Spanish were the primary European settlers of this region, building missions in an early eighteenth-century attempt to Christianize the Caddo people, the Native Americans whom they found living there.

To get to Toledo Bend State Park from I-49, take LA 6 (Exit 138) west to the town of Many, where the road junctions with US 171. Follow US 171 north to Zwolle, where you want to turn left onto LA 475, following the signs to North Toledo Bend State Park. Turn right onto LA 191, then left onto LA 482 after 1.6 more miles. Finally, after another half mile, turn left onto LA 3229. Approximately 4 miles later, a sign will direct you to turn left into the park. The trailhead for the Dogwood Trail Nature Walk is on the right, just before you reach the park office and visitor center, about a mile past the park entrance. You can park at the park office, near the trailhead. Because this is a self-guided interpretive trail, you'll want to pick up the park's informative trail map, along with the lists of area birds and trees, at the office.

The Dogwood Trail Nature Walk begins by descending a sandy slope to a small footbridge. Along with the plentiful loblolly and shortleaf pine, look for hardwoods, such as American holly, red maple, sweet gum, white oak, mockernut hickory, and of course dogwood in the understory. After crossing the footbridge, the trail forks to begin the loop. Bear to the right, heading up an incline. You'll notice that certain trees are labeled along this trail.

You'll walk beside three types of magnolias on this hike: cucumber, sweet bay, and southern. The most distinctive of the three is the southern magnolia; if you've hiked anywhere in central and southern Louisiana,

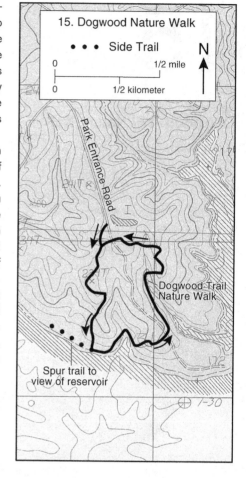

you've probably come across this tree. The two other magnolias are perhaps less distinctive but no less interesting. In fact, sweet bay magnolia, also known as swamp magnolia, is a particularly beautiful small tree with aromatic flowers and bright red, fleshy fruits that mature in late summer or early fall. American colonists, who used the fleshy tree roots as bait in their beaver traps, actually called sweet bay magnolia "beavertree." Cucumber magnolia, or cucumber tree, is generally smaller than its two cousins, as are its flowers, which are greenish-yellow, unlike the milky white petals of the other magnolias.

Trailhead at Dogwood Trail Nature Walk

At 0.2 mile, an unofficial trail to the right leads about 100 feet to an old road. Simply bear left, continuing the Dogwood Trail. Reach a small bench at 0.4 mile. If you sit unmoving for a few minutes, you might notice the quick-flitting ruby-throated hummingbird, common in these woods. These diminutive creatures' backs are bright green, but the bright red throat and black chin band of the male hummingbird are particularly distinctive.

At 0.6 mile, the massive Toledo Bend Reservoir begins to come into view. After crossing a couple of small footbridges, you'll reach a sign at 0.7 mile pointing you to a view of the reservoir. Go to the right for about 100 yards, and you'll also see the beautiful, gnarled cypresses that border the reservoir.

Back on the main trail, you'll soon cross another footbridge. The reservoir is still in view, but the many trees to your right may

obscure it. You might notice several cypresses that have made their way into the higher, dryer woods—a sign that this section probably floods on a regular basis. The trail should be dry, even though you approach the edge of the reservoir again at 0.9 mile. Cypress knees, so plentiful in some parts of Louisiana, are less common here, but several rise out of the water at this spot. Cross another footbridge at 1 mile and begin heading up a very slight incline, winding through the woods. You head back downhill soon afterward, and at 0.7 mile is a scenic little gully to your right. In spring, this area is full of wild azaleas and dogwoods.

After crossing a few more footbridges on the downhill incline, the trail levels out at a larger footbridge. The remainder of the loop is mostly level. Bear right at 1.5 miles, crossing the footbridge that leads to the road and the trailhead.

Dogwood Trail Nature Walk

16

Caroline Dormon Trail

Total distance (one way): 10.5 miles

Hiking time: 6 hours, or overnight

Habitats: Longleaf pine forest, mixed pine and hardwood, small-stream forest, cypress swamp

Maps: USGS 7½' Bayou L'Ivrogne, Kisatchie Ranger District Recreation Opportunities flyer

As a Louisiana hiker, I tend to view Kisatchie National Forest as a big playground: a boundless, wide-open space of rolling hills, clear streams, and picturesque bayous made even more beautiful by spring-blooming wild azaleas, dogwoods, and other wildflowers. Hiking trails meander beneath a canopy of pines, beeches, magnolias, and oaks and occasionally pass swampy sloughs that give rise to cypresses and dwarf palmetto. While its trails are not particularly long or rugged, Kisatchie plays a definite role as the backyard escape for Louisiana hikers, as well as the stomping ground for novice backpackers with longer, more challenging treks on their horizons.

Hiking trails are *not* the primary purpose of this working, heavily managed forest, of course. But Kisatchie does offer a handful of hiking opportunities, including the 10.5-mile Caroline Dormon Trail. With its smooth sandstone rocks, miniature waterfall, sandy creek beds, and grand finale at Kisatchie Bayou, the Caroline Dormon Trail ranks as a favorite among Louisiana hikers and backpackers. The varied path twists along Bayou L'Ivrogne, climbs into hilly pine and mixed pine and hardwood forest, and descends to scenic pockets of beech and magnolia forest—crossing up to a dozen or more small-streams and rivulets on the way, the exact number depending on how much rain the trail has seen recently. The Caroline Dormon Trail's length and moderate terrain make for a good day hike for an experienced group. For an 18-mile weekend trek, backpackers can link this trail to the rugged

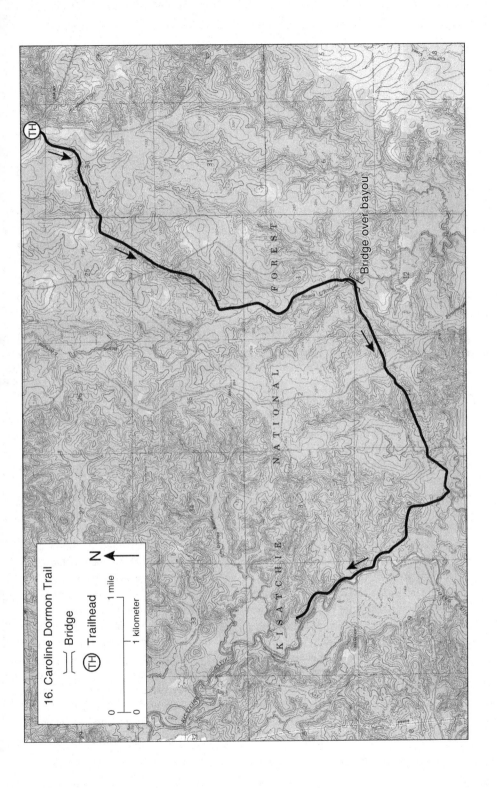

16. Caroline Dormon Trail

Bridge

TH Trailhead

N

0   1 mile

0   1 kilometer

Bridge over bayou

FOREST

NATIONAL

KISATCHIE

This miniature waterfall is one of the highlights of the Caroline Dormon Trail.

7.5-mile Backbone Trail. Although this guide does not cover the two trails as a single backpacking trip, it does highlight potential campsites and water sources.

The Caroline Dormon Trail begins at the Longleaf Trail Scenic Byway and ends at Kisatchie Bayou Recreation Area. From I-49, get onto LA 119 at Derry (Exit 119) and drive south for 5.1 miles to the Longleaf Trail Scenic Byway. Turn right onto the Byway and travel 5.5 miles to the trailhead and parking area on your left. (The Backbone Trail terminus is just across the road.) To reach the south Dormon trailhead at Kisatchie Bayou, stay on the Byway and turn south onto Forest Road 360, approximately 1 mile west of the Dormon/Backbone trailhead. This gravel road will take you about 4 miles to FS Road 321. Following the signs to the recreation area, turn right onto FS Road 321, then left onto FS Road 366 after about a mile. FS Road 366 dead-ends at the recreation area.

The trail begins to the left of the road.

Beginning at the Byway trailhead, follow the orange blazes that mark the Caroline Dormon Trail into the woods. Because this trail is popular with equestrians as well as hikers, parts of it may be rutted. To prevent further degradation of the trail, allow these other users the right-of-way if you encounter them on your hike. In the past, trail travelers of all stripes have expanded the rutted areas by walking around them—making the damaged portions grow even wider. With this damage, wet weather can turn parts of the trail into a quaggy morass. Hikers struggling through this section will be happy to learn that the Louisiana Hiking Club, using a state-funded grant, will be working to improve this trail in the near future. After a couple of muddy stream crossings, you reach a springtime abundance of dogwoods and wild azaleas 0.3 mile into the hike. Although fall and winter are both good seasons to hike this trail, the March and April blooms argue for hiking this one in spring.

By the time you've hiked a mile, you'll have already crossed at least four streambeds. To a great degree, the Caroline Dormon Trail parallels water: Steep Branch for the first segment of the hike, Bayou L'Ivrogne for the second, and Kisatchie Bayou at the end. Your hike will braid back and forth across the erosion-formed ravines and the shallow, sometimes soggy creek beds along the sandy banks of Steep Branch and Bayou L'Ivrogne. These gentle dips in the trail are the primary elevation changes on this first section of the hike, which is mostly flat. Because this section is low and often muddy, you may be hard-pressed to find a comfortable campsite—despite the abundance of water available.

Speaking of water, one of the trail's highlights is a miniature waterfall at 1.7 miles. This shady spot, with its gentle stream flowing over colorful sandstone rocks, is one of the small jewels of Kisatchie. This is a great place to stop for a break; try to hear the musical chipping of a yellow-rumped warbler over the gurgle of the waterfall. If you're on a Backbone/Dormon backpacking trip, you'll definitely want to stop and soothe your feet in the cool water. Note how the water has eroded smooth holes and dips into the rocks surrounding you. One even looks like a face, with two hollow "eyes" and a low, round "mouth" carved out of it! Be careful when crossing these smooth rocks, which can be slippery.

After leaving this scenic spot, the Caroline Dormon Trail winds up and down several gentle slopes before reaching the sandy, rocky banks of Steep Branch at 2 miles. Many small trees, shrubs, and vines characterize this section: yaupon, American holly, wild grape, and common sweetleaf can be seen here. Towering overhead are large,

majestic pines. Listen for the musical, prolonged trill of the pine warbler here. Among the most common warblers in Louisiana, pine warblers are plentiful in Kisatchie's pinewoods. These birds, which are olive green above and yellow beneath, typically wedge their cup-shaped nests between two cones close to the top of a tall pine.

The trail reaches FS Road 360 at 2.4 miles. Cross the road and follow the orange blazes back into the woods. The trail continues to parallel Steep Branch. While there are no clearly established campsites in this area, it is possible to set up camp in one of the wider areas of the "beach" to your right. The sandy trail is narrow and mostly flat through here.

Still following the winding contours of Steep Branch, the Caroline Dormon Trail crosses several more wet areas before veering to the left—and into a low spot—at 3.2 miles. You're nearing the junction of Steep Branch and Bayou L'Ivrogne. If you've been slogging through mud from the start, you'll be happy to know that the trail gets a little higher and dryer at 3.9 miles when it swings left (away from Bayou L'Ivrogne), heads uphill, and takes another sharp left. You'll find yourself on a pleasant low ridge that affords a few scenic winter views. In spring, this section is colorful with red buckeyes, several species of violet, and flowering dogwood. This is also one of the few areas on this trail where you'll find the umbrella-like mayapples so common farther north.

As you hike in and out of Kisatchie's pine forests on this trail, you're likely to see evidence of controlled burns, which are an important management tool for working pine forests. If the trail must go through a recently burned area (as it sometimes does), the Forest Service temporarily marks the path with orange tape tied around the trunks of charred pines. Signs of previous burning include abundant ferns and young saplings and a lack of full-grown understory trees such as dogwood and red maple.

The trail soon descends a slope into an area of large longleaf pines. After crossing another low, wet area at 4.3 miles, the trail takes a sharp right onto a rutted old roadbed. Watch for the blazes, as it is easy to miss this turn. The trail takes another sharp left at 4.4 miles; again, look carefully for the blazes. The Caroline Dormon Trail winds for another mile, paralleling Bayou L'Ivrogne and passing through several low, potentially muddy areas. You will reach FS Road 360 once again at 5.4 miles. When you get to the road, turn right to cross the bridge over Bayou L'Ivrogne. Follow this road for about 0.1 mile before turning *right* to return to the woods. Note that the trail does not actually cross the road, as you might expect. Back beneath the trees, the trail leads away from Bayou L'Ivrogne and climbs a slope at 5.6 miles, only to head back downhill shortly thereafter. A relatively level walk follows as you parallel FS Road 360 to your left.

At 5.8 miles, the trail leads away from the road, crosses a small stream, then swings left. You'll soon see the Bayou L'Ivrogne again to the right. Hike over several small, gentle inclines to cross FS Road 321 at 6.3 miles. The trail is mostly flat and potentially muddy through this next section. After about a half mile of on-and-off slogging, you will ascend a short but steep uphill. At the top of the hill, take a sharp left, then head back downhill soon afterward to cross yet another small stream.

At 7 miles, the trail ascends once more, this time at a pretty good clip. This is one of my favorite sections of the Caroline Dormon Trail, where pine needles cover the ground and elms, white oak, maple, holly, and wild azaleas grow alongside the path. Tall pines

tower over the hardwoods. The brief ascent soon levels out to descend and wind through woods of magnolia and dogwood. In spring, look for Carolina jessamine, bird-foot violets, and wild azaleas.

The trail reaches the dirt FS Road 389 at 7.3 miles. Watch for the orange blazes as they lead you through this somewhat rutted area. The Caroline Dormon Trail recrosses this road at 7.6 miles, then descends slightly into a wetter area in which beech, sycamore, and magnolia thrive. Take a sharp right at 7.8 miles to head slightly back uphill. The trail soon reaches a huge magnolia, where it veers to the left, following along a ridge and a stream. You could camp in this area, but a better campsite lies just ahead at 8 miles. If you're low on water, you'll want to fill up your water bottles here before heading up the ridge. *Remember to filter or treat all water on the trail.*

Soon, you'll begin to see tupelo, eastern hophornbeam, and ironwood among the beech and magnolia. Although these species are indicative of low, wet areas, you'll soon notice that you're actually in an elevated spot with an overlook! Reach this broad, open area at 8 miles, where there are plenty of places to set up a tent and a nice view of a branch of Kisatchie Bayou below. Note that the water is not easily accessed from this spot. Upon reaching the open area, the Caroline Dormon Trail arcs back to the right to return to the woods. This section can be confusing; it almost looks as if the trail crosses the water just ahead by way of a fallen tree. Rest assured that it does not. The first time I hiked here, I was ready to scoot across the tree before I realized, thankfully, that the trail goes in the *other* direction!

The Caroline Dormon Trail winds through a forest of beeches and magnolias, crossing several more creeks before reaching an old road at 8.4 miles. Cross this road, taking a sharp right shortly afterward. When you reach another old road at 8.8 miles, the trail seems to split. Bear left, following the blazes. When it seems to split again shortly afterward, bear right and go downhill. Although the Dormon Trail may be a little hard to follow in this section, the area surrounding it is just beautiful. At 8.9 miles, notice a swampy area on your left, full of cypress and tupelo—a real change from the previous piney woods.

You will encounter another slough to the right at 9.2 miles. After swinging around it, the trail meanders peacefully through the woods. You're beginning to approach Kisatchie Bayou and will soon pass a fire ring and a small campsite immediately to the right. At 9.4 miles, keep a sharp eye out for orange blazes, as the trail suddenly veers to the left, descending a steep slope. This path brings you next to the water and winds alongside it for some time.

At 9.6 miles, you will gain a view of the mesalike banks of Kisatchie Bayou to the left. These vertically eroding sandstone bluffs look a little bit like miniature versions the desert mesas in the American West.

Kisatchie Bayou's strikingly scenic banks are part of a larger geologic band called the Catahoula Formation, the sandstone evidence of which is intermittently visible from the Sabine River east to the Kisatchie Ranger District, and as far as Sicily Island. In fact, Louisiana's waterfalls—the ones in Kisatchie, as well as those in Sicily Island Hills—are all the result of sandstones of the Catahoula Formation, which occurred during the Oligocene Epoch of the Tertiary Period, between 24 and 37 million years ago.

The Caroline Dormon Trail leads away from the view. Don't be disappointed, though; you'll soon return to the bayou, exiting the woods to walk along Kisatchie's sandy shoreline for 0.1 mile. Once you're on the "beach," note the cypresses growing, uncharacteristically, on the sandy shore.

After the short beach walk, reenter the woods to the right again at 10 miles. Where the trail seems to split at 10.1 miles (at the *Posted* sign), bear right. You are entering the Kisatchie Bayou Recreation Area and will start to see picnic tables, campsites, and other signs of civilization. Continue walking along the bayou to the trailhead, where your hike concludes at 10.5 miles.

17

Backbone Trail

Total distance (one way): 7.5 miles

Hiking time: 5 hours

Habitats: Mixed pine and hardwood, longleaf pine forest, cypress swamp

Maps: USGS 7½' Flora; USGS 7½' Cloutierville, USGS 7½' Gorum, USGS 7½' Bayou L'Ivrogne, Kisatchie Ranger District Recreation Opportunities flyer

A favorite among Louisiana hikers, the linear Backbone Trail through the Kisatchie Hills Wilderness features scenic campsites, rocky outcrops, and some downright rugged hiking. At only 7.5 miles, this trail is good for a full-day hike, though its beautiful, secluded campsites make it an ideal route for a short, one-night backpacking trip. For a full-weekend backpacking trip, you can connect the Backbone to the Caroline Dormon Trail (Hike 16) for an 18-miler that ends (or begins) at Kisatchie Bayou. Be aware that most of the Backbone Trail is dry trail. Carry in plenty of water, particularly if you're planning to camp overnight. This guide treats the Backbone as a day hike beginning at FS Road 339 and ending at FS Road 329 and the Caroline Dormon trailhead. Campsites along the trail are noted for backpackers.

To reach the FS Road 339 trailhead, take I-49 to LA 119 at Derry (Exit 119). Go south on LA 119 for 5.1 miles, then turn right onto the Longleaf Trail Scenic Byway and drive approximately 7 miles to FS Road 339. Turn right into the small parking area and Backbone trailhead. The Backbone Trail begins to the east (right) of FS Road 339; you'll see a sign marking the beginning of the trail. To the west (left) of FS Road 339 is the Sandstone ATV Trail.

After registering at the trailhead, begin hiking east on the orange-blazed Backbone Trail. This sandy, well-worn segment passes through longleaf pines above and ferns below. The level trail can get gloppy and unpleasant after a rain—and some

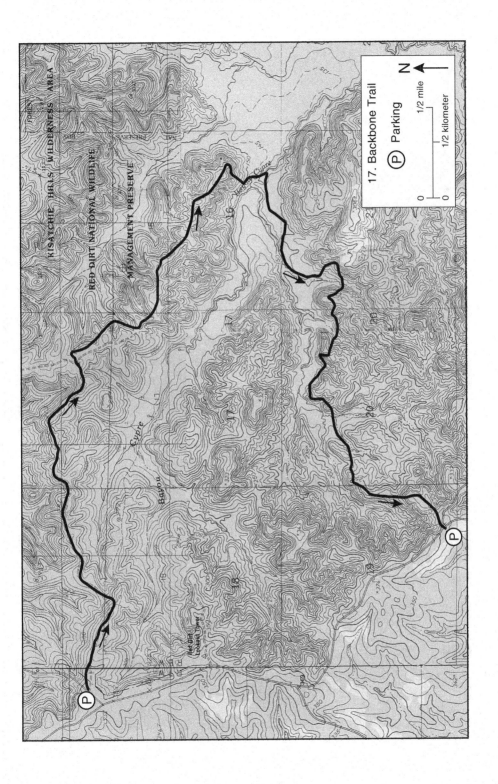

N

17. Backbone Trail

Ⓟ Parking

| 0 | | 1/2 mile |
| 0 | 1/2 kilometer | |

The Backbone Trail features rugged hiking through sandy pine forests.

parts never quite seem to dry out. This mucky soil will grab hold of your boot soles with a vengeance, and can make for frustrating hiking. If this is your experience starting out, rest assured that the entire trail is not like this.

Before long, you'll find yourself on a ridge—and you haven't even had to climb it! This skinny ridge you're hiking is actually part of Louisiana's original "flat" elevation. The entire area consists of eroding clays, mudstones, shales, and sandstones formed from sediments deposited by rivers and streams over millions of years. Over time, streams eroded the softer sediments down into surrounding valleys and carved out gullies and ravines to create even more topographical relief. The erosion-resistant sandstones—including this ridge—barely changed in elevation, and they now tower over the eroded valleys.

The Backbone Trail descends toward the valley at 0.4 mile. In March, look for blooming wild azaleas in the next 0.3 mile. You'll continue downhill for much of this section, leveling out at 0.6 mile, where you'll find an accumulation of interesting sandstone fragments. Head down a gentle incline at 0.8 mile, passing several gullies choked with common sweetleaf and wild azaleas. At 0.9 mile, the trail turns to rock—actual rock in Louisiana! Look for the purples, grays, and browns of the surrounding sandstones.

The sandy, well-drained soil of this area is ideal habitat for pines, particularly longleaf, which is native to this area. As you hike the Backbone Trail, you'll see longleaf in various stages of growth. In the grass stage, or seedling phase, the tree is a mere tuft of green pine needles on the ground. This stage alone can last for more than 7 years as the seedling builds a sturdy taproot, which will ultimately make the longleaf more wind

resistant as it ages. Although longleaf does not take any longer than other pines to grow, it clearly takes a long time to *start* growing. Sometime after the nearly 90 million acres of the South's virgin longleaf were felled for timber—and their resin-soaked stumps tapped for pitch and turpentine, then blasted by dynamite—the denuded lands were replanted with loblolly and slash pines. Although those pines are of poorer quality, they were preferred for their seeming ability to grow faster—because they *started* growing faster. While you'll see plenty of loblolly, slash, and shortleaf pines in different parts of Louisiana, you'll get a good taste of longleaf here on the Backbone Trail. My favorite stage of longleaf growth is the sapling phase. To me, the trees look like skinny, overgrown adolescents in dire need of a haircut!

The views begin at 1.1 miles and improve as you hike. At 1.3 miles is a vista overlooking the pine-studded hills of Kisatchie to your right. This open spot is a great dry campsite for weekend backpackers who aren't able to hit the trail until after work on Friday. Throughout this area, look for blooming huckleberry, Carolina jessamine, and birdfoot violets in spring. The trail, which has been mostly straight, wide, and flat, swings left at 2 miles and narrows as it begins a slight ascent. This is Louisiana, so the uphill doesn't last long; instead, you'll have begun the series of small ups and downs that characterize many of Kisatchie's trails. At 2.4 miles, a side trail to the left leads about 0.2 mile to a beautiful campsite carpeted with pine needles, complete with an established fire ring and room for several tents.

The Backbone leads past sizable clumps of mildly fragrant wild azalea bushes before reaching a sandstone outcrop with an expansive view at 2.5 miles. The trail soon descends a gradual slope. In wet weather, the foot of this slope can get particularly muddy. This low area doesn't last long, though. At 2.7 miles, the Backbone ascends along a small ridge with a gully to the right. This scenic segment winds beneath tall pines that shade the path on either side.

At approximately 3 miles, the habitat changes from primarily pine to a mix of pines and hardwoods. You'll start to see magnolia, oak, hickory, red maple, sassafras, and sweet gum among the pines. At 3.3 miles you'll see another new plant—prickly pear cactus! This spiny plant's bright yellow flowers can be seen from mid-spring to early summer.

Following a very pleasant, winding walk through mixed forest, you'll reach another rocky outcrop with a view—and a spot to set up your tent—at 3.9 miles. Bear to the right after this, heading downhill, past more potential campsites. The Backbone Trail gets more rugged as it heads steeply downhill over a jumble of rocks. As the elevation decreases, note how the trees change. You are entering an area of large, healthy, moisture-loving magnolias and elms—though you'll still see plenty of pines. Off to the left at 4 miles is a pleasantly shaded spot overlooking a small creek. At 4.2 miles, the trail crosses Bayou Cypre. At the time of this writing, there was no bridge, but crossing could be accomplished via a fallen log that conveniently straddles the narrow bayou.

The next mile of the Backbone Trail is particularly pleasant. When the trail seems to split at 4.7 miles, bear right, following the orange blazes. You'll soon reach a low, wet, cypress-filled slough, where a bridge takes you over a nearby stream. Wild azaleas are plentiful here in spring, and the large, dark-leaved magnolias provide shade—a perfect spot for a short break. Head uphill after crossing the bridge to reach an area surrounded by very tall pines, and with numerous ridges all around. At 5 miles, it seems to split; the left fork leads up a badly eroded hillside, so you'll want to take the right fork, following the orange blazes. Head uphill and rejoin the original trail shortly afterward. At 5.1 miles is a junction with a short spur, the Turpentine Hill Trail. Unless you want to explore this side trip, continue uphill on the Backbone Trail.

The trail descends to cross a stream at 5.3 miles. Walk briefly alongside the stream, then ascend to a scenic, rocky area. At 5.5 miles is an established campsite with a fire ring, room for several tents, and a bit of a view. From here, the trail resumes its characteristic small ascents and descents as it leads past interesting sandstone fragments. Be aware that this segment can get very muddy and sticky, particularly as it leads back uphill. You will reach a scenic view at 5.9 miles before descending the rocky trail once more. The path soon flattens out and crosses a small stream, then leads through several low, potentially muddy areas and streams before returning to sandy, pine-dominated forest at 6.6 miles. At 6.8 miles is a rocky area to the right—a good spot for tenting or just taking a lunch break.

The remainder of the trail is mostly downhill, and you'll reach a KISATCHIE HILLS WILDERNESS sign at 7.4 miles. At 7.5 miles, exit the trail at the Longleaf Trail Scenic Byway. The parking area is just across the road, as is the trailhead for the Caroline Dormon Trail.

18

Longleaf Vista Nature Trail

Total distance (circuit): 1.5 miles

Hiking time: 1 hour

*Habitats: Mixed pine-hardwood
with stands of longleaf pine*

*Maps: USGS 7½' Gorum,
Kisatchie Ranger District
Recreation Opportunities flyer*

Sandstone outcrops. Rocky climbs. The soft trickle of a distant waterfall. Miniature mesas that provide expansive vistas of the Kisatchie Hills Wilderness for miles around. No, this doesn't sound like a Louisiana trail—but it is. Considered one of the state's most scenic hikes, the 1.4-mile Longleaf Vista Nature Trail elicits "oohs" and "ahhs" from just about everyone who hikes it. Are people really impressed with the views? I like to think so. But I think they're also pleasantly surprised to see that modestly flat, swampy little Louisiana has an actual overlook of the landscape. Several overlooks, in fact!

Like the rest of Louisiana, this generally rugged area of Kisatchie was once the smooth, sandy floor of the future Gulf of Mexico. Over millions of years, streams and rivers farther north carried sediments southward, dumping layer after layer onto the primordial Gulf Coastal Plain. The land sloped oceanward as Louisiana grew in elevation. The coastline stretched farther and farther south. Meanwhile, the layers of sediment accumulated farther north, slowly giving rise to sedimentary rocks: mudstones, shales, sandstones, limestones, and gravels. Even as these rocks formed, the force of erosion took its toll as flowing water carved out a distinctive landscape. The erosion-resistant sandstones stood firm and formed hills, while the more malleable mudstones and shales eroded into the valleys. Today, the sandstone hills that characterize this region are known collectively to geologists as the Kisatchie Wold. Within the Kisatchie Wold are slope-sided, flat-topped buttes, or small mesas. You'll ascend several buttes on this hike, all of which provide impressive views of the 8,700-acre Kisatchie Hills Wilderness.

The Longleaf Vista Nature Trail begins and ends at the Longleaf Vista Recreation Area, west of Alexandria. To get there from I-49, take LA 119 at Derry (Exit 119) and travel west for 5.1 miles to the Longleaf Trail Scenic Byway. Turn right onto the byway and drive 3.1 miles to the Longleaf Vista Recreation Area on the right. By the way, the Longleaf Trail Scenic Byway is an interesting 17-mile drive along a natural ridge. If you have time, you'll want to explore this driving tour a bit more after your hike.

The recreation area features a large parking lot, picnic tables, a water fountain, and a restroom. A stone walkway leads about 200 yards from the parking lot to a gazebo and a wide view of the Kisatchie Hills Wilderness. Redbuds and dogwoods make this short walk particularly beautiful in early spring, when the breezes are still cool and summer's stifling humidity is yet to come.

The Longleaf Vista Nature Trail picks up at the end of the stone walk, to the right of the gazebo and to the left of a plaque that has a trail map embossed onto it. You'll immediately descend a curving flight of irregular stone steps. The trail swings left after leveling out, leading past red-berried yaupons and huckleberry shrubs that have white, tubular flowers in spring and round, black berries ripening in early summer. As you round the tall bluff to your left, observe it from your new standpoint beneath it. Rocky, vertical outcrops like this are rare in Louisiana.

The trail descends a bit more, only to bottom out on a ridge and begin back uphill at 0.2 mile to approach a butte. A spur trail to the right leads to the top of this flat-topped hill. You'll want to take the spur, of course. After all, how often do you get a chance to ascend to an overlook in

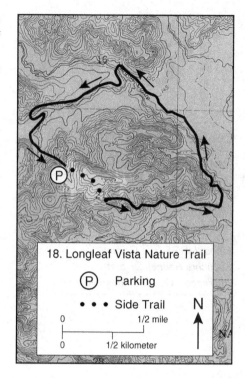

18. Longleaf Vista Nature Trail

Ⓟ   Parking

• • •   Side Trail   N

0   1/2 mile

0   1/2 kilometer

Louisiana? A flight of some 30 stone steps leads to wide views of central Louisiana's piney woods.

Back on the trail, begin a mild descent. Most of the shrublike trees you're seeing here are yaupon and common sweetleaf. Yaupon has small, dark green, dully toothed leaves, while the leaves of common sweetleaf are larger and have smooth edges—similar to those of mountain laurel. This tree, also called horsesugar, is known for its sweet-tasting leaves—though the sweetness changes from season to season. It's also known as yellowwood, for a yellow dye that can be obtained from its bark and leaves. Its Latin species name, tinctora, refers to its dyeing properties as well.

The trail soon changes from stone to asphalt, and it will remain a narrow asphalt path for the rest of the hike. The earth is sandy in Louisiana's piney woods, so the as-

Steps lead to the top of a miniature mesa, or butte.

phalt may be obscured in places by a mix of sand and pine needles.

The descent levels out at 0.3 mile to approach another butte. When the trail forks, you have a choice of detouring to the left (to hike around the butte and avoid the climb) or heading straight for the next flight of stone stairs. If you have time, consider taking both routes. While the view from the top is certainly worth the climb, the sight of the sandstone rock from beneath definitely has its own charm. The two trails rejoin 0.2 mile later, and you'll enjoy a level hike past several interpretive signs before the winding trail begins another descent.

Pines grow well in the sandy, well-drained soil of this region, and you'll see three of the five pines that grow in Louisiana on this hike: longleaf, loblolly, and shortleaf. Although all pines may look alike at first glance, these three species are really quite different, and this hike offers a great opportunity to notice those differences. Appearance-wise, the longleaf is perhaps the most striking tree, with its long, (8- to 18-inch) needles that fan gracefully outward at the ends of its branches and its thin, scaly, reddish-orange bark. Its Latin species name, *palustris,* refers to its preference for moist, swampy soils. Longleaf has the largest cones of any Louisiana pines, some of them up to a foot tall. Shortleaf is easy to differentiate from longleaf, with its 3- to 5-inch needles and 2-inch cones. Loblolly is the most common of Louisiana's pines, having been heavily planted for timber. Loblolly also proved adept at invading abandoned fields throughout the state after the timber industry denuded much of the region in the first half of the 20th century. At only 6 to 9 inches, loblolly needles are not as long as those of longleaf. Measuring between 2 and 6 inches, its cones are markedly smaller, too.

The trail continues its steady descent, passing a bench at 0.6 mile, then leveling out to cross a small stream. After veering to the right, you'll briefly head back uphill. You might notice a creek on your left at 0.7 mile. Ferns add to the beauty of the low, wet area that slopes gently down from this small ridge.

The Longleaf Vista Trail hugs a small hill, curving slightly to the right with the creek below. This segment may be soggy during wet seasons, but the asphalt keeps it from getting too unpleasantly muddy. You'll still want to watch your step, in case parts of the trail are slippery. Begin another descent at 0.9 mile to cross a small footbridge. The trail soon makes a hairpin turn to the left and passes a ravine to the left and some dead pines to the right—the result of a wildfire several years ago.

Cross another low, wet area at 1 mile. The trail remains relatively straight through here and crosses an intermittent creek at 1.1 miles. This area is heavy with undergrowth; notice how the tallest trees are pine, and how the understory comprises smaller scrub oaks, hickories, sweet gums, and red maples.

Pass a bench, then swing to the left to approach the trail's one "waterfall." This whitewater trickle is delightful in early spring, when the banks are bedecked with blooming wild azaleas. Several gnarled old southern magnolias shade this pleasant spot.

The narrow streambed is just a few inches deep, so you should have no trouble stepping across it. After crossing, the trail ascends slightly. The mild, steady uphill gets notably steeper at 1.3 miles; in fact, it climbs a flight of a few dozen stone steps before leveling out. Here, you can bear right for another view of the surrounding pine forests. If the area has seen a lot of rain recently, you may hear another small waterfall. Cascading Carolina jessamine and showy birdfoot violets grace this entire area in early spring.

The trail itself swings left, away from the overlook, to continue uphill. As the elevation increases, you'll gain more views of the surrounding piney woods. Soon the trail approaches the day-use area. At 1.4 miles, a final set of stone steps leads back the stone walkway near the parking lot—and the conclusion of this short but remarkable hike.

19

Fullerton Mill Trail

Total distance (two circuits): 2 miles

Hiking time: 1 hour

Habitats: Mixed pine and hardwood

Maps: USGS 7½' Fullerton Lake

Louisiana has long hosted a thriving timber industry, even though it was a bit of a "late bloomer." In 1869, we had the lowest lumber output in the South. Once the railroads finally started reaching into our extensive pine forests in the 1870s, however, things changed. By 1904, Louisiana's timber output had surpassed that of the other southern states at nearly 2.5 billion board feet. In fact, with huge regions of longleaf and shortleaf pine, plus the hardwoods and cypresses along the Mississippi, Louisiana contained more timber than any other state in the Union, except for those on the west coast. With the coming of the railroads, Louisiana became a major player in the growing country's timber industry.

Lumber companies sprouted up everywhere. With them came the lumber towns, often booming communities built exclusively around the industry. One such town was Fullerton, home of the Fullerton Lumber Mill—at one time the largest pine sawmill west of the Mississippi River. For 20 years in the early 1900s, Fullerton's thriving population hovered around five-thousand. Today, Fullerton—a town that had such modern features as fountains, electricity, indoor plumbing, and a swimming pool—is little more than a memory. Although the town still stood after its timbering heyday, the World War II army engineers at nearby Camp Polk (now Fort Polk) used the site for bombing exercises, further relegating the site to obscurity. The property, which is located in the Vernon Ranger District, has been on the National Register of Historic Places since 1986. You can explore this interesting site by hiking the Fullerton Mill Trail, where you'll see a few small heaps of ruins where timber once brought so much prosperity.

To get there via I-10 or US 190, go west from Baton Rouge and turn north onto US 165. When you get to Oakdale, go west on LA 10 to the small town of Cravens. (You can also get to LA 10 from I-49 by taking Exit 23 at Ville Platte.) At Cravens, turn right onto LA 399, which junctions with LA 458 after 3.1 miles. Bear left to continue on LA 399, following the signs to Kisatchie National Forest and the Longleaf Recreation Area. After approximately 2 miles, turn left onto the gravel road leading to the campground and drive 0.6 mile to find an interpretive sign and marker for the Fullerton Mill Trail on the left. The trail includes a short loop and a long loop. The hike described here takes you on both loops. Because the loops overlap, you'll need to retrace your steps for part of the hike.

Marked by metal signs nailed to trees, the Fullerton Mill Trail begins on a downward slope past southern magnolia and dogwood. After crossing a footbridge, the trail forks into the long loop and the short loop. For now, you want to bear right to begin the short loop, which ascends a mild incline beneath tall pines. After 0.3 mile, a short side trail to the right leads to the ragged remains of Fullerton Mill's alcohol plant. A large cedar rises from the rubble. Resurrection fern grows in places, making this area look lush after a rain, and old and weathered, like the ruins themselves, during dry seasons. As you continue hiking, you'll see clumps of thicketlike undergrowth formed by wild grape, poison ivy, Virginia creeper, ferns, and various decidu-

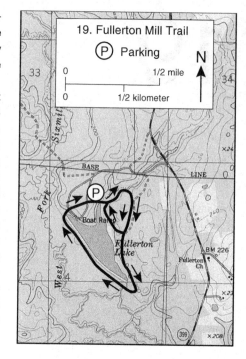

ous saplings. The tallest, oldest-looking trees are mostly pines.

The trail winds around the vegetation-covered ruins before reaching a second side trail, this one leading to what remains of an old water tank. You'll see more of these intriguing ruins on your right, several hundred feet down the path. When the Fullerton Mill Trail splits at 0.4 mile, bear right to conclude the short loop, walking past the remains of one of Fullerton's sawmills. You'll pass the water tank ruins once more, this time from the west. As you continue the short loop, you'll get your first glimpse of the quiet, scenic waters of Fullerton Lake to your left. The trail approaches its shoreline before shifting away from the lake at 0.5 mile to complete the short loop just a few hundred feet farther on. From here, you'll need to retrace your

Ruins at the Fullerton Mill site

steps 0.4 mile to the long/short loop split for a total hike, so far, of 0.9 mile.

When you return to the fork of the long and short loops, bear left to hike the long loop. With an abundance of flowering dog-woods, this little trail is absolutely stunning in spring. The pine needle-carpeted ground seems to wear a blanket of snow once the dogwoods' white flowers have fallen in April. As you follow the trail's lonely mean-der through this once-bustling mill town, look for small, blue violets, along with the maroon flowers and mottled leaves of ses-sile-leaved trillium as these early-spring blooms push their way through the fallen pine needles. Violets are hardy little wild-flowers; you may see them here as early as January, and you'll continue to see them on the trails well into early summer.

At 1 mile, you'll reach the rubble where another sawmill stood. A little farther down the trail is the site of the mill's roundhouse, where locomotives were housed and switched. The trail also passes the site of the mill's machine shop before leaving the ruins behind. The Fullerton Mill Trail bends to the right and crosses an old road trace, winding beneath tall, shade-bearing hardwoods and pines. At 1.2 miles, you will reach an open area. Go straight ahead, along the right mar-gin of this open area, then hike slightly left to encounter the last of the mill ruins on this trail.

You'll reach a road at 1.3 miles. Turn left here to follow the trail as it joins the road for a short time. The trail exits the woods into an open area soon afterward to parallel the western bank of Fullerton Lake for a half mile. Here the hike transforms from an historical walk to a pleasant, scenic hike alongside the lake. Wildflowers adorn the shoreline in spring, and the fallen petals of Carolina jessamine dot the still waters. The remainder of your hike is the short walk around Fullerton Lake back to the trailhead. In fact, if you look across the lake, you'll be able to see the trailhead and your car. The marked trail concludes at the picnic area on the opposite side of Fullerton Lake. The short walk back to the trailhead will complete your 2-mile hike.

20

Wild Azalea Trail

Total distance (one way): 26.2 miles

Hiking time: 2–3 days

Habitats: Mixed pine and hardwood, longleaf pine forest, small-stream forest

Maps: USGS 7½' Woodworth West, USGS 7½' Elmer, Evangeline Unit Recreation Opportunities flyer; brochure and map available at Calcasieu Ranger District office

Located in the Calcasieu Ranger District of Kisatchie National Forest, the Wild Azalea Trail is Louisiana's longest backpacking trail. With its mild, rolling hills, peaceful creek-side campsites, and meandering rambles ranging from sweet-smelling longleaf pine forest to scenic, magnolia-lined ravines choked with blooming wild azaleas, it is the perfect trail for unwinding, relaxing, and simply delighting in the natural world around you. While this is a good trail to hike any time of year (except for late summer), late March and early April are most popular, when the azaleas, dogwoods, and other trees and wildflowers are in bloom.

With an abundance of road crossings for shuttling, the Wild Azalea Trail lends itself to day hiking as well as backpacking. Because forest roads are not always clearly marked, you'll want to obtain a good trail map at the Calcasieu Ranger District Office. Popular short hikes along the Wild Azalea Trail include the following:

- LA 488 Trailhead to Castor Creek Scenic Area (4.8-mile circuit)
- Evangeline Camp to Valentine Lake Trailhead (9 miles, one way)
- Evangeline Camp to Forest Service (FS) Road 212 (11 miles, one way)

This guide will describe an east-to-west weekend backpacking trip from the Woodworth Town Hall to the Valentine Lake Recreation Area. Although you can avoid the road walk and start where the trail enters the National Forest 1.7 miles down, be aware that available parking is minimal at that access point. This hike should be a

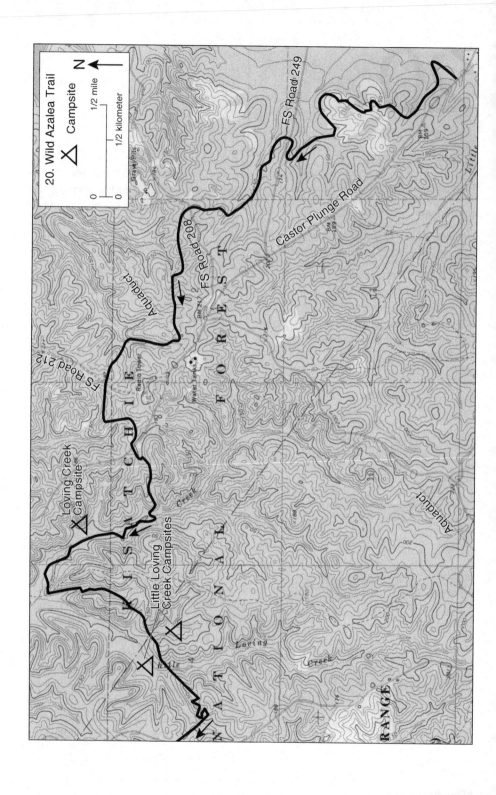

20. Wild Azalea Trail

△ Campsite

N

0   1/2 mile
0   1/2 kilometer

FS Road 249

Castor Plunge Road

Aqueduct

FS Road 208

FS Road 212

Radio Tower

Water Tank

Loving Creek Campsite

Little Loving Creek Campsites

Gravel Pits

KISATCHIE NATIONAL FOREST

Creek

Loving Creek

Aqueduct

RANGE

Little

good 2½-day trek for most backpacking groups. Backpackers may want to pack an earplug or two, as the trail is in close proximity to the U.S. Air Force's Claiborne Range. While the military activities do not pose a danger for backpackers, their nighttime exercises can interrupt a good night's sleep!

Getting to the Woodworth Town Hall:

The official southeast trailhead is at the Woodworth Town Hall on Castor Plunge Road. To get there from I-49, go east on LA 3265 at Woodworth (Exit 73). This road becomes Castor Plunge Road and will lead you the short distance through town to the Woodworth Town Hall. The Town of Woodworth allows hikers to leave their cars in the parking lot, though you'll want to check in with the folks inside before hiking.

Getting to the Valentine Lake Terminus:

If you are traveling *south* on I-49, take Exit 99 at Boyce and go south on LA 1200 for 3.6 miles. Turn left and take LA 121 to Gardner. After 7.1 miles, you'll pass a convenience store and gas station. From there, follow the signs to the Valentine Lake Recreation Area. Just before you cross the cattle grate to enter the Valentine Lake Southshore Campground, you'll see a grassy parking area and the yellow-blazed trail terminus to your left.

If you are traveling *north* on I-49, take Exit 80 south of Alexandria and follow US 71/165 to LA 28. Turn left onto LA 28, which will take you to Gardner. Once in Gardner, turn left onto LA 121 and follow the signs to the Valentine Lake Recreation Area.

Day 1: Woodworth Town Hall to Little Loving Creek
Total distance: 8.6 miles
Time: 4–5 hours

The hike begins with a 1.7-mile road walk down Castor Plunge Road, passing through suburban Woodworth before entering Kisatchie National Forest, where the paved road turns to gravel. At that point, look ahead and to your right for the large Wild Azalea Trail sign and the double yellow blazes that will mark the straight, flat path through pine-dominated forest. As you enter the woods, you'll see heavy undergrowth of poison ivy, wild grape, mayhaw, yaupon, wax myrtle, common sweetleaf, red maple, and sweet gum. Several short side trails break off from the main trail early in the hike; just keep following the yellow blazes. This part of the trail is not considered to be as scenic as later segments, but the spring-flowering dogwoods add to the area's visual appeal.

The Wild Azalea Trail swings to the right at 1.9 miles and soon crosses a dirt road. In late March, you'll start to see the blooming wild azaleas for which the trail is named. Sometimes mistaken for honeysuckle, the wild azalea is a low shrub with spidery pink and white flowers. These distinctive flowers grow in abundance on much of this trail, as well as throughout Kisatchie's pine forests. Speaking of pine, you'll begin to see long-leaf pines at 2.2 miles—in my opinion, the prettiest of Louisiana's pines. Veer to the right at 2.3 miles, through an area that had seen a recent burn at the time of this writing. Ferns and red maples have sprouted at the charred feet of the tall conifers.

The trail crosses a second road at 2.6 miles, then passes a reseeded clear-cut pine plantation at 2.7 miles. Cross a small footbridge at 3.3 miles, then veer to the right to walk alongside a small creek. You'll soon head downhill toward a boardwalk through a wet, boggy area. Perhaps you'll spot the flashing white of a prothonotary warbler's tail feathers as it flits by, low in the understory. Listen for the rising *sweet sweet sweet* song of this beautiful songbird, whose body is a brilliant, citruslike yellow. Since it prefers wet, swampy habitats, this warbler is abundant throughout most of Louisiana during both summer and the migration seasons.

Swing left after crossing a boardwalk to cross your first major road, FS Road 249, at 3.6 miles. The trail descends slightly at 3.7 miles, then cuts through a swath of planted longleaf pines. If you're like me and love these pines, you'll enjoy this peaceful walk. If, however, you're already tired of walking through piney woods, keep hiking. The Wild Azalea Trail has much more to offer.

After crossing an ATV road at 4 miles, you'll wind through mixed pine and hardwood forest to reach FS Road 208 at 4.5 miles. Following the yellow blazes, descend past heavy undergrowth of wax myrtle, sassafras, and wild grape. The trail levels out, crosses an old road trace, and becomes rather hilly and rolling as it meanders alongside pines and dogwoods. You will cross a dirt road at 5.1 miles before entering a low, flat spot teeming with dogwoods. After exiting this low area, you will cross an aqueduct at 5.3 miles. Water towers and a radio tower dominate the view from this clear-cut.

The trail begins a mild, gentle descent past oaks above and ferns below. Although pines still dominate, you'll start to see more hardwoods than previously. At 5.6 miles, the trail contours a small ridge before beginning a mild but steady uphill. As you hike, notice that some of the longleaf pines are marked with painted white bands. If you're familiar with Kisatchie National Forest or have hiked Big Branch Marsh National Wildlife Refuge, you'll recognize these banded trunks as nesting trees for the endangered red-cockaded woodpecker.

At 5.9 miles, the trail swings left to parallel FS Road 212 for about 50 feet before crossing it. Because the Wild Azalea Trail becomes more varied from here, this road is a popular access point for day hikers and for backpackers looking for a shorter hike. Just north of the trail crossing is a small parking area. At the time of this writing, the trail was not well marked for the first few hundred yards following the crossing. Simply go straight across the road and follow the level path through the pines and oaks, looking for yellow blazes on the trees in the distance.

The Wild Azalea Trail descends a mild incline at 6.2 miles, swings left, and levels out soon afterward. After crossing a highline at 6.3 miles, you want to turn right, hike north for about 100 feet, then swing back to the left and reenter the woods. The trail exits the woods soon afterward to cross FS Road 287 (Castor Plunge Road). Look up to see a red-tailed hawk, recognizable by its light-colored underside and distinctive red tail.

The trail soon begins a modest uphill and swings left through a patch of dogwoods. Cross an old woods road at 6.5 miles, then descend to a beautiful area that is filled with southern magnolias and wild azaleas. American hollies, with their dark, waxy green leaves and bright red berries, make this spot quite scenic in the winter, too. This exquisite spot has room for a couple of tents to the left, though another, larger campsite is available in less than a half mile.

As you contour a low ridge on your way to Loving Creek, you'll see lots of magnolia, sassafras, and red maple, along with hundreds of ferns downslope. For now, you've left the sandy, well-drained habitat so preferred by the pines, though pines will grow—and thrive—all along the Wild Azalea Trail. The trail descends at 6.8 miles to reach a level area next to Loving Creek. Swing to the right, then keep hiking past moisture-loving bald cypress, American beech, and water

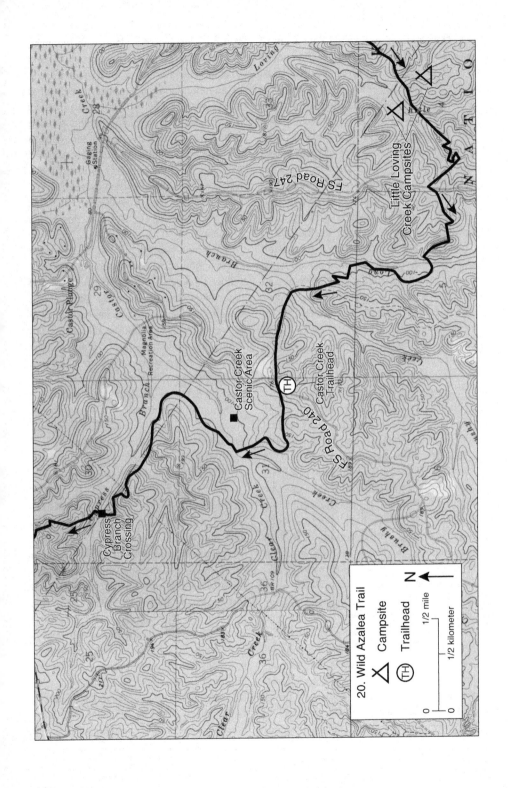

20. Wild Azalea Trail

△ Campsite
(TH) Trailhead

N

0 ____ 1/2 mile
0 ____ 1/2 kilometer

Little Loving
Creek Campsites

Castor Creek
Trailhead

Castor Creek
Scenic Area

FS Road 247

FS Road 240

Cypress
Branch
Crossing

oak. Note the cypress knees jutting out of the ground nearby, indicating that this poorly drained area sees plenty of flooding. You'll also see swamp chestnut oak, also known as cow oak or basket oak. The leaves of this large tree can grow up to 10 inches long and 6 inches wide, though they're more likely to be little smaller. The elliptical leaves have numerous wavy, shallow lobes or "teeth"—up to two dozen teeth per leaf!

Following the yellow blazes, bear left (rather than going straight uphill) to pass through a spongy little spot beside Loving Creek. The trail then ascends a small ridge and passes a small forest of cinnamon ferns. These hardy ferns are Louisiana natives and do well in wet, acidic soils and in areas that receive lots of sunlight. You can recognize them by their size; some grow more than 5 feet tall! The leaves of these ferns seem to wear tattered coats of rusty or cinnamon-colored "wool." In early spring, you'll see their notably large, unfurling "fiddleheads."

The Wild Azalea Trail traverses the mild undulations of this low terrain, passing several cypress sloughs before reaching a bridge and the Loving Creek campsite at 7.2 miles. Be aware that this campsite can get pretty soggy in heavy rains. Moisture-adapted ironwood and sugarberry dominate this area. Both trees have rather smooth, gray trunks. While the sugarberry's thick trunk often has knobby, corky growths, the ironwood's trunk is thin and sinewy, and looks almost like a sculpture of a human muscle.

Cross the bridge over Loving Creek, then hike alongside the water with an often-flooded brake to your left. Beginning at 7.4 miles, you will follow a wide, raised path through a swampy area. As you walk down this clear, easy path, you see huge cypress trunks and plentiful cypress knees just a few feet away, on either side. In spring, this sec-

tion sees mayapples, along with blooming red buckeye, violets, spiderwort, phlox, and of course, wild azaleas. You'll reach the site of an abandoned pine beetle study at 8 miles, where tall, white, siding-like material is attached to numerous trees and is falling down in places. Look at the fern-choked ravine below to see the occasional dwarf palmetto. The trail ascends to reach a low hilltop at 8.3 miles and then crosses an old road. Heading back downhill, you can look over the forest and see flowering dogwoods in spring.

Continue downhill, only to level out and climb another small hill. Once you descend (rather steeply) that second hill, you'll find yourself at your destination: Little Loving Creek. This pleasant campsite has plenty of space for tents and features at least two fire rings. More campsites are available across the creek. Although bears are not a threat in Kisatchie, you will want to hang your food in order to deter the raccoons and other small critters from eating tomorrow's meals.

Day 2: Little Loving Creek to Evangeline Camp

Total distance: 9.6 miles
Time: About 6 hours

To begin today's hike, cross the small foot-bridge over Little Loving Creek, continuing your westward trek of the Wild Azalea Trail. The path soon descends to skirt another campsite with a fire ring, then crosses another footbridge. After a mild ascent at 0.3 mile, the trail meanders over rolling hills through scenic mixed pine and hardwood forest. Be aware that the low stream valleys of these rolling ridges can become flooded—or at least very muddy—during a wet spring. The path crosses FS Road 247 at 0.7 mile, then crosses a couple of creeks, including Little Brushy Creek at 2.8 miles. There are some nice flat spots around Little Brushy for

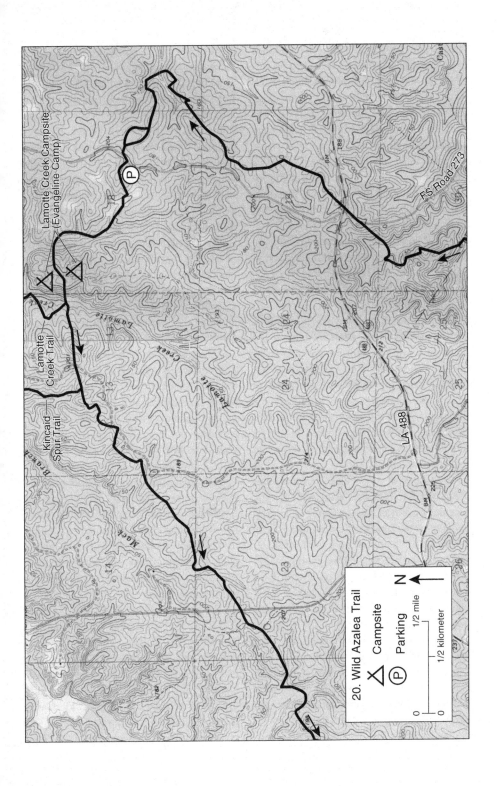

Lamotte Creek Campsite
(Evangeline Camp)

Lamotte
Creek Trail

Kincaid
Spur Trail

Lamotte Creek

Branch

Mack

FS Road 273

LA 488

BM 188

BM 212

20. Wild Azalea Trail

△ Campsite

Ⓟ Parking

N

0   1/2 mile
0   1/2 kilometer

tenting, but I have found that this area tends to flood easily and may be quite soggy.

Reach the Castor Creek trailhead at FS Road 240, 3.1 miles into your hike. Dayhikers can use the small parking area here for a short, half-mile stroll to the upcoming Castor Creek Scenic Area; however, because the space for parking is limited, they might wish to park at the LA 488/FS Road 273 junction. From that junction, the trail distance to Castor Creek and back is about 5 miles.

The Wild Azalea Trail descends immediately after crossing the road, and much of the next segment takes you over low, gently sloping terrain and past beech, southern magnolia, oak, hickory, sassafras, red maple, dogwood, wax myrtle, muscadine, and numerous ferns. Christmas ferns are common here. You can identify their evergreen fronds by their singly pinnate, toothed, dark green leaves, the bases of which are sharply notched. Imaginative folks might liken the notch to the heel of a Christmas stocking. The leaves are evergreen—probably the reason for the common name of Christmas fern.

Cross a small stream at 3.7 miles to enter the Castor Creek Scenic Area. Although the "scenic" aspect of Castor Creek was sadly affected by the pine beetle epidemic several years back, this special spot is definitely on the road to recovery. The sturdy bridge across the clear creek is a great spot for a snack break. This spot also makes for a pleasant campsite. If you do camp here, be sure to hang your food bag.

The next 0.5 mile is through an often soggy area that is full of spring beauties, violets, and violet wood sorrel in March and April. The trail heads uphill at 4.1 miles, winding beneath tall pines and alongside various hardwood saplings—and hundreds of blooming wild azaleas and dogwoods. This segment of the trail is absolutely thrilling when the spring flowers are in bloom.

Cross Cypress Branch at 4.6 miles, then pass through another low, quaggy area before heading back uphill to wind beneath dogwoods and pines. When the trail reaches an old logging road at 4.8 miles, turn right onto the road, then take a sharp left to return to the woods, keeping an eye out for the blazes. The trail descends into a marshy little azalea-filled gully at 5 miles. After crossing a small bridge here, the trail winds through the small-stream woods, which are dominated by American beech, chestnut oak, and other trees that prefer low, claylike soils rather than the sandier soils favored by pine. Parts of the trail here are reinforced with limestone to prevent erosion of the already soft ground.

The trail ascends back into mixed pine and hardwood country at 5.1 miles. It follows an old road trace, then swings right to reenter the woods at 5.3 miles. You'll soon gain a beautiful view of flowering dogwoods to your right. If you like the smell of pine, you'll love this scenic segment of the trail. After a few more ups and downs, the Wild Azalea Trail traverses a footbridge at 5.7 miles and ascends to level out at an old logging road, passing beneath mostly young hardwood saplings and tall pines. Springtime wildflowers are plentiful here and include blue-eyed grass, spiderwort, and wild grape. The wild azaleas, of course, continue to grace the forest.

The junction of LA 488 and FS Road 273 is at 6.1 miles on the Wild Azalea Trail. As you exit the woods, look ahead to see a parking area and trailhead. With plenty of room to park a car, this is an good access point for day hikers or overnight backpackers, whether they are headed for Castor Creek or Lamotte Creek, a little more than 3 miles down the trail. Turn left onto the road and right into the parking lot. Cross LA 488 (a paved road), then reenter the woods at the hiking sign and yellow blazes. The trail descends slightly through an area that, at the time of this writing, had recently seen a controlled burn. Numerous pine saplings and ferns had begun to emerge at the feet of the charred older pines. The trail descends some more at 6.6 miles, passing near a wide dirt path to the left. After hiking through the recent burn area, you cross another dirt road at 7 miles.

Cross this road, following the very straight trail through the flat, recently burned area. In spring, you can see flowering dogwoods in the distance. The trail swings to the right, then begins a gentle descent. At the bottom of the incline, you want to veer to the right as the Wild Azalea Trail winds through woods of full-grown pines and saplings of red maple and other quick-growing hardwoods. At 7.9 miles, the trail passes several more of the white-banded longleaf pines.

The trail forks at 8.2 miles. You can go either way, though the blazes direct you to bear right. The two trails join up soon afterward, shortly before the trail reaches FS Road 273. From the parking area, you can see the Evangeline Camp trailhead straight ahead. Go through the gate at the trailhead and past a pit toilet. The wide, sandy trail forks at 8.4 miles. Bear to the right, past longleaf saplings and ferns. The Wild Azalea Trail soon narrows out and reenters the woods.

The 9 miles between the Evangeline Camp trailhead and Valentine Lake are a popular day hike on the Wild Azalea Trail, and the path is very well worn. The trail follows a series of ups and downs through this scenic area and crosses a footbridge at 9.1 miles. The uphill that follows is overlaid with concrete—an effort to make the trail more maneuverable for mountain bikers while preventing erosion of this often muddy space.

At one point, the trail seems to fork; you want to bear right, following the blazes, and continue uphill. Bear left at the top of the hill, then swing to the right a little as the trail begins to wind again. At 9.5 miles, you'll reach the spur trail on the left, which leads to tonight's destination: the Evangeline Camp primitive campsite on Lamotte Creek.

Because this campsite is a good distance from the road—not too close and not too far—and because it features lots of flat spots, several fire rings, and a crystal-clear water source, it is popular to the point of being overused. If you camp here on a weekend, be aware that you may have human company—as well as an overabundance of night critters looking for peanut butter and beef jerky. That said, I have had countless pleasant experiences camping here: chatting with friends around a small campfire, falling asleep to the lull of Lamotte Creek's clear, flowing waters, and waking up to hear the soft hoots of a barred owl in the early morning.

Day 3: Evangeline Camp to Valentine Lake

Total distance: 8 miles
Time: About 4 hours

After you've hiked the spur back to the Wild Azalea Trail, turn left to resume your hike. You'll soon cross a footbridge and swing to the left, gaining a final view of the Lamotte Creek campsite. At 0.1 mile, the Wild Azalea Trail junctions with the blue-blazed Lamotte Creek Trail, a 2.5-mile hike along Lamotte Creek to Lake Kincaid. Go straight ahead to continue the Wild Azalea Trail.

The next mile of the hike is winding but primarily flat, and you'll soon find yourself on a small ridge that overlooks small pines, red maple, dogwoods, magnolia, and many ferns. The trail descends slightly before reaching the Kincaid Lakeshore Trail Spur, a

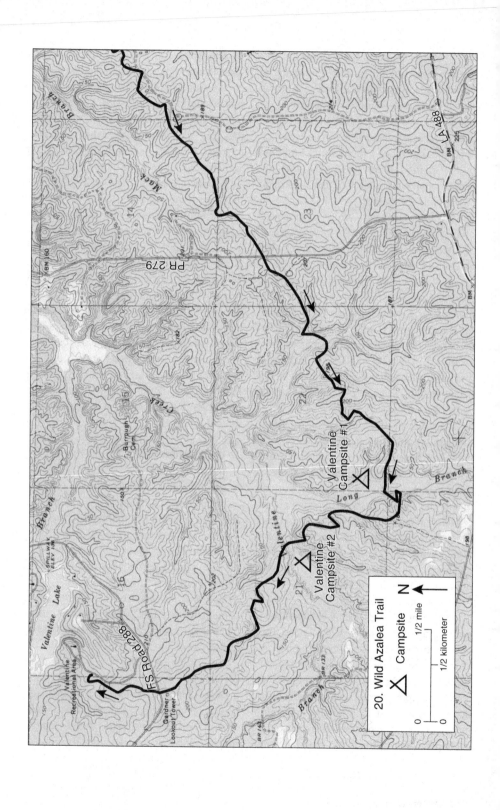

20. Wild Azalea Trail

△ Campsite

N

0   1/2 mile

0   1/2 kilometer

1-mile spur that leads to—you guessed it—the Kincaid Lakeshore Trail.

This next segment of the Wild Azalea Trail is very beautiful as the path winds over the rolling, pine-studded Kisatchie hills. Cross a logging road at 1 mile, then another at 1.2 miles. After traversing a low, potentially muddy area, the trail continues over rolling hills through a thicketed area of low plants clumped beneath a forest of tall pines. Among the vines and shrubs, look for blooming Carolina jessamine, wild grape, and huckleberry. As the trail drops in elevation, you'll see some dwarf palmetto in the lower areas, as well as southern magnolia.

The level, winding trail follows a low ridge at 1.5 miles, then crosses another old logging road and descends sharply into a ravine at 1.7 miles. Yet another old logging road follows soon afterward, and the Wild Azalea Trail winds through a delightful area of spring-blooming wildflowers, shrubs, and trees. Cross a footbridge at 2.3 miles; here, you'll find several flat spots for a tent next to the creek. The trail climbs out of this low area and crosses a road with a parking area at Rapides Parish Road 279. Following the yellow blazes, reenter the woods to exit again at a clear-cut highline at 3 miles.

This segment of the Wild Azalea Trail leads through a forest thick with longleaf pines that dwarf the hardwood saplings growing at their feet. You're also approaching another area where the wild azaleas are thrillingly plentiful. The path descends to cross a bridge at 3.4 miles through a swampy, magnolia-dominated spot. It heads back uphill to level out into a beautiful area that is rife with wild azaleas, red cedar, sassafras, and many colorful wildflowers in spring. In late fall, many of these hardwoods have lost their leaves and provide nice views through the hilly woods.

You will descend to cross another bridge at 3.5 miles. The Wild Azalea Trail's small streams are home to the endangered pearl shell mussel, which has been found only in the sandy creeks of Rapides and Grant Parishes. The mussels are about 4 inches long, 2 inches high, and 1 inch wide and live in small-streambed colonies. You may well see one of these dark brown mollusks as you hike along the streams of the Wild Azalea Trail. The staff of Kisatchie National Forest and the Louisiana Department of Wildlife and Fisheries are making efforts to improve the habitat for this little creature, which has been threatened by a variety of factors, from human logging operations to beaver dams.

The trail winds some more before crossing another forest road at 3.9 miles. You'll see a fence to your left as the trail heads downhill. After a short, mild uphill, you'll cross FS Road 206, and then follow the straight, level trail beneath more towering pines. Pass a few low beeches before heading uphill again and crossing FS Road 2133 at 4.4 miles. The mild ups and downs give way to flat, level walking on a wide, pine needle-carpeted trail at 4.7 miles. Just after that, the trail forks. If you bear right, you'll reach the first of several campsites on Valentine Creek, about 50 feet off the trail. This pleasant spot is a prime area for a hiking break and makes for an excellent campsite. Just walk straight ahead and past the huge, fallen beech.

To continue the Wild Azalea Trail, however, bear left, watching for the yellow blazes. The trail winds alongside the water, and then crosses a bridge (and another potential campsite) at 4.9 miles.

From here, you want to bear left and ascend to a scenic spot at 5 miles—an area graced by wild azaleas, beeches, and southern magnolias. The trail ascends a bit more before leveling out, then veers to the right

Wild azaleas on the trail

onto an old road trace at 5.2 miles. Several downhills follow, and at 5.9 miles, the trail bottoms out in a small-stream forest of magnolia, beech, and countless ferns.

Cross another footbridge at 6 miles, then swing to the left, following the yellow blazes. You're now walking on a sandy trail alongside Valentine Creek. The trail soon swings to the right, away from the water, to continue through beech and magnolia country, though you'll also see some large pines. Other than a few mild ups, downs, and winding turns, the trail stays pretty straight and level for the rest of the hike. By the time you've hiked 7.3 miles, you'll find yourself in pine-dominated woods once more. The wide trail passes the Gardner Lookout Tower and FS Road 288 at 7.4 miles. Following the yellow blazes, bear right when the trail reaches an open area and a gravel road. Hike down this flat, rutted old road, and when the road forks, stay to the right, keeping an eye out for the blazes. At 7.6 miles, the trail swings left, away from the road and back into the woods. It crosses another cleared area, then makes a slight, winding descent. The trail forks one last time at 8 miles. Bear right to exit at the Valentine Lake Trailhead. Valentine Lake—and the short Valentine Lake Loop (Hike 21)—is just a mile farther down the road to your left.

21

Valentine Lake Loop

Total distance (circuit): 1.7 miles

Hiking time: 1 hour

Habitats: Mixed pine and hardwood forest, small-stream forest, nontidal marsh

Maps: USGS 7½' Elmer, Calcasieu Ranger District–Evangeline Unit Recreation Opportunities flyer

The Evangeline Unit of Kisatchie's Calcasieu Ranger District offers trails for just about every hiking level. The Wild Azalea Trail (Hike 20) is Louisiana's longest trail, suitable for backpacking and long day hikes. The Kincaid Lakeshore Trail (Hike 22) is a good day-hike with gentle terrain and beautiful views. The most modest of the Evangeline Unit's trails is a delightful short path that is just a brief road walk from its more famous brother, the Wild Azalea Trail: the Valentine Lake Loop, a 1.7-mile hike around the marshy edges of scenic Valentine Lake. This pleasant ramble will take you through a rolling forest of hardwoods and pines before depositing you on the lakeshore, where you'll see a wealth of yellow irises blooming in April.

On some of the United States Forest Service maps, the Valentine Lake Loop looks like an extension of the Wild Azalea Trail. Indeed, it's just a short drive (or hike) from the Wild Azalea Trail's Valentine Lake trailhead. This loop has no official trailhead, which can cause some confusion. The most obvious starting point, however, is the entrance road to Valentine Lake Recreation Area's Northshore Campground. Another starting point, particularly for anyone camping here, is at the back of the campground, just behind Campsite #12. This campground is closed between October and April, which can limit your ability to park near the trail in winter. You can always park at the Wild Azalea Trail's Valentine Lake trailhead (at the Southshore Campground entrance), or you can park at the nearby day-use area.

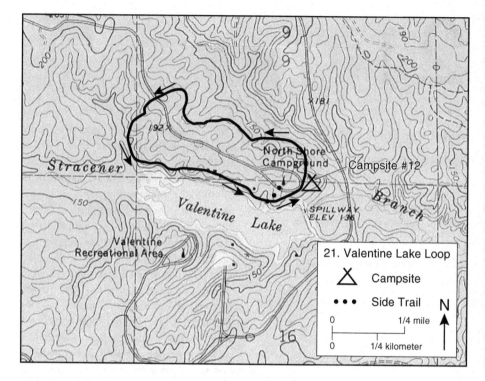

21. Valentine Lake Loop

△ Campsite

••• Side Trail

N

0 — 1/4 mile

0 — 1/4 kilometer

Either of these will require a short road walk to the trail.

To get to the trail from I-49, you can take either Exit 99 at Boyce or exit 80 south of Alexandria to Gardner. You'll take LA 121 past Leavine's convenience store in Gardner, then follow the signs to Valentine Lake Recreation Area and the Northshore Campground. Turn right into the campground. Before you reach the campground proper, you'll see double blue blazes that mark where the Valentine Lake Loop crosses the road. Park at the campground, then walk back down the road. Veer right into the woods at the blue blazes for a clockwise hike of the loop.

Begin by hiking a short, mild descent that parallels the campground road. The trail crosses a small, dry creek bed, then climbs past spring-flowering mayapples and vines of wild grape as it leads away from the campground road. At 0.2 mile, you'll reach an opening in a barbed wire fence. Once you've passed through it, the trail descends once more. You might see evidence of armadillos through this forested section of the hike. Look for small piles of leaves where the armadillos have burrowed with their snouts, rooting at the ground for bugs, berries, and seeds.

The Valentine Lake Loop arcs to the left after that, passing through still more beech, magnolia, and pine, then crosses a dry wash at 0.3 mile. It meanders into a mild downhill shortly afterward—one that soon levels out when the trail swings left around a large pine. Make a sharp right turn at 0.4 mile, passing beneath a profusion of flowering dogwoods. After heading uphill a bit, you'll find yourself in a stand of loblolly pines.

The mostly flat trail reaches a disturbed area with lots of undergrowth at 0.6 mile,

The Valentine Lake Loop offers numerous pleasing views of Valentine Lake.

then winds sharply before crossing a gravel road. The trail straightens out after reentering the woods, then begins a sloping descent at 0.9 mile, one that lasts about 200 yards—a major downhill for this hike! The path levels out at an intermittent creek, then swings to the right, beneath large beeches and alongside a scenic gully to the right.

Cross a highline at 1 mile, then reenter the woods and bear left. The trail swings to the right a bit at 1.1 miles; here, you'll start to see the marshy edges of Valentine Lake. As you walk along the shore, you'll see more beech, palmetto, yaupon, wax myrtle, sassafras, and cane, all of which seem to grow just about anywhere in Louisiana but especially love to border the low, marshy transition zones between land and water. Notice also that there are fewer pines here than along some other sections of this trail—though you still have enough pines to

carpet the path somewhat with their fragrant needles.

You'll soon pass through another opening in a barbed wire fence. The trail swings left at 1.2 miles, and you'll really start to get a good view of the lake, no matter the time of year. The plentiful yellow irises growing along the shore are usually at the height of their beauty in mid-April. As you hike, you'll have more views of the lake, some of them winter-only vistas. At 1.3 miles is an old, rotted pier. A newer, sturdier-looking pier is just ahead.

Pass an old camp to your left at 1.4 miles. The Valentine Lake Loop reaches a small, knoll-like peninsula—and a beautiful view of the lake—at 1.5 miles. Look for wading birds along the lake's edges and wood ducks and green-winged teals on the water's surface. After leaving this scenic spot, the trail swings left and back downhill.

After a few small ups and downs, the trail bottoms out at a thrilling stand of irises and a small cove to the right at 1.6 miles. Just after this, a spur trail leads to the larger pier and a view. The Valentine Lake Loop veers to the left, soon to reach another spur trail, this one leading to the campground off to the left. Continue to follow the blue blazes along the lakeshore. You'll reach a short flight of steps to Campsite #12 at 1.7 miles.

Following the double blue blazes from Campsite #12, you'll reenter woods of beech, magnolia, and pine after about 100 feet. As you hike, you'll be able to see the campground on your left. The mildly furrowed land leads you over a few slight ascents and descents before passing an outhouse. After passing beneath a stand of red maple, the trail reaches the campground entrance road where you started.

22

Kincaid Lakeshore Trail

Total distance (circuit): 9 miles

Hiking time: 4.5 hours

Habitats: Mixed pine-hardwood forest; non-tidal marsh

Maps: USGS 7½' Rapides, USGS 7½' Elmer, USGS 7½' Gardner, Kisatchie Ranger District Recreation Opportunities flyer

Kincaid Reservoir, managed by Kisatchie's Calcasieu Ranger District, is among central Louisiana's most popular recreation spots. In addition to campgrounds and boat launches, the Kincaid Recreation Area features a 9-mile hiking and biking trail along the reservoir's ragged southern shoreline. Bathrooms, water fountains, picnic tables, and trash cans are all available at the day-use area, roughly a quarter of the way into the hike. If you want a longer hike and have the means to shuttle cars, the Kincaid Lakeshore Trail has a 7-mile extension that skirts the reservoir's eastern shoreline and ends at FS Road 210. The hike described here covers only the 9-mile loop.

To reach the trail from the north, take I-49 to LA 1200 at Boyce (Exit 99), and drive south 3.6 miles to LA 121. Turn left here and drive approximately 7 miles to the small town of Gardner. (Be sure to follow the signs and stay on LA 121). Shortly after you pass a convenience store and gas station, you'll see the brown sign for the Valentine Lake and Kincaid Lake Recreation Areas. Turn left at this sign onto Valentine Lake Road (Parish Road 279). After about 4 miles, turn left onto FS Road 205 to enter the recreation area. Approximately 2.5 miles down this road, you'll find a parking lot, a pay station ($3 per vehicle), and a convenient point to access the Kincaid Lakeshore Trail.

From the south, you can take I-49 to US 71/165 (Exit 80) and drive north to LA 28, which will take you to Gardner. Once in Gardner, turn left onto LA 121 and follow

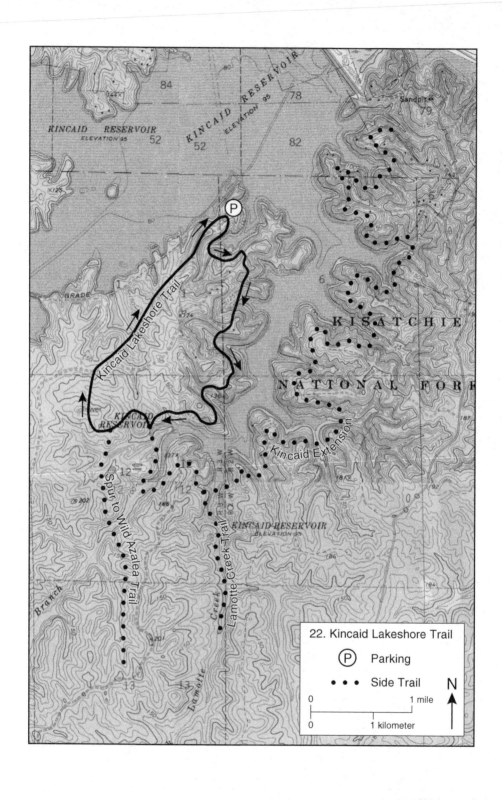

RINCAID RESERVOIR

RINCAID RESERVOIR
ELEVATION 95

KINCAID RESERVOIR
ELEVATION 95

Sandpit

GRADE

Kincaid Lakeshore Trail

KINCAID
RESERVOIR

Kincaid Extension

K I S A T C H I E

N A T I O N A L   F O R E

Spur to Wild Azalea Trail

Lamotte Creek Trail

KINCAID RESERVOIR
ELEVATION 95

Branch

Lamotte Creek

22. Kincaid Lakeshore Trail

Ⓟ Parking

• • • Side Trail

N

0   1 mile

0   1 kilometer

the signs to the Kincaid Recreation Area. Unless you're staying at the campground, the most convenient starting point for the 9-mile loop is just before the entrance station. Look closely as you drive in, and you'll see the blue blazes of the Kincaid Lakeshore Trail just a few hundred feet before the parking lot and pay station. No sign or kiosk marks the trail access point at this time. You can also access the trail from the Kincaid Recreation Area and the Wild Azalea Trail.

Begin hiking at the blue-blazed tree on the west side of the road (the trail entrance to the right as you drive in). The trail immediately drops downhill but soon levels out. As you hike through this relatively low, mixed pine and hardwood forest, look for dogwood, American holly, southern magnolia, and white oak. You'll also see plenty of loblolly and longleaf pine. The path meanders gently through the forest and forks at 0.7 mile. The spur to your left goes to the boat ramp, so you want to bear right, following the blue blazes. Kincaid Reservoir should be clearly visible to your left, unless the leaf cover in late spring and early summer blocks the view.

The trail bends sharply to the left at 1 mile and begins providing wide views of the reservoir to your left. At 1.3 miles, you'll reach the scenic shoreline, where beautiful old bald cypresses thrive, along with willow oaks, white oaks, and loblolly pines.

The Kincaid Lakeshore Trail swings right at 1.4 miles and then passes several girdled trees, which are evidence of beaver activity. Beavers tend to prefer Louisiana's sweet gum and loblolly pines—both of which grow in abundance here. These industrious rodents are not uncommon in the state, though their dams and lodges along our lazy bayous and creeks tend to be much smaller than what you'll see farther north.

Follow the blue blazes to where the trail exits the woods at the day-use area and campground at 1.7 miles. This section can be a little confusing, as the route through this open spot is not clearly blazed. Once you exit the woods, turn left onto the paved walkway just ahead and walk along the reservoir's shore, passing the small beach and several picnic tables. If the area is not too crowded, this is an ideal spot to stop for a snack break.

Pass a flight of steps to your right before the paved walkway ends at 2 miles. There is no obvious trail at this point; you can either take the steps, or you can take a sharp right where the sidewalk ends and hike back about 50 feet until you spot blue blazes in the woods to your left. Reenter the woods, where the trail is low, flat, and potentially soggy. Private homes have been built along the opposite bank.

At 2.5 miles, a spur to the right leads uphill to the campground. Stay on the Kincaid Lakeshore Trail, which leads away from the reservoir but soon returns to pass a fishing pier at 2.9 miles. Along the water's edge, you'll see many large American beeches, along with common sweetleaf and wax myrtle shrubs.

The trail meanders between the reservoir and the campground, passing several more spurs to the camping area before it leaves this often-crowded spot behind. The trail leads downhill—a steep one, by Louisiana standards. Thus begins a series of small ups and downs. You'll pass a few more piers over the next half mile, always with a view of Kincaid. At 6.3 miles, the trail junctions with FS Road 205, marked with double white blazes. Simply stick to the blue-blazed trail, which swings to the right at 6.4 miles. A scenic little gully to your left is stuffed with Virginia chain fern and Christmas fern, and you'll encounter more moisture-loving plants over the next mile. In

Egrets in flight

fact, parts of this segment may be flooded as you skirt several sloughs with wetland plants: sundew, irises, and spider lilies. The woods throughout this low segment of the trail are open, with the largest trees being pine, beech, and magnolia. You'll also see some cypresses, particularly as you look to the opposite bank at 7.4 miles.

This sometimes-flooded section ends when the trail leads uphill at 7.6 miles and junctions with the 3-mile Lamotte Creek Trail at 7.7 miles. Bear right to remain on the Kincaid Lakeshore Trail, which is generally straight and level at this point. The trail crosses a highline at 7.9 miles, then junctions with the Wild Azalea Spur Trail before crossing a dirt road. Listen for the falling *tiw tiw tiw* song of the northern cardinal. These beautiful birds are plentiful along Louisiana's wooded trails. You'll recognize the male, which is red with a black face and orange bill. With a grayish body, the female of

this species may be a little harder to spot, but she does have an unmistakably reddish-orange tail and crest. To me, she looks like a little punk rocker with her Mohawk-like "hairdo" dyed bright orange! Like the male cardinal, the female has a thick orange bill.

The blue-blazed Kincaid Lakeshore Trail now leads through a stand of longleaf pines. Few understory trees grow in this relatively mature stand. As is typical with this miniature habitat, ferns and ground vines carpet the earth below. Both emerge rather quickly following a controlled burn. The trail crosses another dirt road at 8.6 miles and continues to meander through the open woods.

At 8.8 miles, the trail leads through a fence opening, then veers to the left, heading uphill. After hiking this low, level segment of trail, you'll exit the woods at 9 miles to complete the loop and return to the parking area.

23

Indian Creek Trail

Total distance (circuit): 3.3 miles

Hiking time: 1½–2 hours

Habitats: Mixed pine and hardwood forest, small-stream forest, nontidal marsh

Maps: USGS 7½' Lecompte

The Indian Creek Trail is a little-known hike in Alexander State Forest's Indian Creek Recreation Area. This pleasant loop east of Woodworth skirts the ragged northern edge of Indian Creek Reservoir, leading hikers beneath large beech and magnolia, through a wildflower-filled spring forest, and past several views of the reservoir from its marshy banks. Most hikers will be able to complete this interesting walk through mixed pine and hardwood forest in just a couple of hours or less. Late fall, winter, and early spring are perhaps the best times to hike at Indian Creek. The adjacent recreation area and campground, heavily populated with vacationers in the warmer months, is much quieter and more peaceful once school starts and the weather cools. In addition, you'll have scenic views in winter, when the deciduous trees along the lake have shed their leaves.

To get to the trail, take I-49 to Woodworth, just south of Alexandria (Exit 73). Go east off the interstate for approximately 2 miles to Woodworth, then turn left onto Indian Creek Road. Following the signs to Indian Creek Recreation Area, go 2.5 miles down paved Indian Creek Road, which makes a sharp left turn halfway to the entrance station. A $3 fee is charged to enter the area. Campsites range from $10 to $17 per night.

Parking is available behind the entrance station. The loop trail, which begins and ends nearby, is blazed with red paint. Small hiking signs designate the trail's two access points on either side of the entrance road.

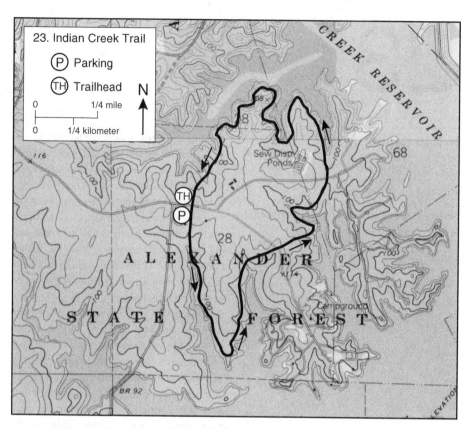

23. Indian Creek Trail

ⓟ Parking

⟲ Trailhead

N

0   1/4 mile

0   1/4 kilometer

You want to hike south, starting to the right of the entrance station as you drive in. This hike will lead you through a mixed pine and hardwood forest that includes sweet gum, red maple, and various oaks and hickories among the loblolly and longleaf pines so common to this part of the state.

Begin by walking through a planted row of tall, thick, widely spaced pines, then enter the woods after about 100 yards. In spring, look for bluets and blue-eyed grass among the violets and wood sorrel at your feet. At 0.1 mile, the trail begins a brief, gentle descent. As is typical of Louisiana's trails, you'll go downhill before heading back up, as our "hills" are generally the result of naturally flat land eroding downward—not of rocks being pushed up from below. The

Indian Creek Trail soon levels out, and a short, unofficial spur trail to the right leads to a muddy wash.

The trail's first 2 miles are mostly level, though you'll cut across numerous low washes that can get muddy. A quarter of a mile into the walk is an interesting sight to your right: a sideways dogwood! The ravages of Louisiana's storms may have shaped the mostly horizontal trunk when the tree was younger, and its branches now grow vertically skyward. Although you'll see plenty of dogwoods, the trail itself, thickly cushioned with fragrant pine needles, clearly tells which trees are dominant in this forest.

The trail becomes more meandering after reaching the banks of Indian Creek Reservoir

A view from the marshy shore of Indian Creek Reservoir

at 0.4 mile. At 0.6 mile it bends gently right to afford a scenic winter view of the reservoir. As you follow the red blazes, look beyond the shoreline to catch sight of a pair of green-winged teals as they glide swiftly and agilely above the water's surface before landing with a quiet splash. These common winter residents are smaller-than-average ducks. As with most ducks, the males have more distinctive markings than the females. The male duck's face is a rich chestnut color with an emerald-green patch that spreads from its eye to the back of its head. If you look imaginatively at this beautiful duck in profile, you'll see that the two colors are arranged in a kind of yin-yang pattern on its face, with a thin, white swirl separating them. Although Louisiana's true mecca for wintering waterfowl is a little farther south, you might also see northern pintails, canvasbacks, ring-necked ducks, hooded mergansers, and ruddy ducks at Indian Creek. In

spring and fall, look up to see hundreds of snow geese squawking overhead as they make their twice-yearly migratory journeys. If you're hiking in late spring or summer, you may be disappointed at the lack of a view, as the leaves obscure the sight of the reservoir in most places.

At 1.1 miles, a spur trail to the right leads to the camper hook-up sites. Continuing on the Indian Creek Trail, you'll cross a low wash and a drainage area before reaching a paved road at 1.2 miles. From here, the campground entrance is several hundred yards to your right, and the recreation area's entrance station is down the road to your left. The trail crosses the road and winds very little after reentering the woods. Although the reservoir is off to the right, it isn't always visible, even in winter. Descend a slight incline at 1.4 miles. Once the trail levels out, you'll gain another winter view of the water.

The latter half of the trail traces the ragged, often scenic inlets of Indian Creek Reservoir. You might catch a few winter views of the lake, but you're more likely to see the tall grasses growing in the marshy transition zone between water and land. In March and April, look for the brilliant purple and yellow irises that ornament these boggy patches. The trail passes an old, shaggy-barked southern magnolia at 1.5 miles, then makes an unexpected hairpin turn to the right. This turn is easy to miss, so watch for the blazes. After this sharp turn, the trail becomes more predictable as it once again traces the reservoir's contours.

The Indian Creek Trail reaches a dirt road at 1.8 miles. Keep following the red blazes to descend an incline shortly afterward. You're now entering an area that Alexander State Forest staff use for outdoor education and environmental awareness training, and you'll pass several cleared outdoor "classrooms." At the time of this writing, spur trails to the left had been blazed to these temporary learning stations. Whenever you reach a fork in the path, simply bear right to avoid the spur trails—which can have you walking around in circles. The Indian Creek Trail soon crosses a small footbridge over a gully and affords another view of the reservoir at 2 miles. The trail ascends to the top of a little bluff to begin the final stretch, which is characterized by a series of brief, rather steep ups and downs, making for quite a change from the first part of the trail.

After several small climbs and descents, cross a small footbridge at 2.4 miles. The surrounding ferns make this bridge very scenic on a small scale. Next, swing to the right, heading slightly uphill. The trail continues to go up and down as it traces the shoreline and provides views of the reservoir from small bluff tops. Be aware that the "valleys" can get muddy at times. Look for great egrets and great blue herons wading in the nearby shallow waters of the reservoir. Soon, you'll be able to see the entrance station's American flag waving ahead—and you'll probably be able to hear the traffic as people enter and leave the recreation area. The trail exits the woods at the entrance station, concluding the 3.3-mile hike.

24

Glenn Emery Trail

Total distance (round trip): 3 miles

Hiking time: 1.5 hours

Habitats: Mixed pine and hardwood forest, forest gaps, and edges

Maps: USGS 7½' Pollock, Catahoula Ranger District Recreation Opportunities flyer

Located in Kisatchie's Catahoula Ranger District, the Glenn Emery Trail is a pleasant 2-mile hike through mixed pine and hardwood forest. At one end of the trail is the Stuart Lake Recreation Area, and at the other end is the Pollock Athletic Complex, which is a 17-mile drive from Alexandria. The Glenn Emery Trail shares a trailhead with the Stuart Lake Interpretive Trail at the Stuart Lake Recreation Area, a level, half-mile walk that you might want to tack onto your total hike.

To get to the Stuart Lake Recreation Area trailhead, take US 165 north from Alexandria. Once you reach Pollock and the junction of US 165 and LA 8, go west on LA 8, driving just under 2 miles to the Grant Dogwood Trail, a designated auto tour. Following the signs, drive about a mile down the auto tour, then turn right into the Stuart Lake Recreation Area. Camping is available at the recreation area, but note that the entrance is closed between 8 PM and 7 AM daily. Turn right toward the camping area, passing a pay station, where a small day-use fee is charged. Look for the Dogwood Forest Walk sign near the small parking area. The trailhead for both the Forest Walk and the Glenn Emery Trail is just down the slope from the parking area. Although the trail officially begins right here, you may need to park in the adjacent day-use area. This will add 0.4 mile to the hike from the campground to Pollock.

To reach the Pollock Athletic Complex by car, take US 167 out of Alexandria to LA 8. Turn left onto Howell Road and travel 0.1

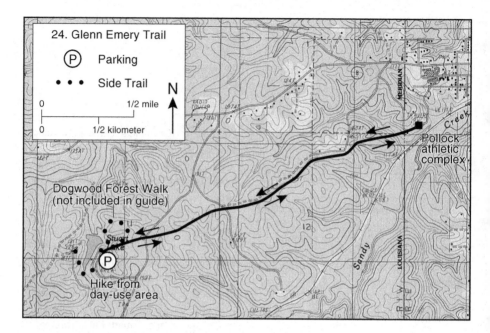

24. Glenn Emery Trail

(P) Parking

• • • Side Trail

N

0 ——————— 1/2 mile

0 ——————— 1/2 kilometer

Dogwood Forest Walk
(not included in guide)

Stuart Lake

Hike from
day-use area

Pollock
athletic
complex

Sandy Creek

mile to the trailhead. Limited parking is available at the trailhead, but you can also leave your car in the parking area for the adjacent baseball field.

Beginning at the kiosk downslope of the Stuart Lake parking area, hike the short distance to the boardwalk just ahead. Once you've crossed the boardwalk, bear right, following the yellow metal diamonds that mark the Glenn Emery Trail. The Dogwood Forest Walk, blazed with blue metal diamonds, goes straight ahead. The Emery Trail touches the edge of the Forest Walk once more in about 100 yards, just as it approaches the edge of the recreation area. The terrain of this hike is gently rolling. In spring, this pleasant spot will be graced with flowering dogwoods. Most of the forest is pine, however, along with ferns, hardwood saplings, various vines, and other low plants.

At 0.3 mile, cross the Grant Dogwood Trail (FS Road 144) and continue the mild, winding descent that began before the road. You'll soon pass a split log bench before heading uphill through tall pines and open woods. The trail crosses another road at 0.7 mile and leads you beneath a power line several hundred feet beyond.

The Emery Trail begins a slight descent at 0.9 mile before reaching a covered picnic shelter on the right. Shortly afterward, still continuing the descent, you'll pass a wooden 1-mile marker. If you started at the day-use area, you'll actually have walked 1.4 miles at this point. At the time of this writing, the undergrowth on either side of the trail was thick, in contrast to the tall pines that dominated the forest. Look for blackberries and muscadine ripening here in late spring and early summer. This is also a great area for birding in spring and fall. Regular breeding birds in this region of Louisiana include great crested flycatchers, pine warblers, white-eyed vireos, yellow-billed cuckoos, and downy woodpeckers. The diminutive downy woodpecker is a delight to spot—and

Central Louisiana

Glenn Emery Trail

it's not so difficult to find, being among the most common woodpeckers in the state. Look for a small, dark, gray-and-white bird with a white back. You might hear its soft, high-pitched *peek* as it flits unwarily through the woods.

Perhaps the best thing about hiking through pine forest is the smell of a pine forest, and the Glenn Emery Trail is no exception. The trail continues straight and mostly level and is covered with pine needles for much of the year. By the time you've hiked 1.3 miles, however, you might notice that more oak and hickory leaves carpet the trail. You've moved from a pocket of pine forest to one of primarily hardwoods. You'll also see a few magnolias as you begin another mild downhill.

At 1.4 miles, reach a bottom area that can get quite muddy. A barbed wire fence to your left marks a property line. Soon afterward, the trail passes a bench for contemplation, or just listening for warblers and marveling at the large American beeches and southern magnolias surrounding you. Because this segment of the Glenn Emery Trail is lower and wetter than the previous piney woods, you may also see a few ferns. Dogwoods are plentiful all along the trail. When not in bloom, dogwood is easily identifiable by its gray, pebbly bark and its opposite leaves that look like perky dog ears to someone with a bit of imagination.

You've been following a small creek for a short time, and at 1.6 miles, you'll cross it via a footbridge. The trail heads uphill after this crossing, but not for long. Cross another bridge over a usually dry creek bed at 1.7 miles, then swing right. The trail continues to roll up and down alongside young hardwoods and older, fatter pines. You'll cross a power line past a thicketed area at 1.8 miles. Look for moths and hummingbirds flitting among the abundant Japanese honeysuckle in this area. This vine, which is considered a weed in many areas, is a native of Asia and tends to grow quickly and crowd out native vegetation. Deer often browse the evergreen leaves of honeysuckle, and fruit-eating birds, such as quail, wild turkeys, and cedar waxwings feed on its small, dark berries. The yellow-and-white flowers are a favorite of some butterflies and hummingbirds.

You'll soon reach the entrance sign for the trail. Here, you'll exit the woods at the parking area behind the baseball field of the Pollock Athletic Complex. Just a few yards north is a picnic area with a water fountain. If you have a car waiting in Pollock, then you're finished with your hike. Otherwise, you'll need to retrace your steps back to the Stuart Lake Recreation Area. If you haven't hiked the Dogwood Forest Walk yet, you may want to add this small loop to your hike once you return to the trailhead.

25

Water Hickory Trail

Total distance (circuit): 1.1 mile

Hiking time: 40 minutes

Habitats: Bottomland hardwood forest, cypress swamp, nontidal marsh

Maps: USGS 7½' Bird Island Point, refuge brochure

The Water Hickory Trail is one of Louisiana's few trails located in the remnant bottomland hardwood forests along the Mississippi River floodplain. Like the Rainey Lake Trail (Hike 12), this short, mostly flat footpath at Catahoula National Wildlife Refuge (NWR) traverses a land of ridge-and-swale topography, where the low-lying streams and bayous give rise to cypress and tupelo and the contrasting ridges are home to overcup oak, willow oak, and pecan. A spur trail leads to a scenic view of Duck Lake, where you can view thousands of ducks and geese that feed on the refuge's abundant stores of chufa flatsedge and call this region home in winter. Bald eagles are occasionally spotted here, as well.

Located approximately 30 miles northeast of Alexandria, the refuge is a 25,000-acre haven for all types of wild creatures; in addition to the wintering waterfowl, the refuge sees a host of migratory birds in spring and fall. Its year-round residents include white-tailed deer and bobcat, which occupy the higher, dryer ridges of the bottomland region.

Because this is bottomland, these lands are often flooded for part of the year. Hikers should always contact the refuge staff before planning to visit Catahoula's trails. This guide focuses on the 1.1-mile Water Hickory Trail. However, if you're planning a trip to Catahoula NWR, consider taking some of the other available walks. Besides the Water Hickory Trail, the refuge features a 3-mile trail alongside lazy Cowpen Bayou. If this trail is flooded (as it often is), an alter-

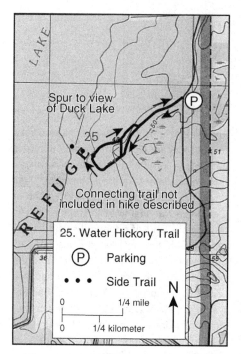

Spur to view
of Duck Lake

25

Connecting trail not
included in hike described

25. Water Hickory Trail

(P) Parking

• • • Side Trail N

0   1/4 mile

0   1/4 kilometer

native is to walk the northeast spur of Wildlife Drive, which also parallels the bayou. In addition to ascertaining water levels, hikers should also check hunting schedules, as hunting is allowed at the refuge. Even though the Water Hickory Trail is off limits to hunters, you should always wear hunter orange on your clothes or pack when hiking during hunting season.

To reach the trail from I-49, take US 167 out of Alexandria, then go east on LA 28 at Pineville, just a few miles out of Alexandria. LA 28 will take you approximately 25 miles to US 84 at the Little River. Turn left (west) onto US 84 and follow the signs to Catahoula NWR. Bear left onto Wildlife Drive. Drive approximately 1 mile to the Water Hickory trailhead, which will be on your left. On your way, you'll pass the refuge shop area and headquarters building on the right. You may want to stop in at the headquarters to pick up a refuge brochure.

The Water Hickory Trail begins at the gate on the right side of the road, just beyond the parking area. As you begin hiking, notice some of the trees characteristic of bottomland hardwood habitats: water oak, willow oak, sugarberry, and water hickory. The footpath has been well named, for you'll see plenty of water hickories out here. These shaggy-barked trees can grow to impressive heights; in fact, they are among the tallest of the hickories. If you're hiking in mid-spring, you might also notice that the water hickories tend to be among the last trees in the forest to leaf out. As you hike, you'll also see a lot of wild grapes, their vines trailing from low trees and snaking along the ground.

Approximately 0.1 mile into the hike, notice Lower Paul Brake off to your left. A brake is a low, poorly drained area that holds water during periods of flooding. During periods of dry weather, moisture-loving plants grow in the soil of the brake and provide food for wildlife. Unless central Louisiana is in a severe drought, this stretch of clumped hardwoods usually holds some water.

At 0.2 mile, the trail forks at a bench. Bear to the left; you'll return by the other trail toward the end of your hike. The Water Hickory Trail passes several bald cypresses—suggesting that the elevation has lowered just a tad. The trail splits once more in the next quarter mile; just keep going straight (bearing left), sticking to the wide path. At 0.4 mile, the Water Hickory Trail swings right, then reaches a T intersection at 0.5 mile. Take a left onto a spur trail that leads about 500 feet to a view of Duck Lake, the refuge's 1,200-acre impoundment for waterfowl. This is a great viewing spot between November and January, when thousands of waterfowl descend on the refuge. In late summer and early fall, look for migrant shorebirds on the mudflats. Catahoula NWR has an abundance of chufa, a sedge with

Duck Lake

spiky yellow flowers that is a favorite food for waterfowl, particularly the mallards, pintails, and canvasbacks that nest on the refuge each year. Although farmers treat chufa as a pesky weed, others consider it a culinary delicacy. It is certainly an important food source for the waterfowl, as it brings so many thousands to the refuge annually. Be aware that the spur trail to Duck Lake can get very muddy. In fact, heavy rains may temporarily submerge it.

Once you've retraced your steps back to the T intersection, bear left to continue the trail. You'll walk beside large cypress and sugarberry. Notice a number of interesting hollow trees here—the possible hideaway of a fox squirrel. These woods are also home to a slightly more dangerous creature, but one you're not likely to see on your hike: the bobcat.

The trail passes a bench at 0.7 mile, then forks. Bear left to complete the short loop.

When you reach another fork at 0.9 mile (also marked by a bench), bear left there as well. You'll reach the trailhead at Wildlife Drive soon afterward, at 1.1 miles. To travel from here to the Cowpen Bayou Trail, continue driving south on Wildlife Drive, past the observation tower, until you reach the Cowpen Bayou trailhead on your left after approximately 4 miles.

If the Cowpen Bayou Trail is flooded, you can continue the drive past a boat launch until you reach a second boat launch and a gate blocking vehicular traffic. Park here and walk down this 1.5-mile spur of Wildlife Drive, which parallels the northern third of Cowpen Bayou. Because the spur is open to vehicles only in October, hikers have it to themselves for much of the year. A good circuit hike is to walk the entire length of 9-mile Wildlife Drive, which leads around the Duck Lake impoundment and along Cowpen Bayou.

26

Big Creek Nature Trail

Total distance (two circuits): 1.4 miles

Hiking time: 1 hour

Habitats: Upland hardwood forest, small-stream forest

Maps: USGS 7½' Harrisonburg, Sicily Island Hills WMA map

Sicily Island Hills Wildlife Management Area (WMA), site of the Big Creek Nature Trail, rises sharply above the surrounding flood-plain of east-central Louisiana and provides nature lovers with miles of rugged, scenic hiking. Wait a minute, you ask. There are *hills* and an *island* along the Mississippi River floodplain? Aren't floodplains sup-posed to be . . . flat? True, but one aspect of the land here has resisted the easy culti-vation characteristic of this region. The Sicily Island Hills are part of an "island" of loess-topped sandstone and occupy the southern end of Maçon Ridge—a wedge-like ridge of sand, silt, and gravel that was dumped by the Mississippi during the last great Ice Age. In the north, Maçon Ridge separates the Ouachita from the Mississippi River east of Monroe; in fact, you can clearly see the ridge's upward slope at Poverty Point (Hike 11). At the south end of the ridge, erosion has carved out the area we know as Sicily Island Hills into a Louisiana hiker's mecca of small waterfalls and sharp elevation changes.

The Big Creek Nature Trail, a 1.4-mile path through the southern end of the WMA, scrambles up rugged climbs, crosses clear creeks, and comes within view of two small waterfalls. Adventurous hikers will also want to explore the area's creek beds and ATV trails when hunting is not in season. If you do hike in the WMA during hunting season, be sure to wear your hunter orange, even though hunting is not permitted on the na-ture trail. Check regulations for specific

Central Louisiana

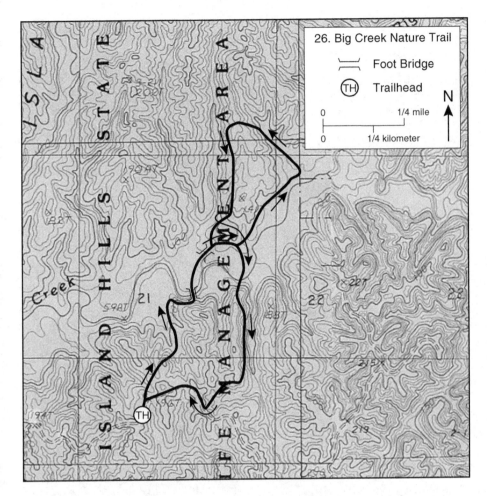

26. Big Creek Nature Trail

Foot Bridge

(TH) Trailhead

N

0   1/4 mile

0   1/4 kilometer

hunting dates. Remember, a hunting license, fishing license, or Wild Louisiana Stamp is required to hike on management area lands. As at Tunica Hills WMA, hikers should also obtain a WMA map from the Louisiana Department of Wildlife and Fisheries and a United States Geological Survey topographic map. Always hike this isolated area with a partner or group.

To reach the trail from I-49, take US 167 north, to LA 28, then travel east on LA 28 until it ends at US 84. Go east on US 84 to Jonesville, then turn north onto LA 124, tak-

ing it all the way to Harrisonburg. Once in Harrisonburg, go east on LA 8 until you see the Sicily Island Hills WMA sign on your left. Turn left here at Williams Road, which will take you into the WMA. Be sure to register at the self-clearing station. You'll pass a road to the camping area after 0.8 mile. Bear to the right, driving another 1.9 miles on gravel road to reach the nature trail sign on the right side of the road. No parking is available at the trailhead, but if you drive several hundred yards farther, you'll find a few areas to pull over.

The Big Creek Nature Trail features one of the tallest waterfalls in Louisiana.

If traveling from the southeast, your best bet is to take US 61 north out of Baton Rouge. At Natchez, go east on US 84 to Ferriday, then north onto US 65/LA 15 to Clayton. Stay on LA 15, taking it to the town of Sicily Island, where you want go east on LA 8. Once you reach LA 913 at Leland, it is 3.1 more miles down LA 8 to Williams Road and the WMA entrance.

Like so many Louisiana trails, the Big Creek Nature Trail begins by going downhill—in this case, a pretty steep downhill. Hiking sticks are a big help here. The trail is lined with switch cane, and you'll see elm, eastern hophornbeam, yellow poplar, and beech among the oaks and hickories of this upland habitat. The trail is not marked at first, but you'll soon see the characteristic arrows nailed to the trees along the path.

The trail levels out at 0.9 mile, then swings to the right. To the left is a scenic little ravine that features a trickling waterfall. Yes, this is a real waterfall—perhaps the tallest in the state. The trail bears to the right, contouring the ridge. A quarter of a mile after the waterfall, tumbling over a jumble of rocks, is a smaller waterfall, which will be on your right. This little area is particularly beautiful, as ferns thrive among the rocks and alongside Big Creek. Swing to the left to cross a small footbridge, keeping an eye out for the arrows. The trail is relatively straight for a short distance as you walk alongside a ravine. Step across another footbridge at 0.2 mile. You'll soon reach the start of the loop and can either take a sharp left uphill, or go straight ahead and up a more gentle incline. For now, you want to take the gentle incline straight ahead, and you will soon see a sign indicating the long route and the short route. To take the long route first, bear left at the sign. You'll soon return to this junction to hike the short route.

Hike uphill, passing beneath numerous pines, oaks, hickories, and beeches. Those interested in tree identification should look for both loblolly and shortleaf among the pines. Oaks include cherrybark, white, and water. The rather sparse understory consists largely of dogwood and red buckeye. At your feet are huckleberry, smilax, blackberry, and wild grape. Contour the ridge for a short time, enjoying the scenic view of Big Creek downslope to your right. The trail makes a short hairpin turn before working its way closer to the creek. If it's rained recently, look for a trickling waterfall at the creek at 0.3 mile. You'll follow the creek briefly, then bear right and head back up a slope at 0.4 mile. The Big Creek Nature Trail soon levels out, then heads uphill again. Take a sharp left when you level out again to walk along the top of the ridge for about 80 feet. Next, take a sharp left to descend from the ridge, ending this too-short trek on the ridgetop. Catch sight of a long-tailed American redstart as it flits through the understory, chasing small insects.

At 0.6 mile, you'll be able to see a footbridge ahead, at the bottom of the hill. Bear left, toward that footbridge. Before you know it, you will approach the main trail again. Instead of crossing the footbridge (you crossed it earlier), bear left onto the main trail. You'll know where you are when you reach the long route/short route sign once more. This time, hike straight ahead to take the short route, which is actually an exit route for this trail.

Swing right almost immediately after the sign and step across Big Creek. Now begins the longest, steepest uphill of this hike. This beautiful climb levels out at 1.3 miles. Reach the road shortly afterward, turning right to walk the remaining 400 feet to the trailhead.

III. Southwest Louisiana

27

Sam Houston Jones State Park

Total distance (circuit): 4.3 miles

Hiking time: 2½'–3 hours

Habitats: Longleaf pine forest, small-stream forest, cypress swamp

Maps: USGS 7½' Buhler, park map

Hikers may initially be disappointed by the seeming lack of hiking opportunities offered by southwest Louisiana–a land of mudflats and marshes, with an elevation that barely rises above sea level. Although the marshes of Cameron Parish are unquestionably among Louisiana's finest treasures, folks who want a more "traditional" hiking experience will have to go elsewhere. Luckily, hikers in the region won't have to go far. Sam Houston Jones State Park is just up the road from Lake Charles in Calcasieu Parish, and it will be a pleasant surprise for anyone who feared that hiking Louisiana's soggy southwestern corner would require, at the very minimum, a good pair of waterproof hip boots.

To get to the park, take I-10 to LA 171 (Exit 33) and drive north out of Lake Charles for 3.8 miles to LA 378. Turn left onto LA 378. After 3 miles, take the LA 378 spur to the right. When the spur ends a mile later, turn left, following the signs to the park entrance. You'll go another mile to reach the trailhead for your hike.

Sam Houston Jones State Park has three official hiking trails and any number of unofficial bike paths cut by local mountain bikers. The Old Stagecoach Trail, the Longleaf Pine Trail, and the wheelchair-accessible Riverwalk Trail are blazed yellow, blue, and orange, respectively. Because the Old Stagecoach and Longleaf Pine trail can be linked, this guide will direct you down a combination of the two, for a total hike of 4.3 miles (including the road walk back to the trailhead). The Riverwalk Trail is at the

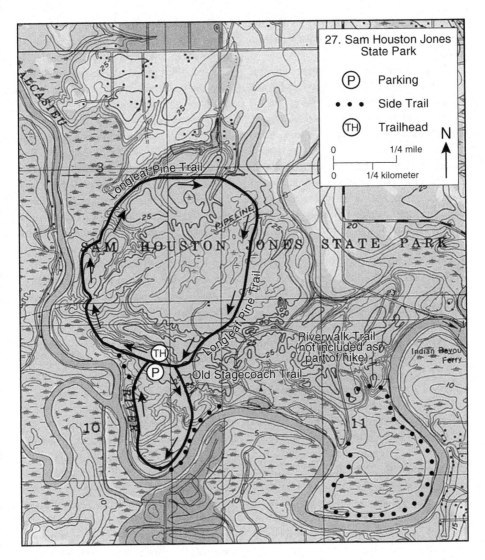

opposite end of the park and is a gentle, paved, 1.7-mile stroll alongside the Calcasieu River.

Pick up a park map at the entrance station. The trailhead for the Old Stagecoach and Longleaf Pine Trails is about a mile past the entrance, just beyond the deer pen. Follow the blue and yellow blazes for about 100 yards, then turn left when the trail forks, following the yellow-blazed Old Stagecoach Trail. This path, named for an historic old stagecoach road that followed the banks of the Houston River's west fork, was part of the larger Old Spanish Trail, which ran west from Baton Rouge. Used for travel, trade, and thievery during prerailroad times, it was undoubtedly traveled by such famous figures as Sam Houston and Jim Bowie. That historic route is a thing of the past, however, and the trail leading through the forest, beneath an archway of yaupon shrubs and Carolina jessamine vines, shows little sign of its colorful history.

After 0.2 mile, the Old Stagecoach Trail passes a bench on the left. If you sit still and listen, you might hear the rustle of a small gray squirrel as it nervously sidles through the fallen leaves to scurry up an oak. Soon afterward, the trail forks. The official, blazed trail goes to the right. Straight ahead is an unofficial trail back to the guest cabins and the boat ramp. Follow the yellow blazes to descend a gentle slope and bisect a small slough. The path bends to the right, and you'll soon reach another spur to the left, this one leading to a pleasant hike along the river. Continuing the Old Stagecoach Trail, you'll pass beneath numerous pines, with the river to your left and a slough to your right. Along the ground, you'll see where foraging armadillos burrowed their snouts into the pine needle-carpeted ground.

At 0.5 mile, the Old Stagecoach Trail junctions with the blue-blazed Longleaf Pine Trail. Turn left to begin this 3.5-mile trail, which crosses more than a dozen bridges as it winds through mixed pine and hardwood forest, beneath longleaf pines, and alongside scenic pockets of cypress swamp. Once plentiful throughout the Gulf Coast states, longleaf fell victim to heavy logging and other factors in the 1900s. Today, their numbers are greatly diminished. Longleaf pines grow in three distinct regions of Louisiana: an area northeast of Alexandria, a larger region in Tangipahoa and St. Tammany Parishes (see Hike 45), and in a sizable swath of land covering much of southwestern Louisiana. Sam Houston Jones State Park is toward the southernmost end of this largest area, which also includes the longleaf-rich Kisatchie Ranger District of Kisatchie National Forest.

The trail splits after 0.1 mile. The left fork leads back to the Old Stagecoach Trail, so you want to bear right. After 0.3 mile, pass a marker indicating that you're a half mile from the trailhead where you parked. As you near the next footbridge, note that some parts of the trail are sandy. The park is actually on the eastern edge of a long ridge stretching all the way from Galveston Bay, Texas. This sand ridge, called the Ingleside Trend by geologists, is thought to have originated in the Pleistocene epoch and is an estimated 135,000 years old. During an interglacial period of the great Ice Ages, when the water was higher than it is now, this sand ridge was actually part of a coastal barrier island in the Gulf of Mexico.

The next footbridge is just a few hundred feet farther, at a particularly scenic spot. Ferns grow from either side of the stream, and heavy tree coverage provides welcome shade. The trail slopes upward and leads to a junction, with an arrow directing you straight ahead. The trail soon splits again, only to rejoin itself in a few hundred feet. At 0.7 mile, the trail approaches the river and leads to a bench and a couple of garbage cans. The trail then swings to the right and shadows the west fork of the Houston River. You can see private camps on the opposite bank of this relatively narrow body of water.

The Longleaf Pine Trail continues to wind beneath pines, oaks, beeches, and magnolias, with the river to the left and a swampy backwater to the right. As with many Louisiana trails, it is interesting to see how a tiny change in elevation and moisture can distinctly dictate which trees and shrubs will thrive. The swampy backwater is full of cypress, tupelo, and palmetto, none of which appear in any great abundance in the mixed pine and hardwood habitat nearby.

At 1.2 miles, the trail swings to the right before crossing a footbridge, then splits immediately afterwards. Bear left to cross another bridge. The trail will fork several times in the next half mile. At the time of this writing, the blue blazes were few on this section of the trail, so it can get a little confusing. Just realize that each fork is merely a temporary loop away from the trail and will rejoin the main trail after several hundred feet. To avoid getting turned around, bear left at each fork.

After crossing a few more bridges, you'll reach another arrow pointing you forward. Soon, it should be obvious why this is called the Longleaf Pine Trail. These beautiful, fragrant pines grow in abundance in the north-central region of the park. You'll reach another bench (bench #2) shortly after passing the 2-mile post. This area is like a jungle, with lots of overhanging vines, and is very green, even in the winter. The trail crosses a cleared area, and passes to the right of a small stream. This is a very pleasant, shaded area of the trail; because the evergreen pines grow rather close together, they provide shade throughout the year.

You'll soon reach another arrow directing you to the right. The trail to the left rejoins the main trail a short distance farther up. Cross another bridge before reaching the 2.5-mile post. Within the next half mile, you'll cross seven more footbridges as the trail becomes lower and more swamplike. Dwarf palmetto, cypress, and tupelo become much more abundant as you edge this overgrown pocket of swamp. In spring, hundreds of wildflowers bring color to the forest floor.

Spring also delivers thousands of migrating birds to Louisiana, and the seasonal bird migrations bring this region to life even more. At certain times of year, up to 200 different bird species can be found within a 30-mile radius of the park. If you're a birder, look for yellow-billed cuckoos and spotted sandpipers. Other species commonly seen here are wood ducks, great blue herons, red-shouldered hawks, barred owls, red-bellied woodpeckers, downy woodpeckers, and belted kingfishers.

Also look for white-tailed deer, fox squirrels, and rabbits. You may even spot an alligator as you hike past the park's swampy backwaters. The trail winds through this beautiful area for less than a half mile before ending at a paved road. Once you've exited the woods, return to the trailhead by turning right and walking just under a half mile down the road.

Sam Houston Jones State Park

28

Peveto Woods Sanctuary

Total distance (circuit): 1.3 miles

Hiking time: Varies; 30 minutes to hike

Habitats: Oak and hackberry forest, forest gaps, and edges

Maps: USGS 7½' Peveto Beach

Each spring, millions of diminutive song-birds take flight from their South American wintering grounds and begin their long, arduous migratory journeys up South America and across the Gulf of Mexico, to their breeding grounds in climes thousands of miles north. In clear weather, and with winds blowing from the south, they are able to soar over the United States' southern coast as the wind carries them to lands farther inland. If the weather is poor, or if winds blow from the north, the journey can become difficult for these tiny creatures. Hungry and exhausted, they will drop down at the first land they reach. Peveto Woods Migratory Bird and Butterfly Sanctuary, located on a forested *chenier* at the edge of Louisiana's southwestern coast, is an ideal first stop for these neotropical migratory songbirds; here, they can find the food, rest, and cover that they so desperately need. The phenomenon of *fallout* occurs when hundreds—or thousands—of birds descend on these wooded islands rising up from a sea of wetlands.

The 35-acre Peveto Woods Sanctuary is owned and maintained by the Baton Rouge Chapter of the National Audubon Society. A network of birding trails leads through a variety of miniature habitats within the *chenier* and provide an opportunity to see dozens of different bird species, particularly during the migration seasons. If you plan a hike down here, remember that this is a *birding* trail, as opposed to a hiking trail. Visitors to Peveto Woods are not out here to make miles; they're here to walk at a snail's pace—or sit

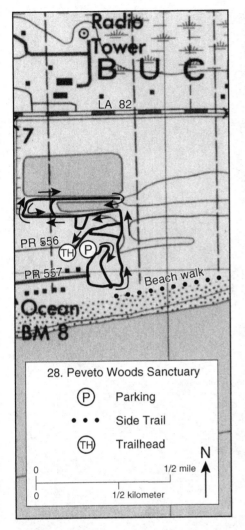

28. Peveto Woods Sanctuary

(P)	Parking
• • •	Side Trail
(TH)	Trailhead

0   1/2 mile

0   1/2 kilometer

N

miles. Watch for the Peveto Woods Sanctuary sign, which will be on your left when you reach Cameron Parish Road 528. Go south on PR 528 for 0.3 mile, then turn left onto gravel PR 556. This road dead-ends at the sanctuary. The trail begins to the left of the small kiosk near the parking area. No admission is charged, but there is a box in the kiosk for donations, which are requested of all visitors. The sanctuary depends entirely on funds donated by volunteers. The best times to visit the sanctuary are in fall, winter, and early spring. Be aware that as spring progresses and the weather warms up, the deerflies in this region can become unbearable.

The trail system begins at the gate to the left of the kiosk and forks almost immediately. Bear to the right, walking past majestic sugarberry and live oak trees, listening for the wealth of songbirds that are often heard here: buntings, flycatchers, grosbeaks, orioles, tanagers, thrushes, sparrows, and vireos. This route takes you to the sanctuary's southern border at 0.1 mile. The path goes left to follow along a wire fence. As you walk, notice the thickets to your left; if you look closely, you're sure to see any number of perching birds. Since you're just a stone's throw from the Gulf of Mexico, you'll be able to hear the waves beyond the birdsong. The trail is almost perfectly straight as it follows the fence line. Then it turns left with the fence line at 0.2 mile. If you look to your right, you'll see a meadow, on which grow numerous wind-shaped live oaks.

You are hiking on a ridge known as a *chenier*, or "place of oaks." These ridges stretch 200 miles from the east Texas coast to Louisiana's Vermilion Bay. Up to 30 miles long and quite narrow, these *cheniers* rise above the surrounding marshy shore and support woody vegetation of live oaks and

on the benches beneath live oaks–and *look,* preferably through binoculars. If you want more of a walk, you can extend your hike to the beach, which stretches for miles down the southwestern Louisiana coast. The hike described here introduces you to the trail system by tracing its perimeter.

To get to Peveto Woods, take I-10 to LA 27 in Sulphur (Exit 20), traveling south for approximately 36 miles to LA 82. Turn west (right) onto LA 82, driving approximately 9

Flowering prickly pear cactus

sugarberries, in addition to black willow, American elm, toothache tree, green ash, and honey locust. Among the smaller trees, shrubs, and vines are red mulberry, dwarf palmetto, wax myrtle, elderberry, and smilax. You'll see all of these—as well as prickly pear cactus, which flowers in spring. At one point, you'll encounter an opening in the fence that allows you to walk along the beach. If you take this side trip, you'll have the opportunity to see dozens of shorebird species.

The trail forks at 0.3 mile. The path to the left leads to a bench and an opportunity to walk among the shrublike trees and gnarled live oaks. Go straight ahead for now, still following the thicketed fence. When the trail forks again soon afterward, bear to the right. The trail itself soon swings left at a large clump of spiny-trunked devil's walking sticks.

The trail forks again at 0.4 mile. Bear right; this route will take you to the pond segment of the sanctuary, where you may spot wading birds or even shorebirds. Continue bearing to the right wherever the trail forks, and at 0.5 mile, you'll find yourself walking between two ponds. Here, the trail is grassy and mowed, and thickets and brush grow on either side. Watch for fire ant piles as you walk. This section dead-ends at the preserve's northwestern border. Turn around to retrace your steps, keeping a sharp eye out for any number of colorful birds in the underbrush. Nesting birds at Peveto Woods include the brilliantly colored painted bunting and the white-eyed vireo, whose body is yellowish-green.

Once you've retraced your steps to the trail junction at the beginning of the pond, keep going straight, continuing your walk alongside the pond to your right. On your left will be a stand of young live oaks, where volunteers replanted 1,600 live oak seedlings in 1994. In addition to providing much-needed shelter for countless songbirds, the canopies of these trees will serve as nesting sites for orchard orioles and northern parulas.

Turn left when you reach the sanctuary's northwestern border at 0.7 mile. The trail briefly parallels Little Florida Road, then turns left to circle the seedling segment. You will reach the information kiosk and trailhead after approximately 0.6 mile if you bear right whenever the trail splits after this.

29

Sabine National Wildlife Refuge

Total distance (one circuit and one round trip): 2.5 miles

Hiking time: 2 hours

Habitats: Fresh marsh, intermediate, and brackish marsh

Maps: USGS 7½' Browns Lake, (Blue Goose Trail), USGS 7½' Holly Beach (Wetland Walkway), refuge maps

One of Louisiana's most prized attractions is an expansive marsh and waterfowl haven known as Sabine National Wildlife Refuge (NWR). Like the refuges at Lacassine and Cameron Prairie, Sabine comprises extensive marshes in extreme southwestern Louisiana and is a birder's paradise. What makes Sabine different is its unique mix of salt and fresh marsh. Although they may look the same to the untrained eye, salt and fresh marsh are actually worlds apart—despite their proximity within this fascinating 124,511-acre refuge. Sabine's continued preservation of this unique habitat is vital, as marsh is considered one of the ten most endangered habitats worldwide.

Hikers can see various types of marsh up close by exploring Sabine's two hiking trails. Established in 2003, the 1-mile Blue Goose Trail leads past a grit site, provides open views of tidal brackish marsh, and ends at the western edge of Calcasieu Lake. The Wetland Walkway, formerly the Marsh Trail, is a 1.5-mile paved loop that provides a chance to view fresh marsh and see its typical inhabitants, including alligators. In fact, more than one-thousand alligators nest on the refuge annually. Interpretive stations along the Wetland Walkway make it easier to understand and appreciate the surrounding landscape. Trails are open year-round from sunrise to sunset. Camping is not permitted on the refuge.

To get there, take I-10 to the LA 27 exit in Sulphur, 7 miles west of Lake Charles. Go south on LA 27, also known as Holly

Beach Highway, for approximately 27 miles. The refuge headquarters will be on your left. After you've stopped there to pick up a brochure/map and view the exhibits, you can head several hundred yards north to the Blue Goose Trail. To hike the Wetland Walkway, you need to drive four additional miles south on LA 27.

Because the Blue Goose Trail is built on a levee, the path is a mostly straight line from the trailhead to the Calcasieu Lake. Still, this humble pathway offers a lot to see—if you know where to look and what to look for. For example, as you begin the hike, look to the left, and you'll see the refuge's constructed grit site for snow geese. Requiring grit for digestion, thousands of geese descend on this spot during the winter months, fueling themselves up for the long flight back to the high arctic tundra. At the time of this writing, plans were in place to build an observation deck here.

Another interesting sight can be found along the spur trail to the right at 0.1 mile, where a boardwalk will lead to a view of a tidal salt marsh. Back on the trail, you'll begin to climb a hill—in marsh terms, at least. You'll know you've gained a foot in elevation when you start to see actual trees, such as sugarberry, oak, and toothache tree, growing on either side of the trail. These larger trees need some ground in which to take root and grow—and this extra foot in elevation provides just that. Other, smaller plants you'll see include spring wildflowers: evening primrose, scarlet pimpernel, and Cherokee rose. A common shrub through this area is marsh elder, which thrives in salty soils.

At 0.4 mile is an overlook of the marsh to the left, then at 0.5 mile the trail opens up onto the sandy shoreline along an estuary of Calcasieu Lake. Because the ship channel comes in directly from the Gulf, Calcasieu is saltier than the typical Louisiana lake. Can you smell the salt in the air?

Numerous shorebirds seek refuge in this small, wind-protected cove. Watch for a pair of slender black-necked stilts, their sticklike red legs treading delicately across the shallow cove. These black-and-white, needle-billed shorebirds often lean forward as they walk, looking for food. They spend their winters south of Louisiana, but can be seen at Sabine throughout the spring, summer, and fall. In August and September, you're likely to see fiddler crabs along this trail—or at least you'll see their small burrows in the sand. Other animals at the refuge include white-tailed deer, coyotes, bobcats, otters, rabbits, raccoons, and opossums—though this may be hard to believe, considering the dearth of solid ground. This is a great spot to sit, relax, and look for wildlife . . . but Sabine's Wetland Walkway beckons. Retrace your steps back to the parking area, for a total hike of approximately 1 mile.

The paved Wetland Walkway leads through fascinating fresh marsh habitat. From the refuge headquarters, head south on LA 27 for approximately 4 miles. As you drive, you'll see marsh on either side. However, the impounded, rain-fed marsh to the west is fresh and the open marsh to the east is brackish and receives water from Calcasieu Lake.

You will see a shelter to the right of the road, where parking is available, along with a couple of restrooms. The Wetland Walkway begins to the right of the shelter. Head northeast, with LA 27 to your right and the enclosed fresh marsh to your left. In this marsh, you'll see numerous aquatic plants: pennywort, duckweed, and alligator weed, to name a few. Black willow and mulberry thrive along the edge between the solid walkway and the low, soggy marsh.

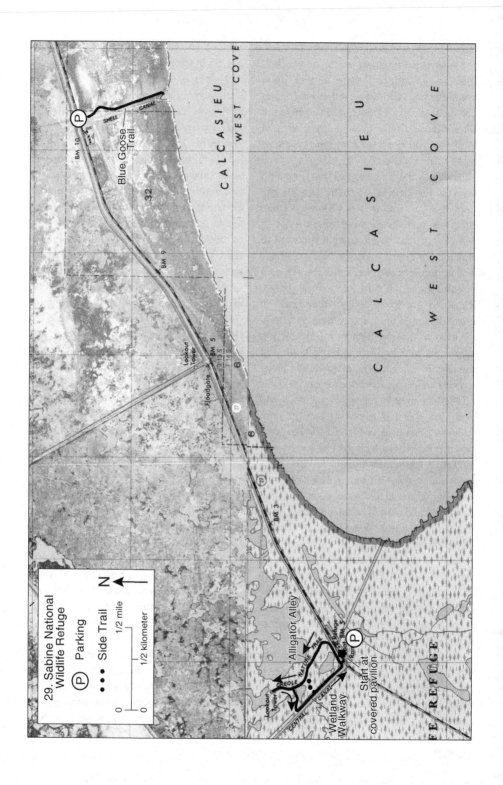

29. Sabine National Wildlife Refuge

Ⓟ Parking

••• Side Trail

0   1/2 mile
0   1/2 kilometer

N

SHELL   CANAL

Blue Goose Trail

BM 10

32

BM 9

Lookout Tower

BM 5

T 14 S

Floodgate

6

CALCASIEU   WEST   COVE

CALCASIEU

WEST   COVE

BM 3

"Alligator Alley"

NATURE TRAIL

CREOLE

Lookout Tower

CENTRAL   CANAL

Bridge

BM 5

Wetland Walkway

Start at covered pavilion

Ⓟ

FE REFUGE

The Blue Goose Trail leads to a salkty view of Calcasieu Lake.

The trail turns to the left and becomes "Alligator Alley" in less than 0.2 mile. Here, you'll find a bench and a small shelter to the left. Look for alligators, swamp rabbits, and nutria, all common marsh inhabitants. Plant species that favor this habitat include roseau cane, maiden cane, cattails, bullwhip, spike rush, and saw grass. The dominance of one species over another changes from year to year, depending on the previous year's weather conditions. One year, the marsh might seem to be nothing but bright green bullwhip, and another year you might see a dominance of giant roseau cane, or it may seem as if the rusty brown cattails have taken over. Most likely, you'll see a mix of the many plants that thrive in fresh marsh conditions.

As you walk, look for the diminutive common yellowthroat in these marshes. You're most likely to spook one out of its place among the reeds as you walk by. These small birds are mostly olive and have yellow throats, and the males wear a distinctive black mask.

Pass a shelter with a bench at 0.3 mile, watching as a red-winged blackbird forages through the marsh for seeds and invertebrates. The male of this common species, with its jet-black feathers and handsome red-and-yellow epaulettes, is easy to identify. A shell-paved trail goes to the left, leading about 100 yards into the marsh. Southern blue flag irises bloom here in March and April. This is an interesting and sometimes scenic little side trip, but be aware that cottonmouths are often seen on this stretch. If you choose to brave the snakes and hike the side trail, you'll add approximately 0.1 mile to your total hike.

Back on the main trail, you will cross a footbridge at 0.6 mile and reach the spur trail to the observation tower and rest area soon afterward. "Alligator Alley" ends here. Go straight ahead for 0.1 mile and climb a short flight of steps for an expansive marsh view. From here, you can see alligators, turtles, and numerous birds, particularly egrets, herons, common moorhens, and purple gallinules. Watch as a secretive king rail runs rapidly across the marsh, or as a pair of white ibises wade through the shallow muck, their long, slightly curved bills ready to pick an invertebrate out of the mud.

Back on the Wetland Walkway, the trail becomes a boardwalk. When the water is high, you may see alligators floating lazily nearby. At 1 mile, notice the patch of shade-giving Chinese tallow trees. This small ridge or "island," like the tree-filled spots on the Blue Goose Trail, is slightly higher in elevation than the surrounding lands—just high enough to support tree growth.

You are back at the cement walkway at 1.1 miles. Pass another shelter and bench, then turn left to walk alongside Starks Central Canal, soon reaching a small observation deck. The water in this canal is brackish, with the salt level varying throughout the year. Both drought conditions and end-of-summer tides can cause the salt level to rise, while heavy rains will cause a salt decrease. Tiny variations in salt content affect which plants will thrive and which will not. As a result, minute changes in salinity affect which critters will feed in an area, and will likewise determine which predators will feed on them. You'll want to return to Sabine NWR at a different time of the year to see how drastically the area changes from season to season.

This sheltered observation deck is a good spot to sit, rest, watch, listen for migratory songbirds, and simply marvel at the wonders of this fascinating place. When you're ready to leave, follow the trail the remaining 0.2 mile to the parking lot.

30

Lacassine Levee Walk

Total distance (circuit): 3.1 miles

Hiking time: 1.5 hours

*Habitats: Cypress swamp
(birding trail only), fresh marsh*

*Maps: USGS 7½' Lake Misere,
USGS 7½' Latania Lake,
USGS 7½' Thornwell,
USGS 7½' Hayes,
refuge brochure*

Some of Louisiana's most memorable views are of those sights that are most fleeting: here-today, gone-tomorrow migratory songbirds at Peveto Woods Sanctuary; crumbling loess hillsides in the Felicianas; thousands of acres of fresh marsh that are literally struggling to survive. Lacassine National Wildlife Refuge (NWR) is one of three federal refuges in southwestern Louisiana where survival of endangered marsh habitat is of prime concern. Lacassine's 35,000-acre marsh is intensively managed and closely monitored for its capacity to sustain a fragile habitat and continue to support abundant wildlife.

Located at the southern extreme of the Mississippi and Central Flyways, Lacassine NWR has long been a favored wintering ground for thousands of waterfowl, particularly northern pintails, white-fronted geese, and snow geese. One of the most awesome sights you'll find here is a fleeting one: thousands of waterfowl nearly blocking the sunrise as they return from a night of foraging to light on the Lacassine Pool. Another fleeting sight: snowy egrets, gracefully adorned in downy breeding plumage, nesting in a small clump of black willows. Or, a month or two later: an adult egret crouched over its large, flat nest, feeding its scrawny young. While Lacassine's 30-plus miles of levee trails are hardly the traditional woods walks associated with hiking, the ephemeral sights they offer are definitely in a class of their own. In addition to birds, you're also likely to see alligators, turtles, snakes,

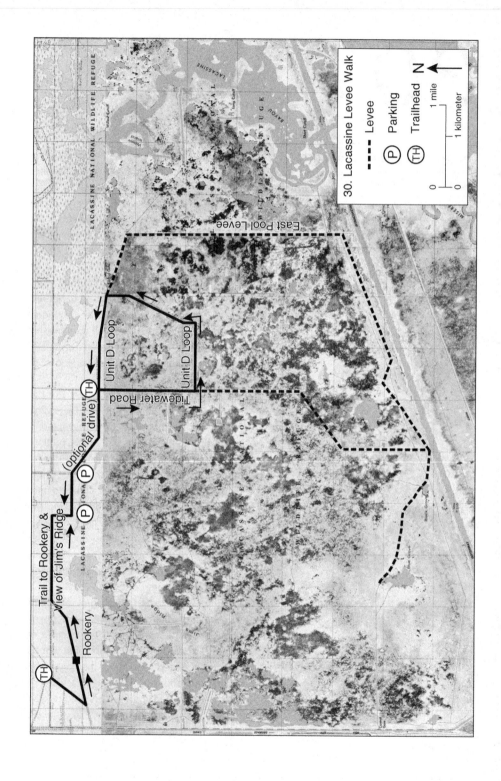

30. Lacassine Levee Walk

- - - - Levee
Ⓟ Parking
TH Trailhead

N

0   1 mile
0   1 kilometer

LACASSINE NATIONAL WILDLIFE REFUGE

East Pool Levee

Unit D Loop

Unit D Loop

Tidewater Road

(optional drive)

Trail to Rookery &
View of Jim's Ridge

Rookery

swamp rabbits, nutria, and many other small creatures.

This guide suggests a short, easily accessible hiking sampler of Lacassine, the Unit D Loop. Using a refuge brochure and map (available at the refuge visitor center), you'll want to make your own, longer adventure through this fascinating area. To get to the visitor center, take I-10 to LA 26 (Exit 64) and drive south to the junction with LA 14 at Lake Arthur. Turn west onto LA 14 and drive 7 miles to LA 3056, then turn south onto LA 3056, which dead-ends off of Nature Road at the headquarters. On your way there, you'll pass the Unit B Birding Trail, which is approximately 3.5 miles down LA 3056 on Parish Road 127 (Streeter's Road). This half mile linear trail through cypress swamp and fresh marsh was in the early stages of development at the time of this writing. Check with the refuge on the progress of this short hike.

The Unit D Loop is located near the refuge's 16,000-acre fresh marsh impoundment known as The Pool. To get to the trailhead, drive approximately 15 miles down LA 14 from Lake Arthur, then turn south (left) onto Illinois Plant Road. Go 4.5 miles to the observation pier, then turn left, driving another 1.1 miles to a small parking area at the beginning of the Tidewater Trail—a shell road and auto tour that will form part of your hike. "Unit D" refers to the roughly rectangular span of marsh enclosed by an old ring levee that was previously used for oil exploration.

Begin your hike by walking south along the Tidewater Trail, which leads straight into the popular Lacassine Pool—popular with birds and birders alike! In the mild winter months, particularly November through January, this large expanse of marsh is the daytime sanctuary for hundreds of thousands of ducks and geese. The sheer sight of the countless waterfowl resting on this rain-fed expanse is enough to leave you speechless.

Interested in identifying the birds out there? Look for greater white-fronted geese, snow geese, and Canada geese in abundance, as well as green-winged and blue-winged teals, fulvous whistling ducks, mallards, gadwalls, American widgeons, and ring-necked ducks. See if you can spot the ducks less commonly seen on the refuge: black-bellied whistling ducks, American black ducks, cinnamon teals, and buffleheads. You might spot a Ross's goose, which looks a little like a miniature snow goose. Regardless of the individual birds you can name, the sight of these creatures as they blanket the marsh horizon is simply thrilling.

After approximately 1 mile, you will reach a boat launch and another parking area. Turn left here, away from the Tidewater Trail. As you hike these levees, look in the nearby ditches for alligators, turtles, and snakes as they soak up the warm sun. Another creature you're likely to see here is the cattle egret. I think of this pink-billed bird as one of the "red-headed stepchildren" of the egret family. Its breeding plumage includes orange feathers on its crown, back, and neck. Originally an Old World bird, this stocky white heron eventually reached Florida in the 1940s and spread quickly through North America. In fact, the first sighting of cattle egrets in Louisiana was at Lacassine NWR in 1955. The bird's Latin name is *Bubulcus ibis*—although it is not an ibis. *Bubulcus* is Latin for "plowman," and refers to the egret's tendency to frequent cattle pastures, following the cows and feeding on the insects unearthed by their hooves. You're likely to see cattle egrets in abundance at the refuge, as well in the fields you pass on your drive back home. Unless

The walks at Lacassine National Wildlife Refuge include patches of cypress swamp.

you're hiking here during the migration seasons of fall and spring, you're not likely to see its red-headed cousin, the reddish egret, which is also pink-billed but has a gray body and pale red head and neck.

After another mile, the trail turns to the left again and reaches an observation tower that allows you to view the marshes from another angle. Look up to catch a rare glimpse of a bald eagle, a northern harrier, or a Mississippi kite. Continuing the levee walk, notice the difference between the marsh vegetation and the trees and plants that grow on the levee. The constructed levees host a variety of vegetation that cannot survive in the squishy marsh soil only inches away. Clumps of black willow grow along the raised ground; in other parts of the refuge, these trees serve as rookery sites for ibises, egrets, herons, anhingas, roseate spoonbills, and neotropical cormorants. The levees are also a prime spot for the hardy, rapidly growing Chinese tallow tree, which changes soil quality and outcompetes native plants. The encroachment of this species is also thought to be a factor in the recent decrease of vireos, warblers, and other neotropical migrants seen at the refuge.

A T intersection after another mile is a great starting point for further exploration. Approximately 0.2 mile to the right is a gate that blocks all vehicular traffic. From here, a grassy levee can serve as your trail for the 6-mile loop that heads south toward the Intracoastal Waterway and eventually rejoins the Tidewater Trail. To complete the short Unit D Loop, however, you want to turn left and walk another 1.7 miles to the parking area.

Back at the parking lot, consider extending your hike to the refuge's western boundary along the northern edge of the Lacassine Pool. Hiking (or driving) west from the parking area, you'll reach another parking lot, boat launch, and kiosk after 1.5 miles. From here, it is a 3-mile hike past more open water to the refuge's western boundary. On the way, you'll pass a heron rookery on the right—a clump of black willows that sees the springtime gathering of nesting herons, egrets, roseate spoonbills, and anhingas. These graceful creatures may flee when they first notice your approach; if you're willing to find a quiet spot and sit still for a while, however, you might be lucky enough to watch them return to their nests.

To the south, look for Jim's Ridge, a stretch of high ground frequented by hundreds of migratory birds in spring and fall. Closer to the trail, you'll probably spot numerous chickenlike marsh birds, such as the secretive king rail. You'll also see common moorhens, American coots, and purple gallinules—all of which nest at the refuge. The purple gallinule's gaudy colors are strikingly beautiful; its bright orange bill contrasts with its bold blue forehead and shimmering green wings. Common moorhens and American coots look similar to the gallinule, but they don't sport such bright colors. During breeding season, the common moorhen has an orange bill and an orange forehead, also known as a facial shield. You can identify the American coot, known as the *poule d'eau* in Louisiana, by its white facial shield.

You may want to keep walking after you reach the rookery and the view of Jim's Ridge. It is not much farther to where this road ends at the refuge boundary. If this is your first visit to this refuge, plan your next visit for a different month, preferably in a different season. You'll be pleasantly surprised at how drastically the marsh and its inhabitants change from season to season. Keep in mind that it is a good idea to contact the refuge staff before making the trip to this unique area. Although trails are open to the public year-round, from an hour before sunrise to an hour after sunset, access to some areas may be limited, so you'll want to check on hiking possibilities. In addition, because heavy rains can render the low trails unhikable, you should request an update on trail conditions. Camping is not allowed on the refuge; however, refuge staff can provide information on nearby camping areas if you want to stay in this area overnight.

31

Cameron Prairie Levee Walk

Total distance (circuit): 4.2 miles

Hiking time: 2 hours

Habitats: Prairie, fresh marsh

Maps: USGS 7½' Boudreaux Lake, brochure map available from refuge

Cameron Prairie National Wildlife Refuge (NWR), consisting mostly of fresh marsh and old rice fields, is one of the few places in Louisiana where you can find wet prairie habitat—the original habitat of this region. This area has since been heavily cultivated, particularly for rice, and today most of our prairie has been lost. The United States Fish and Wildlife Service is currently working to restore the prairie lands at Cameron Prairie, and you can see some native prairie grasses and wildflowers as you travel to the trail. To provide a taste of what the refuge has to offer to hikers, this guide suggests a there-and-back trek of only 4.2 miles, but it is just that—a suggestion. Pick up a refuge brochure at the visitor center to see the wealth of choices for walking the network of levees and dikes through this remarkable area.

To reach the refuge from I-10, take the Chloe exit east of Lake Charles, and go south on LA 397 for 4 miles to its intersection with LA 14. Take LA 14 east until it junctions with LA 27 in Holmwood (about 3.5 miles). Drive south on LA 27 for about 11 miles to reach the visitor center, where you'll find an impressive exhibit and several brochures on the area. Approximately 2 miles south of the visitor center, turn left onto the Pintail Wildlife Drive auto tour. As you drive in, be aware that some of the prairie remnants, such as eastern gama grass, a relative of corn, grows near the Pintail Wildlife Drive sign. This is just the first interesting feature of Pintail Wildlife Drive. The 5-mile auto tour route swings left

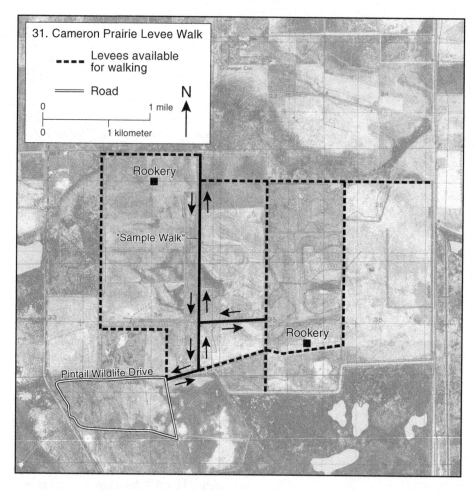

31. Cameron Prairie Levee Walk

- - - Levees available for walking

=== Road

N

0   1 mile
|——————————————|
0   1 kilometer

Rookery

"Sample Walk"

Rookery

Pintail Wildlife Drive

at 3 miles, then reaches a T intersection at 3.5 miles. The auto tour continues to the left, but you want to turn right here and park near the gate, which marks the beginning of the levee walks. Take care not to block the gate with your vehicle.

Begin by hiking straight ahead on the low levee, past the gate. At 0.1 mile, another levee will branch off to your left. Keep going until you reach a second levee to your left at 0.2 mile. Turn left here to begin hiking due north.

As you advance northward between two enclosed marshes, you might notice that the two marshes look different from each other—or maybe they don't! It is difficult to describe what you'll see on your hike at any given time of year, as the many faces of the fresh marsh change from season to season. Because the marshes' only water source is rainwater, their fragile habitat is highly influenced by weather, temperature, and human management, all of which play a major role at the refuge.

At the time of this writing, the marsh to the east (or to your right) had been drained recently. That, along with its slightly lower elevation, made it more watery than the

Red-eared slider turtles in marsh

marsh to the west. For these reasons, it was filled with bullwhip and flowering American lotus—both species that are typically associated with low, standing water. To the west grew a variety of grasses typically associated with the slightly higher, dryer ground of the marsh, including maiden cane and saw grass. Depending on the weather during the previous months, you may see very different conditions when you hike this trail.

One common management tool that drastically changes the face of the refuge is the draining and flooding of Cameron Prairie's 9,000-plus acres of marshes. In spring, as the migrant birds head to more northern climes, the refuge staff opens the water control gates and drains the marshes. The dryer land and greater access to sunlight facilitate germination of moist-soil seeds. The plants, which include such wetland species as smartweed, Walter's millet, and cyperus, are then allowed to grow throughout the spring and summer. When

autumn rolls around and the migrant birds start to return, the refuge staff close the water control gates, flooding the marshes again. The newly flooded expanses of marsh are ideal wintering grounds for waterfowl, and the healthy plants become easier for them to find.

If you're hiking between November and January, you're likely to see tens of thousands of waterfowl visiting from as far north as northern Canada. Look for American widgeons, blue-winged teals, fulvous whistling ducks, gadwalls, green-winged teals, lesser scaups, mallards, pintails, ring-necked ducks, ruddy ducks, shovelers, and wood ducks. Among the geese, you might see snow geese, white-fronted geese, and Canada geese. You might also spot red-tailed hawks and northern harriers, two other species that winter here.

You may have already gathered that Cameron Prairie—indeed, all of Cameron Parish—is a birder's paradise. Birders, there is even more in store for you on this trail! At 1.1 miles, a spur levee leads to the right for 0.3 mile to a heron rookery. Black willow is the dominant tree species here, though you'll also see quite a bit of Chinese tallow tree in places. Look also for pickerelweed growing alongside the levees. Although it can be confused with water hyacinth, this tall plant has large, heart-shaped leaves and deep blue flowers growing in spikes. A very aggressive plant, pickerelweed is considered a problem for rice farmers. However, it is native to the fresh marsh habitat and is a favorite plant for the palatka skipper—a small, rare butterfly with black and pale orange wings that sometimes strays from the eastern United States into Cameron Parish.

From early spring through early summer, a variety of wading birds nest at the rookeries. The first to arrive, usually in February, are the great blue herons, followed in early spring by the great egrets and roseate spoonbills. April is the peak season for bird migrations, and May is the peak season for nesting birds, so you're in for quite a treat if you're hiking here in the spring. You may also hear the loud, deep bellowing of alligators as you hike!

Back on the main trail, you'll reach another spur at 1.6 miles. From the actual trail, you can see another rookery, this one larger than the first. This rookery is the beginning of a series of nesting sites to the west. The birds especially seem to love the old oil well locations, where trees grow in circles and clumps around the abandoned wells, allowing the birds to live in small colonies.

The levee ends at a T intersection at 1.9 miles. From here, you can take a left to see more of the large rookery, or you can go to the right to walk through more marsh habitat. Either way will take you in a loop back to the trailhead, for a minimum hike of 6 miles. Of course, you can make the loop longer if you wish—up to 15 or more miles! The shortest route would be to turn around and hike back the way you came, for a total hike of 4.2 miles.

IV. South-Central Louisiana

32

Louisiana State Arboretum

Total distance (circuit): 2.2 miles

Hiking time: 1 hour

Habitats: Upland hardwood forest with mature beech and magnolia stands, mixed pine and hardwood forest, small-stream forest, cypress swamp, forest gaps, and edges

Maps: USGS 7½' St. Landry, arboretum map

Louisiana residents will be happy to learn that two of the state's most hiker-friendly trails are probably within two hours' driving time of their homes. And these aren't swamp-only trails, either, though each offers an experience of Louisiana wetland habitats—among their other treasures.

The Louisiana State Arboretum and Chicot State Park (Hike 33) are located in Evangeline Parish, which is only a few hours (or less) from just about anywhere in the state. And their trails offer something for just about everyone. The budding naturalist will find several different habitats and varied wildlife within a small area. In fact, the Arboretum, with its hilly topography, contains nearly every type of vegetation native to the state, except for coastal marsh and prairie flora. For the hiker who likes to make miles and work up a sweat, both trails have terrace ridges and hills formed by loessal erosion (similar to the rugged Tunica Hills). For the avid backpacker who wants to spend a night or two on the ground, Chicot has a 22-mile loop trail with several scenic backpacking sites. Dayhikers can hike part of Chicot's trail, or they can explore the 3-plus miles of hiking trails at the Arboretum.

The Louisiana State Arboretum was founded in 1961, following the efforts of Caroline Dormon, the first woman forester in the United States. A gifted artist, naturalist, and educator whose love for Louisiana's natural beauty—and desire to preserve its forests—was unparalleled, this remarkable woman spearheaded the effort to start the Arboretum. The result was the first state-

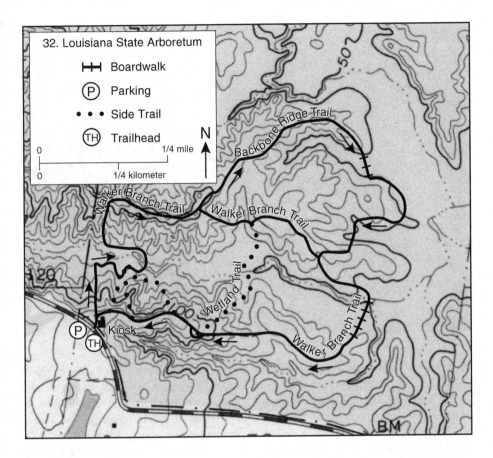

32. Louisiana State Arboretum

⊢⊣ Boardwalk

Ⓟ Parking

• • • Side Trail

Ⓣ Ⓗ Trailhead

N

0 _____ 1/4 mile

0 _____ 1/4 kilometer

funded arboretum in the United States as well as the first "tree museum" in the entire South. The interpretive center is named the Caroline Dormon Lodge in honor of Miss Carrie, as she was called by those who knew her. If you are interested in learning more about Caroline Dormon, you might want to visit the Briarwood Caroline Dormon Preserve (Hike 14), where peaceful woods surround a log cabin that she built and called home for much of her life. You can also check out the Caroline Dormon Trail (Hike 16) in the Kisatchie District of her beloved National Forest—the one trail that has been named in her honor. In fact, without her indefatigable efforts, the present-day Kisatchie National Forest would certainly not exist. You can, of

course, check out the many resources at the Arboretum's Caroline Dormon Lodge. Their permanent exhibit includes books on Louisiana's flora that she wrote and illustrated. You'll also want to pick up a hand-drawn map of the Arboretum's trails here. New paths are constantly being built, and old ones rerouted, so a current map of the Arboretum is a must.

To get to the Arboretum, take I-49 to LA 106, then travel west toward the town of St. Landry. After approximately 9 miles, turn left onto LA 3042 and drive 2.5 miles to the Arboretum, which will be on your left. Parking is available by the road. If you are coming from the south, an alternate route is to take I-49 to LA 167 (Ville Platte), then,

Yellow poplar saplings, with their distinctive tree trunks, are plentiful at the Arboretum.

after 17 miles on LA 167, to get on LA 3042 going north. You'll skirt the western edge of Chicot State Park before the Arboretum appears on your right.

This guide will direct you on a counter-clockwise hike of the trail system's circumference. As usual, do not feel obligated to limit yourself to the trail described here. The connecting trails within are excellent, particularly the Wetland Trail.

The hike begins at the kiosk just outside the Caroline Dormon Lodge, not far from the parking area. You'll immediately notice that the gravel, wheelchair-accessible trail is well manicured and features signs labeling the many trees along the first part of the trail. Amateur naturalists will appreciate the fact that so many trees are identified. For those who prefer the wilder feel of "non-interpretive" hikes, be assured that the trail will soon change from gravel to dirt, and the signs are not so abundant once you leave this central area.

At the start of the trail is a small clump of red buckeye trees, easily identifiable by their leaves, which are divided into five (sometimes seven) leaflets ranging from 3 to 7 inches long. In spring, a spike of dark red flowers rises from the center. These spring flowers, along with Carolina jessamine, which is abundant throughout Louisiana in early spring, are important early humming-bird plants.

Start by hiking Path A, which begins to the left of the red buckeyes. In spring, the ground is accented with a variety of wild-flowers: violets, false garlic, sessile-leaved trillium, and spring beauties, to name a few. In less than 100 feet, reach a downhill flight of steps. As is typical in Louisiana, you'll begin the trail by going downhill first—into the eroded ravines—and then climbing back uphill to level ground. If you've hiked the Tunica region of Louisiana, you might see a similarity between Tunica's terrain and this one. Both are characterized by deposits of loess (windblown silt), which erodes vertically, leaving a series of scenic terraces and bluffs. Not only are these landforms extremely fertile, but they also make for excellent hiking terrain and can afford beautiful views.

Once you reach the bottom of the steps, the trail continues to slope downhill. Giant cane and poison ivy are two plants that you'll see here and throughout your hike. Understory trees include eastern hophornbeam and American hornbeam. Both members of the birch family, these two species are sometimes confused, perhaps because they share the name hornbeam. Also, a common name for both of them is ironwood, in reference to their tough wood. Although both trees have toothed, oval-shaped leaves, the two are easy to differentiate. To tell them apart, just look at the bark. The American hornbeam's bark is gray, smooth, sinewy, and "musclelike," while the eastern hophornbeam's bark is more fissured, and broken into long, thin, scaly ridges.

After 0.1 mile, the trail curves sharply to the right. You are heading toward Paths B, C, and D—all of which lead back to the gravel-paved trail that you just left. When you reach the sign pointing to Paths C and D, take a sharp left, away from those trails. First, however, be sure to notice the magnificent old-growth beech and magnolia gracefully adorning either side of Path C.

You are now on the Sudie Lawton Walk, which will soon become the Walker Branch Trail. There are several bridges along these trails. After crossing a small bridge at 0.3 mile, the trail heads uphill and swings to the right onto a ridge, from which there are views to either side, particularly in winter and early spring. In March, flowering dogwoods embellish the new, bright green of the surrounding oaks and hickories.

Parts of the Arboretum are classified as a mature beech and magnolia forest. Look around. Unless you are in one of the trail's forest gaps, where one or more large trees have recently fallen, you'll see mostly large beech and magnolia, along with dogwoods and yellow poplars. The largest beeches and magnolias were here before logging operations commenced in Louisiana. Some of them are an estimated 300 years old! The smooth bark of magnolias grows shaggier with age, while the ancient beeches retain their smooth bark. Look for the interesting, sculpturelike root systems of the old beeches. Another interesting fact about beeches: It is often difficult to estimate their age simply by their girth. When beeches fall, they're often discovered to be hollow inside. As you hike, you may see one or more recently fallen beeches that have hollow trunks—and are now probably home to an opossum, squirrel, or other small forest creature.

At just under 0.5 mile on this rolling trail, you'll find yourself standing on Backbone Ridge, the highest point of the Arboretum at 125 feet above sea level. Even after the trail slopes downward and levels out again, you will continue to have nice views, due to the unusual terrain created by loessal erosion. In fact, you'll soon approach an overlook on the left. In the spring of 2003, much of the view was blocked by damage from Hurricane Lili, but there were still dogwoods visible in the distance and soon-to-bloom oak leaf hydrangeas gracing the forest floor.

Following the overlook, the trail takes a downhill slope to intersect with the Backbone Ridge Trail. Bear right onto the Backbone Ridge Trail, which traces the circumference of the trail system. You'll walk through several forest gaps, where huge canopy trees have fallen and left large, cleared areas in their wake. At 0.7 mile is once such cleared area. In these spots, you're likely to see devil's walking stick, a common Louisiana plant that grows well in recently disturbed areas. This sun-loving small tree has a thorny, often branchless trunk. Devil's walking sticks tend to grow in clumps.

After some minor ups and downs, the trail levels out at a bench. There is a view to your left, and to your right is an ancient cherrybark oak, estimated at around 200 years old. You'll soon cross a bridge, then reach another bench at 1 mile after some more up-and-downing through beech and magnolia territory. At 1.3 miles, the Backbone Ridge Trail rejoins the Walker Branch Trail. Bear left onto the Walker Branch Trail, which soon heads down a slope toward Ferguson's Gully.

At 1.4 miles, cross the bridge over scenic Ferguson's Gully. Heading uphill after that, you'll see common sweetleaf and numerous ferns. The trail has leveled out at this point. At 1.5 miles, a boardwalk takes you through a low, wet area of the trail. Notice the dwarf palmettos—a relatively uncommon plant on upland hardwood trails like this one. If you're interested in seeing more wetland vegetation, you can turn right onto the Wetland Trail where it meets the Walker Branch Trail at 2 miles. On the Wetland Trail, which basically bisects the Walker Branch Trail, you might see herons and egrets feeding in the water. You'll also see cypress and pawpaw trees, and beautiful irises blooming in April.

Shortly after passing the Wetland Trail junction, the Walker Branch Trail heads up the hill to where the dirt trail becomes a gravel trail. The gravel trail includes a wheelchair-accessible loop that soon branches to the left. Keep going straight, passing the junctions with Paths D, C, and B. This final leg of the hike affords some nice views, as it is situated on one of the many small, steep ridges running through this part of the state. At 2.2 miles is the Caroline Dormon Lodge and the end of your hike.

33

Lake Chicot Trail

Total distance (circuit): 22 miles

Hiking time: 10 hours or 2–3-day backpacking trip

Habitats: Upland hardwood forest, mixed pine and hardwood forest, cypress swamp, forest gaps, and edges

Maps: USGS 7½' St. Landry, park map

Few Louisiana trails offer the opportunity to move from loess-topped bluffs to miniature cypress swamp habitats, and Lake Chicot Trail is one of them. A primary highlight of this 22-mile backpacking trail is its system of extensive boardwalks that cut across large swaths of swampy waters, allowing you to stand, literally, in the midst of cypress swamp habitat. While the trail does not go through a full-fledged swamp, these cypress-filled arms of Lake Chicot are enough to silence you as you stand in awe of the surrounding beauty.

Described below is a 2–3 day backpacking trip—a perfect hike to start after work on Friday and finish in time to take well-deserved nap Sunday afternoon. After hiking 5.5 miles northward, you'll camp at backpacking site #5, then hike 10.1 miles to Campsite #1 the next day. Your final day will be a short 2-mile trek back to the South Landing. Because the terrain is relatively flat, and because water sources are few, hikers may decide to complete the trail in 2 days, covering a full 12.1 miles on Day 2. Suggested day hikes include:

- South Landing to Walker Branch (1.8 miles; 3.6 miles round trip)
- South Landing to North Landing (4.3 miles; 8.6 miles round trip)
- South Landing to East Landing (11.3 miles, one way)

If you're planning to backpack part or all of the trail, be aware that all backpackers are required to use the park's designated campsites and must obtain a free backcountry camping permit and a copy of Chicot's camping regulations. You can get both at the entrance station.

To get there, take I-49 to LA 106, then travel west toward the town of St. Landry. After approximately 9 miles, turn left onto LA 3042 and drive approximately 3.5 miles. The entrance to the park will be on your left. If you are coming from the south, an alternate route is to take I-49 to LA 167 west (Ville Platte). After 17 miles, turn north onto LA 3042. The park entrance will be on your right. The entrance station is open between 6 AM and 9 PM.

Day 1: South Landing Trailhead to Campsite #5

Total distance: 5.5 miles
Time: 2–3 hours

The South Landing trailhead, and the beginning of your hike, is less than a mile farther down the entrance road. Park at the trailhead and begin by walking north (to the left of entrance road as you drive in), watching for the orange blazes that mark the path. The flat trail leads beneath elm, dogwood, red maple, white oak, and other hardwoods. At your feet are various vines—Virginia creeper, muscadine, and, of course, poison ivy. Cross a small footbridge at 0.1 mile, then head slightly uphill to meander through the forest. This early section of the Chicot Trail winds over rolling terrain with some low, wet areas off to the side. In spring, look for phlox, violet wood sorrel, and the scarlet spikes of red buckeye.

At 0.4 mile is the first of many views of Lake Chicot's jagged, swampy edges. Although the trail circles the lake, it does not strictly follow its banks, so you won't have a constant, unchanging view of the water. Instead, you will have a sense of being in deep woods one moment, then will be standing among small pockets of cypress swamp the next.

At 1 mile, an emergency access trail shoots off to the left. Continue hiking straight ahead on the orange-blazed trail, which arcs broadly to the right before reaching the blue-blazed side trail to campsite #2. (Campsite #1 is to the south of where you started; you'll reach it tomorrow evening.) The wide spur trail leads to the small, secluded campsite, which has room for just one or two tents. This shady site affords a beautiful view of Lake Chicot.

Back on the trail, you'll hike along the rolling terrain and descend to cross a footbridge at 1.4 miles. Reach another footbridge at 1.5 miles, this one in the midst of several majestic old southern magnolias. Head back downhill, skirting a picturesque small cove on the right. The trail rolls alongside this little cove for a little while before exiting the woods at Walker Branch. Cross the bridge to the right, looking for purple gallinules and American coots feeding on the water.

When you reach the Walker Branch trailhead at 1.8 miles, reenter the woods to the right, heading downhill. This next section is particularly scenic, with many huge cypresses. You're likely to spot a great blue heron feeding here. This large, blue-gray creature with a sharp, pointed bill is particularly graceful in flight. Herons and egrets, which are both members of the same family, fly with their great wings outstretched and their necks hunched back between their shoulders. You might also see small perching birds in the shrubs to your left. Spring sees the brief visits of transient warblers: yellow, magnolia, hooded, and yellow-rumped warblers can be seen at Lake Chicot in March and April.

At 2.3 miles, hike uphill to a pocket of piney woods on sandy soil. Keep going straight when you reach another emergency access road to the left. The trail heads

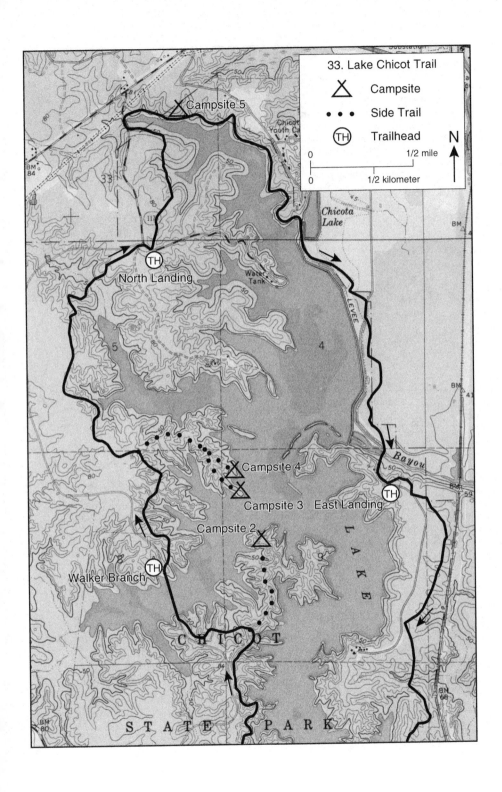

33. Lake Chicot Trail

△ Campsite
••• Side Trail
(TH) Trailhead

N

0   1/2 mile
0   1/2 kilometer

× Campsite 5

Chicota
Lake

(TH)
North Landing

Water
Tank

Bayou

× Campsite 4

× Campsite 3   East Landing   (TH)

Campsite 2 ×

(TH)
Walker Branch

C H I C O T

L A K E

S T A T E   P A R K

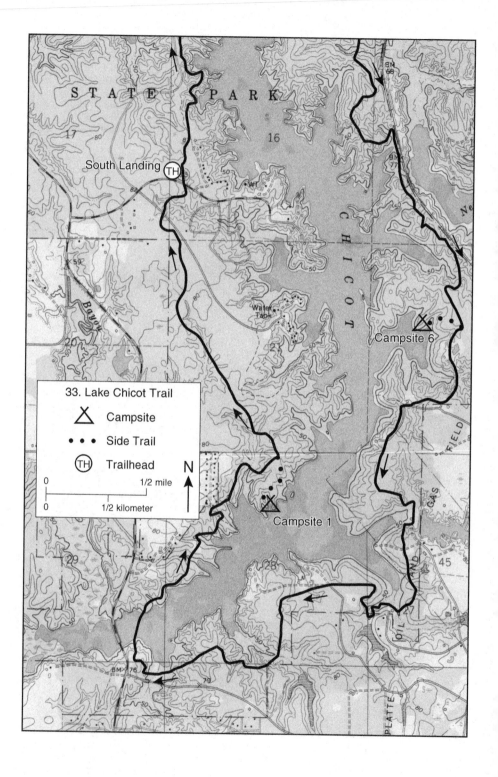

17   80

16

South Landing (TH)

82   50   WT

X 59

CHICOT

50

Bayou

50

Ne

80

Water
Tank

20

21

33. Lake Chicot Trail

⚕ Campsite

• • • Side Trail

(TH) Trailhead   **N**

0   1/2 mile

0   1/2 kilometer

Campsite 6

FIELD

GAS

Campsite 1

80

28

29

45

OIL

LAND

BM 76   78

50

PLATTE

80

down a rather steep slope as it traverses the region's small, rolling hills. You might notice numerous fallen canopy trees in the vicinity of the trail as you hike. The entire trail was closed in the winter of 2002–2003, compliments of Hurricane Lili. At 2.4 miles the trail crosses the green-blazed horse trail, another victim of the hurricane that had not yet been repaired at the time of this writing. Keep following the orange blazes down the level, straight path.

This mixed pine and hardwood area is home to various oaks and hickories, young pine saplings, red maple, and parsley hawthorn. You can recognize the thorny-branched parsley hawthorn, a small tree, by its deeply lobed leaves, which look like the parsley that restaurants use to enhance your dinner plate. Its small, showy white flowers bloom in early spring, and its oblong, bright red fruit ripens in autumn. Also known as parsley haw, this tree is a member of the rose family, along with apple, plum, cherry, peach, and pear trees.

At 2.6 miles, the trail skirts a scenic little gully and soon reaches the spur trail to campsites #3 and #4. Each site is approximately 0.7 mile off the trail. Like campsite #2, they are both small and situated to overlook the scenic, swampy edges of Lake Chicot. Back on the main trail, follow the orange blazes to cross the green-blazed horse trail again at 2.9 miles. This section features towering beeches and slightly hilly terrain and gives way to cypress and tupelo straight ahead as you skirt another swampy slough and cross the horse trail once more.

The trail swings to the right when it meets the green-blazed horse trail again. When it seems to fork with an old road at 3.7 miles, bear right, following the orange blazes to begin a slight downhill slope. As the trail descends, you will enter another beech-dominated area. In spring and summer, this section is lined with giant cane. Cross the horse trail again at 4 miles, then descend a gentle slope to a low, often wet area populated with southern magnolia and American holly. The trail crosses a footbridge at 4.1 miles, then winds through the woods to cross the horse trail once more. You'll exit the woods at 4.3 miles to reach the North Landing trailhead.

After crossing the parking area, bear right to reenter the woods on the well-marked path. The trail crosses a road, a footbridge, and another road within the next half-mile, remaining level as it winds past tall pines, hickories, and oaks. In spring, the dogwoods make this section particularly scenic. At 5.2 miles, head downhill to reach the first of five long footbridges through a lovely pocket of cypress and tupelo forest. Chicot's scenic bridges are maintained primarily by Americorps volunteers each summer. After crossing the bridge, you'll hike a path with cypress and tupelo forest on your right and hardwoods and giant cane on your left. The trail soon reaches the spur trail to campsite #5—your destination for the night. Although only 0.1 mile off the main trail, this site has an isolated feel to it and a nice view of the lake—particularly in winter, when the leaves are off the trees.

Day #2: Campsite #5 to Campsite #1

Total distance: 11.6 miles
Time: 6.5 hours

Return to the main trail, bearing right to continue your hike. You'll soon cross your first long footbridge of the day through an island of cypress and tupelo forest. The next mile winds back and forth as it skirts the water's edge. The majestic cypress and tupelo trees are never far from sight. Cross the next long footbridge at 1 mile, looking for herons, egrets, and ibises perched in the trees.

Hurricane Lili crippled parts of the Lake Chicot Trail in 2002.

When the bridge ends, the trail leads uphill toward the grassy, wildflower-covered protection levee, built when this lake was developed and dammed in the 1930s. Bear right onto the levee top, continuing along it for the next half mile. To your left is a swampy area, and to the right is open water. Bear left at 2.5 miles to reenter the woods at the hiker sign and orange blazes. This segment borders the park's property line, so you may see signs of civilization just beyond the trees to your left. The trail continues to wind through the woods; because it is low and flat, this area can get pretty muddy in wet seasons. Look for deer, raccoon, opossum, and armadillo tracks as you walk.

The trail reaches the East Landing trailhead at 3.5 miles, where you'll cross the parking area and bear right to reenter the woods. This next segment is quite low and flat; you'll see moisture-loving dwarf palmetto, ferns, and ironwood among the other vegetation in this section. After crossing the next long footbridge through cypress swamp at 4.8 miles, you'll enter a mixed pine and hardwood pocket where the trail is carpeted with pine needles. This pleasant segment reaches the spur to campsite #6 at 6.2 miles. It is a short walk on the blue-blazed trail to the small campsite—and a great lunch spot—overlooking a cove of Lake Chicot.

The orange-blazed Lake Chicot Trail continues to wind a level route through the mixed forest. At 6.9 miles, when you enter a grassy, cleared area, turn left to walk between young pines. This wide section is grassy and meadowlike in places and is particularly nice in spring, when the area is full of wildflowers. Look for violets and blue-eyed grass in spring, and various asters in summer. At 7.1 miles, bear left, back into the woods. The trail crosses another long bridge at 7.7 miles. Although this part of the trail is not as swampy as some previous sections, it can get very muddy once you're off the bridge. Two smaller footbridges follow before the trail crosses a gravel road at 7.9 miles and heads down a slight slope. You'll cross two more short footbridges before reaching another long bridge at 8.1 miles.

At 8.5 miles, the trail reaches a junction with two dirt roads. A lack of blazes can make this spot confusing. Simply hike straight ahead as you exit the woods, and begin an uphill slope in about 0.2 mile. Watch for the sparse orange blazes painted on the trees on either side of the road. A clearly painted orange blaze signals where the trail veers left into the woods after approximately a half mile of the road walk. Cross another footbridge at 9.1 miles. The next mile is flat and winding, though the lake views are not as plentiful as previously. Cross another small footbridge at 10.1 miles, then head uphill as the trail begins to show some change in terrain.

You'll soon reach one of the highlights of the entire trail: a 650-foot bridge spanning the southern tip of the lake. This unbelievably scenic section features another small cypress and tupelo forest and is a favorite spot for herons, egrets, ibises, and other wading birds. When the long bridge ends, head uphill. The remaining 2 miles to your campsite are mostly flat and winding. Because the hike passes through several low areas, you'll cross a few more footbridges before reaching your campsite.

At 11.3 miles is a rather open area at a large beech with a wooden cross attached to it. Turn left at this lone memorial, then bear right soon afterward, following the orange blazes. You're near the park's boundary again and may see private buildings nearby. The blue-blazed path to campsite #1 heads to the right at 11.6 miles. This is your destination for day 2, unless you decide to hike the last 2 miles to the South

Landing Trailhead and your car. Campsite #1 is pleasantly situated beneath the shade of a large beech. As with the other campsites, you'll have a scenic view of Lake Chicot from your tent.

Day 3: Campsite #5 to South Landing Trailhead

Distance 2 miles
Time: 1 hour

Return to the trail, bearing right on the orange-blazed path. The path continues to wind a level route through the woods, crossing several footbridges and skirting numerous hurricane-induced blowdowns over the next mile. At 1.6 miles, cross under some power lines, then hike a little farther to cross a road. Back in the woods at 1.8 miles, the trail is covered with pine needles and features beautiful flowering dogwoods in spring. You'll cross one final footbridge before finally exiting the woods—and reaching the South Landing trailhead and the end of your hike.

34

Acadiana Park
Nature Station and Trails

Total distance (circuit): About 2 miles

Hiking time: 1 hour

*Habitats: Bottomland hardwood,
small-stream forest*

*Maps: USGS 7½' Breaux Bridge,
park map*

Thousands of years ago, a slight change in climate marked the beginning of the end of the last Ice Age. During these volatile times, enormous volumes of glacial meltwater coursed southward down the ancient Mississippi, forcing the swelling river to develop deep trenches in the surrounding land to handle the tremendous flow. In the process, the great river expanded its floodplain by 50 miles as its bulk deviated westward to a course through what is now south-central Louisiana—a course that it kept for more than a thousand years. As the Ice Age faded into distant history and the meltwater gradually subsided, the Mississippi River eventually reverted to its more easterly course. Meanwhile, the deep trenches that remained were suffused with a dark, nutrient-rich, claylike sediment. This slow process, which occurred between 5,000 and 7,000 years ago, resulted in a gray-toned floodplain that reached from the Gulf of Mexico north to Tennessee and supported a vast bottomland hardwood forest.

The Mississippi River has long since abandoned this part of south Louisiana, but it has certainly left its legacy. Although much of the ancient floodplain's original bottomland hardwood forest is lost to us, the winding trails of Acadiana Park provide a small glimpse of that once-abundant forest type. A small body of water, François Coulee, meanders lazily through the park along the old Mississippi River route. The word "coulee," derived from the French *couler*, meaning "to flow," is a common south Louisiana appellation for small streams like this one. Rising in elevation south of François Coulee is an escarpment, or blufflike shelf of land, that was part of the Mississippi's western bank so many years ago. Beyond the ancient riverbank to the south begins what was once the Gulf Coast Tallgrass Prairie—and before that, the coastal plain during the last Ice Age.

These ghosts of Louisiana's natural history are all located, to some degree, at Acadiana Park, a 110-acre facility just minutes from urban Lafayette. The park's nature station provides education and conducts research on this unique geological tract, which is also the only bottomland hardwood forest in the area that is open to the public. The trails wind and loop through the bottomland hardwood part of the park and past the various types of flora it supports, including live oak, cherrybark oak, water oak, sweet gum, pecan, and sycamore. The park's resident birds include cardinals, Carolina chickadees, tufted titmice, downy woodpeckers, and red-shouldered hawks. Acadiana Park is also home to numerous reptiles and amphibians: the Gulf Coast toad, green anole, speckled king snake, leopard frog, and green and gray tree frogs, among others.

To get to Acadiana Park from I-10, take US 167 south for about a mile to West Willow Street. Turn left onto West Willow, and go about a half mile to the Moss Street traffic light. Turn left onto Moss and go just under a mile to East Alexander Street and turn right. The Acadiana Park entrance is located about a mile down East Alexander. It costs nothing to enter the park, though camping is available for a fee.

The parking lot is immediately beyond the entrance. The trailhead is to the right of the parking lot and will lead you to the nature station. Obtain maps and brochures at the nature station, which is a short 0.2-mile hike from the trailhead through woods that have been, unfortunately, partially disturbed by the development of a Frisbee course. Soon, however, you'll see the nature station on your right and a footbridge just ahead. The trail continues across the footbridge to reach the park's 1,100-foot boardwalk. The boardwalk is shaped like a figure eight; you'll walk the left half of the eight first, then return to the rest of the boardwalk later in the hike.

You'll immediately notice how green everything is on this trail—even in winter! Louisiana's subtropical climate makes it ideal for various moisture-loving evergreens, from the ground-dwelling dwarf palmetto, to the nonnative Chinese privet, to the venerable old live oaks. Chinese privet is perhaps the most abundant evergreen in the park. This dense, shrublike evergreen has several trunks, many branches, and small, compact leaves that usually grow in two rows. In late spring, it produces numerous showy, fragrant white flowers. Because it is so attractive and easily handled, Chinese privet is a popular tree for decorative hedges throughout the suburban south. It's also popular with birds, which feed in autumn on its round, black berries—which, by the way, are poisonous to humans. Unfortunately, this introduced tree is an invasive species and takes over areas that once saw native plant growth.

Hiking the boardwalk, you'll soon reach the junction of the figure eight. Continue to the left. This part of the boardwalk soon steps downward to the dirt trail. Take a left to begin the trail system's western loop. Several of the oaks on this part of the trail have an interesting, light red lichen growing on their trunks. This lichen, known scientifically as *Cryptothecia rubrocincta*, is common in both tropical and subtropical climates. Commonly known as scarlet lichen or Christmas lichen (due to its red and green tones), it can be found growing on

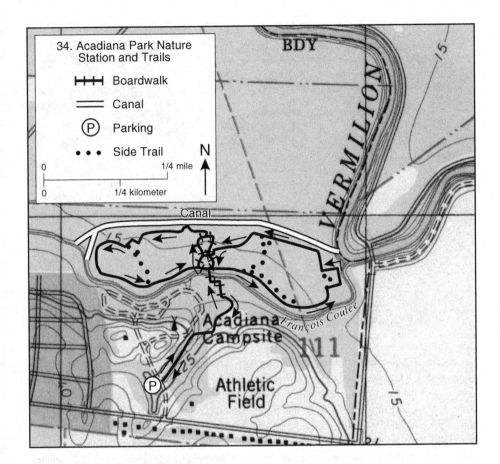

34. Acadiana Park Nature
Station and Trails

live oaks throughout south Louisiana. In fact, sometimes it grows in such abundance that it can make the entire trunk of a tree look like it's been painted pink!

After about 0.1 mile, you'll reach a trail junction. Take the trail to the right, and you'll soon swing left to rejoin the main trail at a junction barely 200 feet after you leave it. Continue on the main trail, reaching François Coulee after several hundred feet.

The trail swings left to meander alongside François Coulee. As you hike this section, the water will be on your right, and its natural levee will be on your left. The levee is evidence that this small body of water was once much larger and more powerful. Note the intricate root systems of the bald cypresses above François Coulee; they are visible as a result of the surrounding erosion. The trail soon crosses over the natural levee, and for a while you'll hike in its inner side. Look for red-shouldered hawks, common in the park all year long, in the surrounding woods.

Almost a half mile into the dirt trail, you'll reach another trail junction. The trail to the left will take you about 500 feet to the northern section that you've already hiked. If you take it, you'll soon see a forest of dwarf palmetto, the result of slightly lower elevations in that section of the woods. For now, go straight ahead toward the boardwalk and

Black-eyed Susans are common summer flowers at the nature station.

the nature station, passing many poison ivy vines and a massive live oak on your left. After 0.1 mile, you'll be back at the boardwalk. Keep going straight to walk the bottom right part of the figure eight. Another dirt trail continues ahead when the boardwalk veers to the left at the center of the eight. Step down onto the new dirt trail to hike the trail system's eastern loop.

In addition to palmetto, you'll also see southern shield fern at your feet. Other common Louisiana ferns in the park include Torres' fern and the intriguing resurrection fern, which grows on the bark of live oaks. Just ahead are two such live oaks on your left. Some of these huge trees have old, hollowed-out branches that serve as homes for various critters, such as raccoons and opossums. Other animals common here are flying squirrels, armadillos, and bats, though you probably won't catch a glimpse of the bats unless you take advantage of one of the nature station's guided night hikes.

Less than 0.1 mile from where the dirt trail began, the trail splits. You can go either way; the two trails actually parallel each other for a short time before rejoining. One trail leads along a levee top, and the other along the ground nearby.

The next trail junction will be 0.2 mile farther. Take a right to ascend a small hillock and gain a view of where both the canal and François Coulee join the Vermillion River at the eastern edge of the park. The trail swings sharply left after affording the view and soon rejoins the original trail at a tall sycamore tree marked with numerous straight lines of small holes. These holes were bored by shy, secretive woodpeckers known as yellow-bellied sapsuckers. Vocally among the quietest of woodpeckers, they bore holes into the inner bark of trees until the sap exudes and oozes down the trunk, where they use their brush-like tongues to collect it. Yellow-bellied sapsuckers, along with other birds, also feed on the insects that are attracted to the sap. Although this red-crested bird is furtive and often moves to the other side of a tree when approached, its even rows of small holes are easy to identify.

Take a right onto the original trail to continue the loop. The trail soon swings left to run alongside the canal that marks the north side of the trail. Several hundred feet later, you'll reach a pipeline clearing that hosts numerous wildflowers in spring and summer. In fact, this whole canal bank is a great place to see wildflowers; look for spiderwort, blue-eyed grass, buttercup, wild geranium, violets, and violet wood sorrel in spring.

After a little more than 0.1 mile, the trail splits once again. Going to the left, you can either head back toward the nature station or meet a junction that allows you to return to the canal, a couple of hundred feet straight ahead. To finish this loop, go straight along the canal bank. After passing the junction just mentioned, the trail swings left, away from the canal, and winds through the woods for a bit. After several hundred feet, the trail rejoins the boardwalk. Go left to return to the nature station. To return to the trailhead, complete the figure eight and return the way you came, crossing the bridge over François Coulee.

The hike covered in this guide is just under 2 miles, but the trail's many loops allow for a much longer hike, if desired. Each time you hike a particular section, you are certain to discover something new, or something you hadn't noticed before—a wildflower, a mushroom, an armadillo, or even a glimpse of a yellow-bellied sapsucker as it retreats from its stores of sap. Don't hesitate to hike and rehike these loops in a single visit; no trail is ever quite the same from hike to hike, and this trail is no exception.

To learn more about the wonders offered by this geologically unique area, be sure to visit the adjacent nature station. Their exhibits and experts are excellent resources for anyone wanting to learn more about bottomland hardwood habitat and the systems it supports. Contact the nature station for its schedule of public tours and night hikes.

35

Lake Martin Loop

Total distance (circuit): 5.1 miles

Hiking time: 2 hours

Habitats: Bottomland hardwood forest, cypress swamp, fresh marsh

Map: USGS 7½' Broussard

Lake Martin, also known as Lake la Pointe, is unquestionably one of the most scenic sites in all of Louisiana. Some of the area is privately owned, but a large part belongs to The Nature Conservancy as Cypress Island Preserve. A natural basin that has been impounded to regulate water levels, the area comprises an open lake, a nearby swamp, and associated wetlands. The site includes a rookery and is a spring haven for egrets, herons, anhingas, ibises, roseate spoonbills, and many perching birds. Another resident is the American alligator; in fact, part of the area is closed during the alligator's summer breeding season. Although this area is beautiful at any time of year, the most popular time to visit is in March and April, when the birds are nesting. You can hike the unofficial, 5.1-mile trail around the lake, or you can explore the bottomland hardwood habitat of the Cypress Island Preserve trail system.

From I-10, drive to LA 328 in Breaux Bridge (Exit 109). Go south on LA 328 for 1.8 miles, then turn right to cross Bayou Teche. At the next red light, turn left onto LA 31. Travel 2.7 miles down LA 31 until you reach Lake Martin Road on the right. After a mile, Lake Martin Road turns into gravel and soon ends at Rookery Road (also gravel). Turn left and drive past the rookery to the parking area at the end of Rookery Road (about a mile). Be aware that this is a very popular area for birders, anglers, and hikers; this stretch, which includes a boat launch, can get very crowded. Following this guide, you will walk the circumference of the lake for a total hike of 5.1 miles.

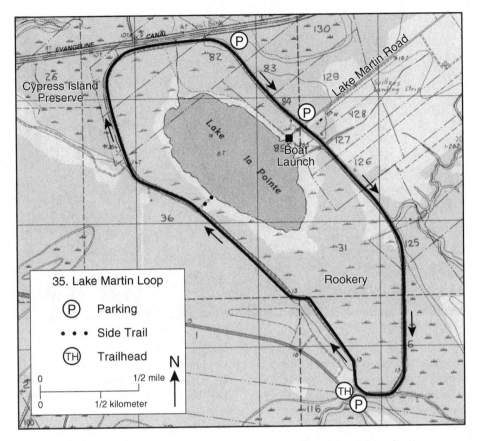

35. Lake Martin Loop

After parking, walk straight ahead and through the gate, hiking with the marshy lake on your right. On this first section, you'll have only intermittent views of the water, as some areas will have quite a bit of undergrowth. The larger trees include honey locust, prickly ash, water oak, buttonbush, and of course, bald cypress. At your feet, you're likely to see poison ivy, as well as fire ant piles. Watch your step!

You'll also see vetch, common blue violets, and various grasses in spring. Views of the lake improve after about a mile of walking. You'll soon reach a small peninsula on your right. If the water is low, you can actually walk to the tip of the peninsula for a clear view of the scenic lake. A half mile past the

peninsula is the Cypress Island Preserve on the left. A delightful tangle of trails, developed by The Nature Conservancy and volunteers, winds for a mile or so through the preserve. If this low-elevation area isn't flooded when you're there, you'll want to explore it for a while. The preserve trails have interpretive signs scattered throughout the area. As a result of recent hurricane damage, however, these trails were closed as this book was going to press.

Back on the levee, it's a mile to the northeast parking lot. To your left is the Evangeline Canal; unfortunately, this canal is the endpoint for bottles, cans, bags, and other trash left by careless visitors to the area. The presence of alligators, red-eared

Cypresses in Lake Martin

sliders, and a variety of birds redeems this area from being a complete eyesore. See if you can spot turtles sunning on a log, or herons collecting branches for their nests. To your right, the lake sparkles as egrets roost in the bald cypresses that seem to rise from the water. The view from here is especially breathtaking at sunset.

Alligators are always a thrill to see, and Lake Martin offers an excellent opportunity to view these large, scaly creatures. Although unprovoked attacks on humans are extremely rare, an alligator will attack if provoked or if its nest is approached too closely. Don't let the presence of alligators discourage you from visiting areas like Lake Martin; simply remain aware of your environment and use care and common sense when hiking.

As you hike this 1 mile stretch, you might notice that parts of the lake—and even some of the alligators—seem covered with a car-

pet of green. Two aquatic plants are primarily responsible for this: duckweed and water hyacinth. Duckweed can make a lake look like a well-manicured golf course. Although many people mistake it for algae, duckweed is actually a flowering plant. The sizable mats of green actually consist of millions of tiny duckweed plants, each with its own roots, pistils, stamens, and blooms. Duckweed is native to Louisiana and thrives in still waters that are high in nitrogen and phosphates. Although it's easy enough to skim duckweed from the water's surface, this little plant has become a nuisance for numerous bodies of water in the United States—including Lake Martin. Because duckweed absorbs nutrients from the water, it becomes difficult or even impossible for other, nutrient-requiring species to thrive.

Water hyacinth is another invasive flowering plant. It has been known to cover entire lakes, preventing fishing and other water activities. It can even block boat traffic on rivers. You can easily identify the showy lavender flowers when they're in bloom; just look for clumps or mats of flowers on the water's surface. These heavy clumps (an acre can weigh more than 200 tons) block sunlight, reduce oxygen levels in the water, and kill fish and other plant communities that depend on these nutrients.

Once you reach the western parking area, the trail changes from a walking path to the gravel Rookery Road. This road is heavily used during the nesting season, when birders, photographers, and other nature enthusiasts flock to Lake Martin in droves. If you're hiking in spring, you'll begin to see the graceful egrets, herons, anhingas, and other species that make this lake so popular. In March and April, the sheer numbers of these gorgeous creatures are apt to leave you speechless. Watch as they fly across to the woods on your left to gather sticks for their nests—and as they fly back to their nesting spots, carrying the branches and twigs they require. The birds begin nesting as early as February; these winter arrivals get the choice nesting spots in the majestic, moss-laden cypresses. Spring latecomers nest wherever they can—often in the smaller buttonbush shrubs closer to the lakeshore.

This remarkable stretch of the walk extends more than a half mile. When the road eventually bends to the right, you'll know the hike is almost complete. About 0.2 mile after the road bends, you'll reach the gate and your car.

36

Lake Fausse Pointe State Park

Total distance (circuit): 5.7 miles

Hiking time: 3 hours

Habitats: Bottomland hardwood forest, cypress swamp

Maps: USGS 7½' Jackass Bay, park brochure, park map

Tucked away in a quiet nook along the western edge of the Atchafalaya Basin, Lake Fausse Pointe State Park is a treat for hikers of all levels. Its trail system winds through beautiful bottomland hardwood forest, skirts the edge of Lake Fausse Pointe, and follows several old canals past swampy cypress sloughs before looping back to the trailhead parking lot. If you're looking for a short stroll, try Trail A—a flat, level walk of only three-quarters of a mile. A longer walk is available along 1.6-mile Trail B, and Trails A and B can easily be combined into a single hike. At 3.3 miles, Trail C offers a few Louisiana-style hills and leads to several isolated backpacking sites. This trail is ideal for both the beginning backpacker and the hiker who desires the benefits of a secluded backpacking site, but doesn't have the time or inclination to hike a full day to get there.

Be aware that parts of the trails can get quite muddy and swampy after heavy rains. If you're concerned about trail conditions, call the park first. You can also call and reserve a backpack site, though reservations are generally not necessary for small groups.

The route to the park is an adventure along Louisiana's back roads. Take I-10 to LA 347 in Breaux Bridge. Going south on LA 347, travel to the second red light. Turn right at the light, following the signs to LA 31. Turn left at the next light onto LA 31, and follow this road to St. Martinville, where you must turn left onto LA 96 (at the Catholic church) and drive for 3.5 miles to LA 679. Turn right onto LA 679, traveling 4.3 miles to turn left onto LA 3083. LA

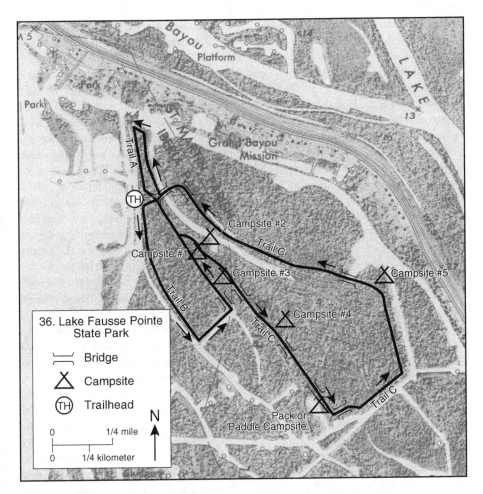

36. Lake Fausse Pointe
State Park

⊐⊏ Bridge

✕ Campsite

(TH) Trailhead

N

0   1/4 mile

0   1/4 kilometer

3083 ends at Levee Road after 4.1 miles. Turning right onto Levee Road, drive 8 more miles to Lake Fausse Pointe State Park, which will be on your right. Note: If you're thinking about taking the Henderson exit (Exit 115), be aware that the Levee Road for much of that route is gravel and is not necessarily a quicker way to get to the park.

Drive past the ranger station, and you'll soon see a sign for the trails on your right. Parking is available across the road from the sign, and restrooms are located adjacent to it. A short approach trail takes you across a canal via a footbridge. Much of the park's geography is oddly molded by numerous canals like this one, all built in the mid-1900s by oil companies to transport materials. These canals were active until the early 1980s and the establishment of the park.

As you cross the bridge, look for a great blue heron or a great egret, either flying overhead or perched along the canal's banks. You'll soon reach the trailhead, where trail maps are available. Trail A, marked with white double blazes, begins to your right. Take Trail A, immediately veering to the right to hike this loop counterclockwise. These trails underwent several minor reroutes after the park took a pounding from Hurricane Lili in October 2002. In addition to knocking down a number of trees, the hurricane left many areas flooded for several weeks in its wake.

Much of the flora along this trail is similar to that of other Louisiana trails: dwarf palmetto, water oak, muscadine, and the ever-present poison ivy. If you're hiking in early spring, you'll see honeysuckle, asters, blue-eyed grass, wild violets, buttercups, spider-wort, and wild geraniums. As for animals, look for deer and opossum. You also stand an excellent chance of spotting an armadillo.

The nine-banded armadillo is a Jurassic-looking creature that populates much of the southern United States, including the whole of Louisiana. This armored mammal is pre-dominantly nocturnal but often feeds during the day by rooting through leaves, brush, and soil with its snout. Its hearing is as-sumed poor, its sense of smell excellent, and its concentration nearly unbreakable—so much so that you can approach and watch an armadillo at close range before it notices you and scuttles rapidly away or magically disappears into a burrow hole. Armadillos wheeze and grunt as they feed, sniffing for beetles, earthworms, snails, and other small critters, as well as berries, seeds, and mushrooms. Many folks con-sider this creature a nuisance because it roots through gardens, takes up residence underneath houses, and digs burrows that can twist the ankle of a human or a horse. Nuisance or not, they're interesting crea-tures to watch from the close distance that they unwittingly allow.

A highlight of Trail A is about 0.3 mile from the trailhead, where the "skeletons" of cypress knees are visible in the water to your right. Normally, only the tops of cypress knees can be seen as they rise from watery surfaces. Here, the ground beneath has eroded away, leaving tangles of connected roots aboveground. This remarkable sight, along with the view of the water beyond, is enough to make you stop for a few minutes and marvel at the unique beauty of south Louisiana.

The trail swings left, away from the water and the cypresses and toward a number of other trees and plants: wax myrtle, dwarf palmetto, bald cypress, tupelo, sycamore, and more poison ivy. At 0.5 mile is a bench that can be converted into a miniature picnic table. About 0.1 mile farther, a view of Lake Fausse Pointe appears on the right. Shortly beyond is the junction with Trail B. To return to the parking area, take the left fork for sev-eral hundred feet. To hike Trail B, go straight ahead. The first 200 feet of Trail B is handi-capped accessible and leads to an obser-vation deck to the right. Early evening is a great time to be here, as the observation deck faces west and allows a view of the sun setting over the tranquil lake.

Shortly past the observation deck is the junction for Trails B and C. Go to the right to continue Trail B, winding alongside the lake. You'll hike past a wood duck box after 0.1 mile. In 1999, numerous boxes were placed throughout the park, both for wood duck breeding and for interpretive purposes. The wood duck is a uniquely beautiful bird; on a single duck, the feathers range from chest-nut, red, and bronze to shiny greens, pur-ples, and blues. These short-necked ducks nest in hollow trees and can often be seen perching in trees. They also use the nesting boxes you'll see along the trail at Lake Fausse Pointe. Nesting boxes were quite successful in the wood duck's recovery from near extinction in the early 20th cen-tury, when its habitat and population were devastated by a combination of deforesta-tion, swamp drainage, hunting, and com-mercial demand for feathers.

View of Lake Fausse Pointe

The trail winds past sugarberry, sycamore, black cherry, oak, cypress, tupelo, and wax myrtle. It leads away from the lake, and soon you'll find yourself walking alongside a canal. At 0.7 mile is a "Louisiana uphill" leading to a sycamore-covered knob that allows a fine view of the water. The hilly terrain that follows is not natural to this part of Louisiana, of course. When the oil companies dredged these canals years ago, the dirt was piled up on either side . . . hence, the "hills" of this otherwise flat trail. The raised areas make for a pleasant change in the terrain and offer several views of the surrounding water.

Further down the trail, look to your left for a slough of cypress and tupelo, and look to the ground in spring for a profusion of wildflowers. A boardwalk begins at 0.9 mile. This boardwalk, an Eagle Scout project built by Boy Scout Troop 350 of New Iberia, takes you through a particularly swampy—and beautiful—pocket of cypress and tupelo forest. At 1 mile is a bench to the right. From

here, look for herons, egrets, pelicans, cormorants, and hawks along the canal. You might even see a bald eagle. Among the nearby tree branches, perching birds are numerous, any time of year.

Three-tenths of a mile past the bench is the junction with Trail C. Go straight ahead to complete Trail B. To continue on Trail C, go to the right. Orange-blazed Trail C is longer than the other two trails, but it's well worth the hike. Winding through a beautiful forest of water oak, cottonwood, black willow, sugarberry, cypress, and tupelo, it leads to six primitive campsites.

Backpack site #1, just short of 0.2 mile down Trail C, is suitable for a small group. Like the other primitive campsites, it features a fire ring. If you opt for a campfire, be aware that it is illegal to cut trees in the park; use only the wood that you find on the ground. Take care to check for poison ivy vines on the wood. Burning releases the poison ivy oils into the air, which can result in extremely painful and potentially dangerous reactions in the lungs if the oils are inhaled.

The next two campsites—Backpack sites #2 and #3—are within 0.1 mile of the first one. Despite their proximity, both offer a welcome sense of remoteness for backpackers looking to get away from it all for a little while. Both are also suitable for small groups.

After crossing a footbridge at 0.3 mile, the trail swings to the right, adjacent to several large tupelos on the left. It winds through the woods, eventually coming to a side trail that leads back to backpack site #3. Keep hiking, and you'll reach a footbridge and numerous cypress knees at 0.5 mile. In warm weather, look for sunning turtles and alligators in the water beyond the trees.

Backpack site #4 is right on the trail at 0.7 mile and is suitable for a larger group, with space for several tents. Less than 0.1 mile down Trail C, keep your eyes open for an unusual-looking tree to your right. This sycamore apparently fell to the ground, then began to grow again, out of the side of its trunk! This is not an uncommon phenomenon in sycamores, amazingly enough—but it is always a fascinating sight.

Reach another footbridge shortly afterward, and the trail continues to wind through a forest of cypress, tupelo, water oak, and sugarberry. At 1.2 miles is the park's "pack-and-paddle" campsite. This beautiful campsite is on a knoll to the right of the trail and has room for several tents.

Trail C continues, climbing a "Louisiana uphill" and riding along a constructed "ridge" between a slough on the left and a canal on the right. After crossing the next footbridge, you'll find a pleasant view of the canal awaiting you. At 2 miles, after hiking along a high bank, you'll reach backpack site #5, suitable for a small group.

Back on Trail C is a boardwalk at 2.2 miles. Look to the left to see another interesting sycamore growing from the side of its horizontal trunk. Taking a left after the boardwalk, you'll enter a near-forest of dwarf palmettos that extends for several hundred feet. You'll also reach an area with many downed trees—the legacy of Hurricane Lili.

Snakes are common in this swampy country. The great majority of Lake Fausse Pointe State Park's snakes are nonpoisonous and include rough green, western ribbon, common garter, and numerous water snakes. Be aware that cottonmouths (water moccasins), copperheads, and pygmy rattlesnakes live here, too. Snakes are beautiful creatures and fascinating to watch from a distance. They generally have no interest in humans and will usually slither away if they hear you coming. Remember that the majority of snakebites occur when the victim is actually trying to handle the snake. Keep your distance and be content to watch this enchanting creature in its natural habitat.

At 2.8 miles, the trail reaches the conference center parking lot. Go straight ahead, along the edge of the parking lot, which is blazed orange like the rest of the trail. The path briefly turns into gravel, crosses a road, then reenters the woods at 3 miles. It swings left and parallels the road you crossed for a time. At 3.1 miles, take a sharp left and cross a footbridge. The hike ends shortly after this footbridge. When you emerge from the woods, walk straight ahead to the parking lot where you started.

37

Sherburne/Atchafalaya Trails

Total distance (three round trips):
17 miles

Hiking time: Varies; half-day and full-day hikes available

Habitats: Bottomland hardwood forest, cypress swamp, forest gaps, and edges

Maps: USGS 7½' Maringouin NW, Sherburne WMA map

A wild turkey crashes through the under-brush. In the distance, a 10-foot alligator floats lazily down Bayou des Glaises while another bellows loudly. A pileated wood-pecker flits secretively from tree to tree, somehow knowing that you are trying to watch it. You hear a whooshing sound as a great horned owl passes overhead. Watch where you step . . . the ground is muddy, and you're definitely in water moccasin country here in the Atchafalaya Basin. The trails of Sherburne Wildlife Management Area (WMA) and Atchafalaya National Wildlife Refuge lead to some beautiful spots and the opportunity to view wading birds and listen to alligators bellow, frogs mate, and warblers chirp. Much of the area's 42,690 acres are remote and wild; the trails here are worth the effort, but they're not for the faint of heart. Travel miles of gravel road to get to your trail, then watch for snakes and 'gators as you walk. And don't forget the bug spray! But if you're willing to accept the risks, this wild place in the heart of the Atchafalaya Basin is worth visiting.

Although the Atchafalaya Basin is best explored by boat, hikers have several op-portunities to experience this unforgettably haunting and awe-inspiring place. Untamed in comparison to some of the other trail sites in Louisiana, Sherburne has several trails of different lengths from which to choose. A trek down the 7.1-mile (one way) Bayou Des Glaises ATV trail ends at a re-mote, scenic spot next to the lazy bayou, where you can see alligators up close, view herons as they glide through the trees, and

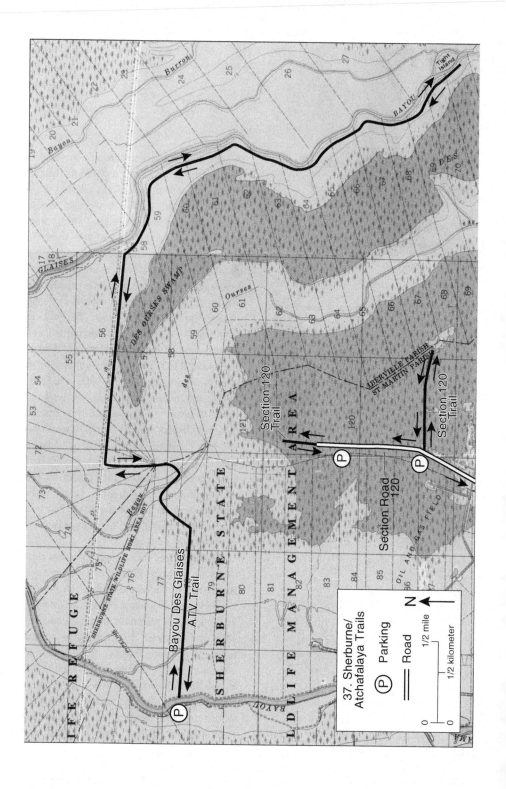

37. Sherburne/Atchafalaya Trails

hear a symphony of warblers all around. If you're feeling a little less adventurous—or if you're more interested in watching wildlife than in making miles—check out the 1-mile nature trail near the refuge headquarters. Or, you might piece together the two short trails on the Section 120 Road for a 2.5-mile hike. Another option is to view wading birds as you explore the South Farm Trail, which leads through an old crawfish farm.

Be aware that this is a hunting area; certain times of the year will see countless hunters crawling through the WMA. Sadly, hiking is not advisable during the busy, late-autumn hunting season. Remember, you'll need a Wild Louisiana Stamp, hunting license, or fishing license to hike and camp here. Check the hunting regulations or contact the WMA for information on the best times for hiking, and always wear hunter orange when hiking in any WMA. You may also want to contact the WMA to check on trail conditions if it has rained heavily in previous weeks.

These trails are couched between US 190 and I-10, approximately 30 miles west of Baton Rouge. The easiest way to reach the headquarters and the 1-mile nature trail from Baton Rouge or Opelousas is to take US 190 to the LA 975 exit at Krotz Springs, then go south on LA 975, a gravel road. After 2.9 miles (0.3 mile past the Sherburne WMA headquarters), you will reach the sign for the Nature Trail on the left. To get to the refuge from I-10, take Exit 127 onto LA 975 north, following the signs to enter the refuge. Directions to specific trails are provided below.

Section 120 Road Trails

No, Section 120 isn't an obscure type of military discharge. It's a gravel road in the middle of nowhere, Atchafalaya Basin, Louisiana. Two short trails begin here; you can combine them for a 2.5-mile hike. Because this area is a popular with duck hunters, you'll want to avoid it during duck season. ATVs are not allowed on either of the Section 120 trails.

From LA 975, turn east onto Bayou Manuel Road. Take a right onto Happytown Road, then drive approximately 1.3 miles to Section 120 Road, which will be the second road to your left. You can also reach these trails by turning onto Happytown Road from LA 975. Parking is available at both Section 120 trailheads, but you want to park at the first one, which will be on your right. The trail—originally built by oil exploration companies in the mid-20th century—begins just beyond the parking area.

As you begin hiking this car-width trail, listen for birds—particularly in spring and fall, when hundreds of migratory bird species are passing through. Ditches on either side provide a fertile habitat for amphibians and reptiles alike; during the spring mating season, you're likely to hear the odd buzzing sounds of bullfrog love. Among the trees in this bottomland hardwood habitat, look for cottonwood, sycamore, red maple, sugarberry, and box elder.

At 0.2 mile, another old road forks to the right, leading to the slough and an old oil well location. Keep going straight, noticing the increase in cypresses as you progress to a slightly lower elevation. At 0.3 mile, a small clearing to the left provides a view of Bayou des Ourses (pronounced "bayou d'zoo"). The view actually changes from year to year; in a drought year, much of the water may dry up and allow you to see a long way into the swamp. Most of the time, the black willows and grasses grow in this area and block any further sight of the swamp.

Wildflowers along the trail

As you continue down the trail, you'll gain more small views of the bayou to your left, and chances are that you'll spot at least a few birds. The one-way trail stops at just under 0.6 mile.

After you've hiked back to Section 120 Road, turn right to walk the short distance to the end of the road and the start of the next foot trail. Similar to the one you just hiked, this short trail is lined with black willow, cypress, wax myrtle, cottonwood, sugarberry, box elder, and red maple. Not quite 0.3 mile long, the path culminates at a pleasant open area that was likely the site of an old oil well. This spot is full of pokeweed, an edible plant whose young leaves and shoots have been cooked and eaten like spinach. The dark purple berries have been used for dyes, and the word "poke" is derived from the Algonquian *pakon*–a dye plant for staining. This vine, which has invaded this area, is na-tive to eastern North America and can grow up to 9 feet tall.

Once you've reached this open space, you'll need to turn back and retrace your steps to your car.

Bayou des Glaises ATV Trail

To reach the Bayou des Glaises ATV Trail from LA 975, follow the directions to Happytown Road. Once on Happytown, turn left onto Refuge Road. When you reach a T intersection; turn left onto Landing Road and drive approximately 1.5 miles to the trailhead.

Although Bayou des Glaises is near a swamp, you will hike along a ridge for the en-tire 7.1 miles. You want to avoid this trail in spring, unless it has been a dry year. The trail along the pipeline can get very muddy and unpleasant for hiking. Early fall is the best time to be out here, if you can catch a pleasant weekend before hunting season starts.

You will feel a refreshing sense of isolation as you begin the long, straight walk down the Bayou des Glaises Trail. This low area is made more beautiful by the huge cinnamon ferns along the path, which leads beneath tall oaks, cottonwoods, sugarberry, and cypress. After the trail swings left at 1.9 miles, it becomes more winding and gets a bit narrower in places. You'll soon reach the highline, which lasts for about a mile. This section of trail may seem less interesting, since you are out of the trees. However, look above you for various hawks. You might also spot an osprey or a bald eagle, both of which are occasionally seen in the vicinity.

At 3.9 miles, the trail swings right, off the highline and back into the woods to lead alongside scenic Bayou des Glaises. This wild, isolated part of the trail stretches for a deliciously long 3.2 miles. Because you are walking on a ridge, the bayou is several feet lower to your left. From this vantage point, you can watch all types of wildlife below and look for birds among the bottomland hardwood trees and cypresses. The abundance of cypresses makes this area seem especially magical.

The trail ends at a small clearing and a nice spot to rest, meditate, watch the bayou for wildlife, or listen and look for birds. Because the trail does not loop, you will need to retrace your steps in order to finish the hike and return to your car. The round-trip hike adds up to 14.2 miles.

South Farm Complex

A popular destination for area birders, the South Farm Complex is great area for viewing wading birds and spotting the occasional bald eagle. To get there from I-10, take Exit 37 (Ramah) and go north on the East Protection Levee. About a mile up the levee, you'll see the sign and parking area for the South Farm Complex. Obtain a map of the management area from the Louisiana Department of Wildlife and Fisheries before exploring this interesting area.

V. Southeast Louisiana

38

Tunica Hills
Wildlife Management Area

Total distance (circuit plus one round trip):
4+ miles

Hiking time: 3+ hours

Habitats: Upland hardwood forest
with mature beech and magnolia stands,
mixed pine and hardwood forest,
small-stream forest

Maps: USGS 7½' Angola,
Tunica Hills WMA (South Tract) map

Tunica Hills Wildlife Management Area (WMA)—with its abundance of red hills, tan loess, meandering bayous, and wildlife-rich upland forests—unquestionably offers some of the most scenic hiking in the state. Consisting of two separate tracts, the WMA also encompasses the historic Old Tunica Trace, which is a portion of the Natchez Trace system the early settlers used for travel. The area has an intriguing geological history as well. Standing up to 360 feet above sea level, these deeply eroded hills are partly the result of the Citronelle formation—colorful sand, silt, clay, and gravel sediments thought to have made their way here over 2 million years ago, just before the start of the great Ice Ages. The fertile soil, along with the flood-resistant elevation, made these hills a coveted area for numerous Native American tribes, particularly the Tunica, Houma, Koroa, and Natchez.

One distinctive element of the Tunica Hills is the loess that mantles the land. This yellow-tan substance is thought to have blown in from the Mississippi River bed during the dry periods of the Ice Ages, when there was little or no plant cover. Up to 35 feet deep in some parts of the Tunica Hills region, loess erodes over time by "spalling off," or shedding large, vertical slabs of soil. The result is the rugged, beautiful bluffs so characteristic of this area. The hills may also result from the gravel that tops the loess in places. The gravel-protected areas were slow to erode, while the loess and other sediments eroded into valleys and ravines. This left the gravel-topped hills of Tunica towering several hundred feet above. This region is actually part of a much larger geological feature called the Loess Blufflands Escarpment, which follows the Mississippi River's eastern bank southward from its confluence with the Ohio River.

Today, the entire area is set aside for public use—primarily hunting. However, hikers are free to take advantage of the nature trail, as well as many miles of ATV paths, all of which are closed to vehicles between February 1 and September 15. Check out hunting season information before heading for these hills. Also, be aware that a Wild Louisiana Stamp, hunting license, or fishing license is required for all management area users. Camping is not allowed on the Tunica Hills trails.

A few words of warning: This trail is not for the novice hiker. It is best for experienced hikers who want a rugged trek on challenging terrain. Steep, eroded gullies can make footing uncertain, and the abundance of quicksand in the creek beds can be dangerous for the unsuspecting hiker. Because most of the hike is unmarked and it is easy to get turned around, the ability to use a map and compass is a must. Obtain a WMA map from the Louisiana Department of Wildlife and Fisheries (LDWF), as well as a United States Geological Survey topographic map before hiking. Consider hiking this area with a partner or as part of a group. If you need a hiking partner, contact the Louisiana Hiking Club. Not only does the club sponsor regular trips to this awe-inspiring trail, but several club members are very familiar with the area and relish the opportunity to introduce this special place to others.

Finally, this area should not be confused with the popular Clark Creek Natural Area, located just over the border in Pond, Mississippi. Known as Tunica Hills to the locals, Clark Creek is a beautiful, developed area that includes a rugged 2.6-mile hiking trail and several waterfalls. Tunica Hills WMA lacks waterfalls, but it is less frequented by the public and provides a greater chance for both solitude and exploration.

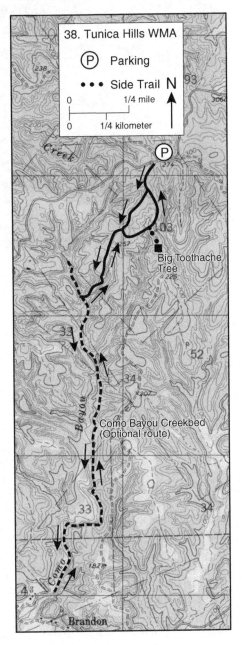

Rattlesnake warning sign

The hike described here is located in the WMA's south tract. To get there from Baton Rouge, take I-110 north to LA 61. Drive north through St. Francisville to LA 66, where you want to turn left. Travel 8 miles to LA 968 and a sign for the Greenwood Bus Route and Greenwood Plantation. Turn left here; within a mile, you'll cross Bayou Sara and turn right onto Old Tunica Road. Old Tunica Road is asphalt at first, but turns into hard-packed gravel after 3.2 miles. About a half mile after that, it bears to the left (away from Parker Road) and becomes loose gravel—which can be difficult to maneuver in wet weather. Stop and register at the self-clearing station, which is a half mile down the gravel road. A mile and a half beyond the self-clearing station is a parking area on the right; park here. The nature trail begins just across the road.

The trail's first quarter mile leads to the start of a loop, marked by a yellow post. The trail may seem to split prior to that; just follow the arrows that mark the path. You'll immediately notice the walls of deeply gullied loess on either side of the trail. Wildflowers will grow right out of these walls. It's also interesting to see the root systems of the magnolias, beeches, oaks, and pines where the soil has eroded.

When you reach the post at the loop junction, take the right fork. After 200 feet, the trail splits once more. Bear right onto the spur trail to Como Bayou. Depending on your penchant for adventure and exploration, it may be a few hours before you return to this spot. Como Bayou offers miles and miles of unmarked "trail"—the creek bed—that lead to some unbelievably scenic sites.

After 0.1 mile, the trail seems to split; take the left fork, which is actually a small gully. If you accidentally take the right fork, you'll soon realize your mistake, as the path peters out after less than 100 yards. The actual trail to the left winds through woods of American holly, yaupon, beech, magnolia, and oak. Arrows mark the route, which follows the ridgeline.

A little less than a half mile after the Como Bayou spur is a shaggy-barked old red cedar. This large, grizzled old tree commands your attention and can serve as a point of reference if you get confused here. After passing the red cedar, the trail begins a slight descent. Notice here that mostly beech and maple trees grow to the right of the ridge, while oaks and hickories are primarily to the left. The ridge narrows, and 0.1 mile after the red cedar, you really begin to head seriously downhill to the bed of Como Bayou.

The nature trail ends at a yellow post just before reaching the bayou, but your hike doesn't have to end here. In fact, for the adventurous hiker, the best is yet to come. The bayou is relatively shallow, and in dry periods the bed is actually dry. Hikers can walk the creek bed, looking for tracks and marveling at the red and purple clays below and the beautiful bluffs above. The bed of Como Bayou, like those of other small creeks in the area, is very sandy. Some parts are actually quicksand; if you do decide to hike the creek, be very careful where you step. It is a good idea to carry a hiking stick to test questionable spots. Warnings aside, the moist, sandy creek bed is an ideal place to look for animal tracks. In addition to white-tailed deer, raccoon, turkey, and opossum, black bear and cougar tracks have been spotted here.

You can hike only a few hundred feet down the creek bed to the right before encountering a boundary marker. If you go to the left, however, you can walk several miles to an abandoned railroad trestle with boundary tape. Approximately 0.4 mile into the hike

down the creek, you'll reach what Louisiana hiker Don Thibodeaux has dubbed the Christmas Berry Junction, marked by a single artesia, or Christmas berry plant. This handsome, albeit invasive, species grows in profusion in some other parts of the Tunica Hills. To see more of them, take a left at the Christmas Berry Junction and follow the side creek bed for several hundred yards. Numerous side trips like this one are available for exploration.

As you continue the hike down Como Bayou, look for moisture-loving magnolia, beech, oaks, cottonwood, and sugarberry. Numerous wildflowers bloom in spring, and woody muscadine vines droop from the trees all around. Around 0.7 mile, you might notice that the trail has descended slightly in elevation. This area is wetter and hosts more moisture-adapted plants, such as sycamore and bamboolike horsetail. If you're able to continue down the creek bed, despite its increase in moisture, you'll see several beautiful, wide bluffs 40 feet high.

When you've walked as far as you want to go down Como Bayou, return to the yellow post that marks the junction of the nature trail and Como Bayou. Turn right, heading back up the hill, until it levels out and you reach the old red cedar. Following the ridge, retrace your steps back to the Como Bayou sign, and then to the post marking the junction of the loop. You can now turn right at the loop to finish up the nature trail. Once again, you'll see arrows on the trees to guide you along the trail, though they are few and far between; if you plan to stick to the actual trail, keep a sharp lookout for them as you hike.

Like many Louisiana trails, this area is very green, even in January. Other colors decorate the forest throughout the year. As early as February, violets begin to pop out of the ground. Another early wildflower is sessile-leaved trillium, also known as toad trillium. This mottle-leaved, maroon flower is the only trillium you'll see throughout much of the state. Bright yellow Carolina jessamine, another early spring flower, grows from the vines above you, though you're just as likely to see these trumpet-shaped flowers strewn at your feet as you hike. Louisiana's brief autumns touch the beech leaves with gold and turn the dogwoods dark red and the poplars yellow. In winter, these brilliant colors are gone, leaving the evergreen magnolia, holly, live oak, pine, and cedar—and countless spectacular views as you crest the small hills.

Less than 200 feet after the split is a makeshift table and a large yellow poplar. If you walk beyond the table, you'll gain another view of the steep loess hillsides. Oakleaf hydrangeas bloom throughout this area in May. To continue the nature trail, turn left at the small table, following the arrows down a slight incline. Several numbered trees correspond to a guide printed by LDWF, but this guide was not readily available at the time of this writing. This section of the trail ends at a labeled cherrybark oak.

To complete the loop, you want to go left and walk between beautiful loess walls before retracing your steps to the parking area. However, a makeshift trail goes to the right and leads to a washed-out bridge. That section can be dangerous, so even the most adventurous hikers need to exercise caution if heading that way. Although you are not advised to explore the path to the right, you might want to go to the right about 100 feet to see an impressively large prickly ash. Also called Hercules'-club and toothache tree, this tree thrives in moist, sandy soils. The name Hercules'-club obviously derives from the spiny trunk; toothache tree refers to its use as a home remedy, in which the bitter bark is chewed to numb toothache pain.

Once you've turned left on the nature trail, you'll reach the yellow post to complete the loop. Take a right at the post and hike approximately 0.1 mile to the trailhead.

39

Blackfork Trail

Total distance (circuit): 2.3 miles

Time: 1-2 hours

Habitats: Bottomland hardwood, cypress swamp

Maps: USGS 7½' St. Francisville, refuge brochure, refuge map

Heavy springtime rains summon the rising—and flooding—of Louisiana's many ponds, lakes, bayous, and rivers. Even the wide Mississippi River can rise several feet in a short time. Throughout most of the state, the rising of the Mississippi has little apparent effect on the everyday life of plants and animals, thanks to an extensive levee system. Not so at Cat Island National Wildlife Refuge (NWR), located on the southernmost unleveed portion of the Mississippi. When the waters rise, Cat Island floods—no questions asked. Cat Island's water levels annually rise well up to 10 feet or more. The only plants that can survive these floods are those that don't mind being saturated from the waist down for months at a time: cypress, tupelo, sugarberry, willow, sycamore, red maple, and the water-adapted overcup, water, and willow oaks. When river levels drop, Cat Island drains, becoming a fertile paradise for herons, perching birds, butterflies, alligators, red-eared sliders, green tree frogs, and various snakes.

Because the water is generally higher in the spring and summer months, Cat Island is a murky underwater refuge for this part of the year. Indeed, the refuge seems an unlikely site for any type of land-based human recreation, much less a hiking trail. Despite the odds, the United States Fish and Wildlife Service, in concert with Friends of Cat Island (a dedicated volunteer organization), maintains not one, but two hiking trails. The Blackfork Trail is a 2.3-mile loop through mixed bottomland hardwood forest

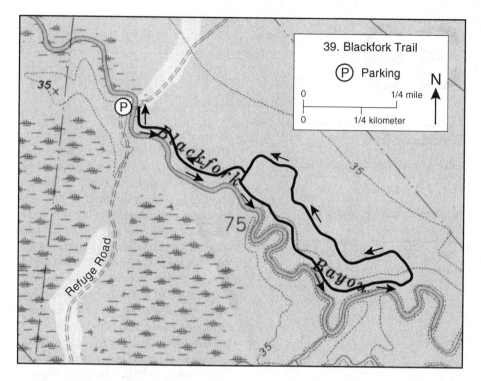

and alongside scenic Blackfork Bayou, and the Big Cypress Trail is a short, straight walk over ridge-and-swale topography to the largest tree east of the Sierra Nevada.

Cat Island NWR, which was established in 2000 to preserve forested wetland habitats and their associated plants and animals, is located north of St. Francisville, though its headquarters are on Commerce Street in that town. To reach this historic town, take I-110 north out of Baton Rouge, then turn right and take US 61, which will take you past Zachary to St. Francisville. North of St. Francisville, turn left onto LA 66, cross Bayou Sara, then turn left onto Solitude Road and drive 3.6 miles. Following the refuge signs, turn right onto Creek Road, which becomes Refuge Road and will lead to the trailhead in less than 2 miles. You can park on the right of the road; the trailhead is on the left. Be aware that vehicular access is restricted when the area is flooded. Your safest bet is to take the all-weather route described above. (A glance at a refuge map will show more than one route to the trail.) In addition, you should always contact the refuge headquarters for the latest flooding reports.

The hiking trail, originally a one-way ATV route that ran alongside the bayou, sees regular reroutes, and you may find that this guide is less than accurate. It is a testament to the power of the river that huge, fallen trees are transported hundreds of yards from year to year. Although the NWR staff and Friends of Cat Island strive to keep the trail cleared and well blazed, Mother Nature sometimes has other plans in mind. In fact, following the flood period of 2002, spring 2003 saw a sizable beaver lodge standing on perfectly dry ground, right in the middle of the trail!

Cat Island National Wildlife Refuge is the home of the national champion bald cypress.

The trail begins across the road from the parking area; look for the hiker sign that marks the trailhead. As you begin the trail, which is blazed with white diamonds, you might notice a profusion of distinctive acorns at your feet. These are the seeds of the overcup oak, a bottomland tree that thrives in southern mixed hardwood swamp forests like this one. The acorn, usually wider than it is long, is nearly enclosed by a rough-scaled cup—hence the common name of "overcup." The botanical name, *Quercus lyrata,* refers to the "lyre shape" of the leaves: oblong, deeply lobed, and narrow at the base.

Although you'll see plenty of overcup oaks, perhaps the most visually impressive trees along this trail are the bald cypresses. Estimated at well over 300 years old, some of these giants are more than a dozen feet in diameter. In fact, Cat Island is the site of the National Champion Cypress—the largest tree of any species east of the Sierra

Nevada. If you're planning a trip to the refuge, you should include the short walk to this famous tree on your hiking agenda. Directions to the Big Cypress Trail are at the end of this write-up.

At 0.2 mile, you'll begin to see Blackfork Bayou to the south. The trail meanders along the bayou's "ridge," which may not seem like much of a ridge, particularly if the trail is muddy. You will gain increasingly better views of Blackfork Bayou as you approach the trail loop at 0.4 mile. Beautiful, awe-inspiring bald cypresses rise from the dark waters. Listen for the rapid, guttural *kuk-kuk-kuk* of the yellow-billed cuckoo, or the rhythmic loud hooting of a barred owl. You're likely to see wading birds at any time of year: great blue herons, green herons, great egrets, and snowy egrets. You may even spot a wood stork, particularly in late summer.

When you reach the loop at 0.4 mile, bear right to continue alongside the bayou.

A cleared area at 0.6 mile tends to be wetter than the rest of the trail. If you're lucky enough to be hiking the Blackfork Trail during a dry spring, you'll see swamp milkweed blooming. This semiaquatic flower colonizes wet areas, particularly streambanks, pond shores, floodplains, marshes, and swamps. Because it's so tolerant of saturated soil, it thrives at Cat Island. The presence of this flower is part of what makes the refuge a great place to look for butterflies. Monarchs lay their eggs on milkweeds, and various adult butterflies, including giant swallowtails, feed on this flower.

Swing to the left at 0.8 mile to reach the bank of the bayou. This beautiful spot, considered the crown jewel of the Blackfork Trail, features dozens of giant cypresses and cypress knees rising from the bayou. You might also see wood ducks, common throughout most of Louisiana. The trail swings right again at 1 mile, curving with the bayou. As you hike, you'll see tupelo and bitter pecan as well as bald cypress.

After this short, scenic walk alongside the Blackfork, the trail veers to the left, reaching the top of the loop at 1.1 miles. You're now hiking away from the water and will start to see more persimmon and sugarberry, as well as a variety of water-adapted trees, including eastern sycamore, swamp chestnut oak, cherrybark oak, sweet bay, and American holly. If the year has been relatively dry with no flooding, March and April witness a sea of yellow-topped wildflowers along this segment.

The second half of the trail is a little harder to follow, since it no longer shadows the bayou; be sure to watch for the blazes and arrows. You might see a white-tailed deer in this area, or you may even hear a wild turkey as it crashes through the distant brush. Another common inhabitant of Cat Island is ladies' eardrop. This thick vine, also known as buckwheat vine, has fragrant, cream-colored flowers that grow in stringy masses. Its pink fruit, which ripens in late summer, has five pointed lobes at the tip and is said to resemble ear pendants. It's such a beautiful vine that you're likely to find it planted in suburban gardens as well as growing wild in the refuge.

Elevation soon drops slightly; the trail may get muckier at 1.5 miles. The reward is an increase in the impressively large cypresses. At 1.8 miles, a birding trail branches off to the right and leads to Refuge Road, several hundred yards northeast of the trailhead. Bear left to continue the Blackfork Trail and complete the loop at 1.9 miles. Bear right onto the original spur and retrace your steps to the trailhead.

You'll also want to hike the Big Cypress Trail, a short, gravel-paved path to one of the largest trees in the east. To get there, drive south from the Blackfork Trailhead, continuing down Refuge Road for approximately 3 miles until you reach the Big Cypress Trailhead.

40

Mary Ann Brown
Nature Preserve

Total distance (circuit): About 2 miles

Hiking time: 1 hour

*Habitats: Upland hardwood forest
with mature beech and magnolia stands,
mixed pine and hardwood, forest gaps,
and edges*

*Maps: USGS 7½' Elm Park,
Nature Conservancy map*

The Mary Ann Brown Nature Preserve is a relatively new hiking trail in southeast Louisiana. Located in West Feliciana Parish, the 109-acre site was donated to The Nature Conservancy by Mr. and Mrs. L. Heidel Brown in memory of their daughter. This beautiful pocket of rolling hills and mature beech and magnolia forest skirts the eastern border of the spectacular Tunica Hills. The preserve doubles as an ecological-education site for youngsters from all over southeastern Louisiana. Although reservations are required to use the picnic area, restrooms, and other group facilities, the hiking trails are open to all visitors from sunrise to sunset. The 2-mile trail system will lead you alongside a stream, past a small pond, and beneath towering old-growth beech and magnolia. You will also see the sad effects of the southern pine beetle on a pine forest.

To get to the preserve from Baton Rouge, take I-10 to I-110, then follow I-110 north until it ends at LA 61. Drive north on LA 61 for 20.5 miles to LA 965. Take LA 965 east for 6 miles. You'll see the preserve's parking area and day-use entrance on your left, about 0.1 mile before The Bluffs on Thompson Creek.

Upon entering the preserve, be sure to sign in at the kiosk just ahead. The Loop Trail begins to the right of the kiosk; look for the first trail marker, a 4-foot brown post. The Loop Trail's unpromising start leads through a corridor of spindly, dead pines—victims of the devastating, but native, southern pine beetle epidemic of the 1980s and 1990s.

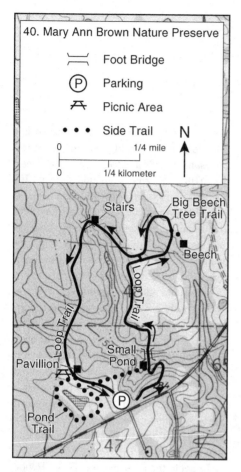

⊏⊐ Foot Bridge

Ⓟ Parking

⊼ Picnic Area

••• Side Trail

N

0   1/4 mile

0   1/4 kilometer

Stairs

Big Beech Tree Trail

Beech

Loop Trail

Loop Trail

Small Pond

Pavillion

Pond Trail

Ⓟ

loess walls of the ravine make the gnarled tree roots clearly visible. You'll pass an identified yaupon tree, with the exquisite classification of *Ilex vomitoria*. This shrublike tree, which is a popular holiday ornamental, can commonly be found growing wild in Louisiana's moist forests. Yaupon is a favorite browse for deer, and its berries are an important food source for birds. The wavy-toothed leaves contain caffeine; they were used by Native Americans to prepare a purgative "black drink"—hence the classification *vomitoria*. In late fall, the yaupon's bright red berries give away its close relation to the American holly.

The trail forks after 0.2 mile. The right fork is a spur trail leading several hundred feet to an overlook of the hilly Feliciana bluffs. Sunny winter days promise a pleasant scene from here, of both the gently rolling terrain and the wintering birds that populate the area. Bearing left at the fork, hike the slightly hilly terrain until the trail forks again at an identified chinaberry tree. To continue the loop, you want to turn right. (The left fork is a short path to a gravel road leading to the pavilion and picnic area.) You'll soon reach a small pond to your left. This peaceful spot is a great area to relax and listen to birds at any time of year. In the early morning, you can sit here to watch for and listen to a variety of warblers, including prothonotary, Swainson's, and hooded. You're likely to see a great egret wading along the pond's shore. Less obvious are the Mississippi kites and red-tailed hawks you might spot in the oaks across the pond. Watch for an eastern chipmunk in the oaks as you resume hiking. This little creature is common farther north; however, its only habitat in Louisiana is the upland forests of the Tunica Hills region.

The trail continues, descending to a bridge across a small stream. As you cross, peer over the bridge to spot raccoon tracks along the stream's claylike banks. This

These tiny insects tunnel through the soft inner tissue of mostly loblolly pines. The only effective way to control this unwanted deforestation was for rangers to cut down the affected trees, preventing further spread of the beetles to surrounding trees. As a result, huge sections of Louisiana's forests were cleared, leaving little more than the sad-looking remnants of once-hardy pines. Although Louisiana is recovering from this devastation, the effects are still quite visible, as you can see here.

Once you've left the pines, the trail dips slightly; notice that you're walking alongside a ravine to your right. The highly eroded

masked creature makes its home in tree hollows 30 to 40 feet high, and generally comes out late in the evening or at night to feed at this stream. Although you may not see a 'coon during your day hike, you'll probably see the evidence of its visit in its track: a distinctive "handprint" with five long, spindly "fingers."

The trail heads uphill from the bridge and follows the creek for 0.2 mile. This is a particularly remarkable section of the preserve; look beyond the creek to see lovely loess bluffs formed as the small creek slowly carves them down. Take a break at the bench atop the hill to view Louisiana's unique natural beauty. As you continue to hike, you may even see a miniature waterfall or two—providing the weather has been wet enough.

Soon afterward, the trail forks at a bench. Take a right to begin the Big Beech Tree Trail, a half-mile loop to a lovely old American beech. En route, the loop borders a sizable stand of beetle-damaged loblollies and skirts the preserve's northeastern boundary. This segment of the trail seems to pass through a virtual pine cemetery before exiting the beetle-damaged woods and leading through a clump of dwarf palmetto.

Reach a labeled ironwood 0.3 mile down the Big Beech Tree Trail. Here begins the spur trail to the Big Beech Tree. Bear right onto the spur and hike the short distance to the highlight of this trail: an enormous granddaddy of a beech, estimated at several hundred years old. Many other trees have smooth bark when young, but as they age, their bark grows more scaly or furrowed. Not true with the American beech—its bark stays smooth well into old age, as can be seen on the one here. Beeches are especially spectacular in the fall, when their leaves change

Looking for animal tracks in the creekbed

from green to blazing gold. Louisiana's leaf season is short and sweet, however; if you're on this trail in November, you might be lucky enough to view this giant in its magnificent autumn attire.

Once you've returned to the Big Beech Tree Trail, bear right, hiking another 0.4 mile to the Loop Trail. Bear right to continue hiking the Loop Trail. You'll soon reach a bridge over the stream that the trail followed for the first part of the hike. After crossing the bridge, continue down the Loop Trail for less than a half mile, where the trail reaches a gravel road to the preserve's picnic area. To return to your car, turn left and walk approximately a quarter mile down the gravel road to the day-use entrance where you parked. If you're not tired of hiking yet, consider heading three miles down LA 965 to the Audubon State Historic Site's Cardinal Trail.

41

Port Hudson
State Historic Site

Total distance (circuit plus two spurs):
3.4 miles

Hiking time: 2 hours

*Habitats: Mixed upland hardwoods, beech
and magnolia forest*

*Maps: USGS 7½' Port Hudson,
park map*

Port Hudson is the site of a 48-day siege in which 7,500 Confederates resisted 40,000 Union soldiers in May and June of 1863. The Confederates found protection in Port Hudson's 4.5 miles of earthen fortifications, which had been built the previous August. Their determination and superior defenses led to the longest siege in American history—one that forced the Confederates, cut off from any hope of resupply, to resort to mules, horses, and rats for food.

In 1863, a primary Union goal was control of the Mississippi River. As the only remaining Confederate bastion on the river, Port Hudson was the Confederacy's last hope for denying them that goal. Under the leadership of Major General Nathaniel P. Banks, the Union first attacked Port Hudson on May 26, 1863. Approximately two thousand Union soldiers perished, including 600 of the African-Americans who comprised the First and Third Louisiana Native Guards. The Union's second attack was less than a month later, on June 13. Nearly as many Union soldiers died as before, in comparison to fewer than 200 Confederates. Port Hudson gave up the fight on July 9, 1863, after learning of Vicksburg's surrender upriver. Without Vicksburg, the South's struggle to control the Mississippi was fruitless.

The Port Hudson State Historic Site rests on 889 acres of the battlefield's northern portion and features a 6-mile gravel trail system. You'll find many natural items of interest on this hike: towering magnolias, bluffs formed by windblown loess, lovely

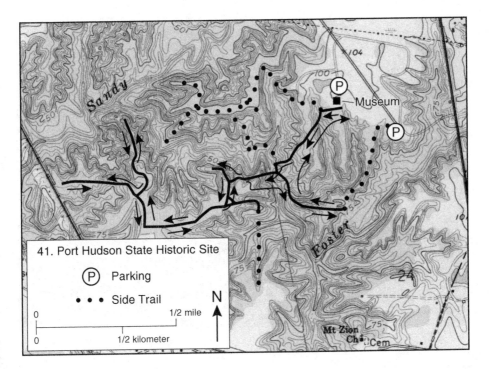

41. Port Hudson State Historic Site

(P) Parking

• • • Side Trail

N

1/2 mile

0

1/2 kilometer

0

stands of pine, and scenic Sandy Creek. Hikers may find it hard to believe that this trail's primary *raison d'être* is as a walk through Civil War history.

To reach Port Hudson, take I-10 to I-110 in Baton Rouge until it ends at US 61. Take US 61 north (toward Natchez) for 12 miles until you see the brown Port Hudson sign on your right. Shortly afterward, turn left into the site and drive a mile farther to the museum, where you'll find a fascinating collection of artifacts from Port Hudson's Civil War days. You might also check out the museum's informative film before hitting the trails. Pick up a trail map marking the historic sites and junction markers along the trail.

Exit the museum through the back door and walk toward the observation tower, originally built to allow visitors a bird's-eye view of the then-cleared site. You can still get a bird's eye view of the site, but the trails themselves provide a much closer per-

spective on the area's history. While the trail itself is not blazed, the gravel path is easy to follow, and periodic posts, labeled A through P, mark your location on the museum map. Take the improved trail to the right of the tower to the first of numerous interpretive signs you'll see on your hike. This miniature history lesson about the 48-day siege marks the beginning of the trail (Point A on the museum map).

Walking past the sign and into the woods, you'll descend a gentle downhill after just 100 feet. Strange as it may seem, the natural landscape of Port Hudson, like much of Louisiana, is actually flat. The area's "hills" of loess (windblown silt) have since been carved into the gullies, ravines, and ridges that the Confederate Army used to their advantage in 1863. You'll never go uphill and then back down on most Louisiana trails; instead, you'll start by descending into an eroded ravine.

Bridge at Port Hudson

In spring and summer, you'll see giant cane along all of the Port Hudson trails. Known locally as switch cane, this plant is the only bamboo species native to the United States. It thrives throughout the state (too well, some would say), from the uplands to the wetlands. You'll also see white oak, cherrybark oak, water oak, post oak, bitternut hickory, and shagbark hickory. Port Hudson boasts several pockets of beautiful beech and magnolia forest, as well.

After 0.1 mile (Point B), the trail forks; take the left fork. After approximately 100 feet, look to your right to see a majestic red oak about 25 feet off the trail. This is the one tree on the Port Hudson property believed to have been here during Civil War times. Most of the trees along the trail are less than a century old—quite young for a tree. The Confederates were the first to deforest this land, since downed trees were effective obstacles to hold off the Union Army. What the

Confederates didn't cut down was eventually shot down during the course of the battles. The federal government deforested this area twice more in the mid-1930s and 1960s. This one red oak has possibly survived all of that.

Some of the younger trees are quite substantial, however. In this section of your hike, notice the grand southern magnolias with their unmistakable smooth, gray-brown bark and waxy, dark green leaves, most of them well over 6 inches long. During the siege, a Union officer referred admiringly to the magnolias as the "monarchs of the forest." If you're hiking in early summer, you'll see their large, showy flowers in bloom. Louisiana has proudly designated this sweet-smelling, cream-colored bloom its state flower.

Continue walking past another interpretive sign and an old crowd-control post from the historic site's earlier days. The trail descends after another 0.1 mile. In late fall and early winter, look to the left for a clear view of a yellow-tan bluff. This bluff is composed of loess, as are many of the landforms in this part of Louisiana. Loess is the name for windblown silt believed to have been collected from the Mississippi River basin during successive Ice Ages millions of years ago. It erodes vertically, hence the near-vertical hillsides of the bluffs. As you walk, you'll see muscadine vines sweeping along the trail's edges and cascading from above in spring and summer. You may also be lucky enough to spot a white-tailed deer, an armadillo, or a wild turkey.

After a short but relatively steep downhill, the trail swings left through a distinctive stand of pine. Here, you'll reach a fork in the trail; just beyond the fork is another magnificent "monarch of the forest," a southern magnolia. Continue to the left and pass bench. If you sit for a while and listen, you might hear the loud, ringing birdsong of a prothonotary warbler, or you even might spot a barred owl perched high in the trees. Keep hiking, and you'll soon reach another fork; here, take the trail to the right. You'll later double back to this spot to take the alternate trail.

Hike about 200 feet to a bridge constructed over sycamore-lined Foster Creek. After crossing, notice how the surrounding forest is temporarily changing from hardwood to pine. The trail swings left to ascend a short flight of steps. Once you've reached the top of the subsequent climb, notice the ravine to your right. In spring, you'll see a profusion of flowering dogwoods in bloom.

After another 0.1 mile, reach a cleared area and trail junction (Point G). The spur trail to the right leads along a ridgelike structure. As you follow it, notice the loess walls on either side of you, remembering that this ridge and the surrounding valley are the result of natural erosion over thousands of years. The trail soon reaches the Fort Babcock site, named for Union Lieutenant Colonel Willoughby Babcock of the 75th New York Infantry Regiment, who fought in the first battle of the siege. The Union soldiers scrambled from the hollow on your right to stand where you now stand, and they fired at the Confederates, who were on a ridge beyond the hollow to your left—only 100 yards away. Because there were no trees standing, the men on each side of the battle would have had a clear view of their opponents. Foster Creek, clearly visible in winter, is in the distance to your right. In March and April, white-flowering dogwoods command your attention in both hollows.

Upon reaching the end of the spur trail, retrace your steps the 0.1 mile back to Point G. At this junction, go straight ahead; this route will take you to the three redoubts on the trail, as well as to an overlook of Sandy Creek. The trail first crosses the naturally preserved Alabama–Arkansas Redoubt, a defensive earthwork built by the Confederate soldiers in 1862. Back then, this "ditch" was a full-fledged moat. During the Civil War, the walls of the moat were much deeper than they are now—up to 8 feet deep! Imagine being a Union soldier in 1863: After struggling through scores of felled trees, with a 10-pound gun and your equipment strapped to your back, you would have to crawl into this moat, then back up the other side— where the Confederates waited expectantly with their cannons and guns.

The trail splits (Point I) after crossing the bridge over the redoubt. Take a right at this junction. The path that follows is straight and leads beneath a mix of pine, beech, and magnolia. A footbridge provides another scenic view of the loess that forms Port Hudson's "hills." The trail veers slightly to the right shortly before you reach Point J, where you'll turn right. From here, the path meanders through the woods, passing through heavy undergrowth on either side that includes muscadine, switch cane, and–at your feet–poison ivy. Before reaching another junction at Point K, you'll skirt the site of quartermaster officer Major William K. Bennett's house and battery. Bear right when you get to Point K. You'll eventually double back to this point and take the other fork to the Mississippi Redoubt.

For now, you are hiking past the "Slaughterpen," which served as a Confederate deterrent during the siege, as you'll learn from the interpretive sign at this site. Several hundred feet farther, Bennett's Redoubt is to your left; the trail actually passes through a kiosk offering information on this spot's historic role. A redoubt, by the way, is a small defensive fortification. The word itself derives from both the French *redoute* and the Latin *reductus,* meaning "a place of retreat." It is also associated with the Old French *redoubter* (to fear), which derives from the Latin *dubitare,* to doubt. It is interesting to think of these old earthen fortifications as places of retreat that most certainly saw fear–and perhaps doubt–in the soldiers under siege.

After passing through the kiosk, the trail turns sharply right to parallels a ravine to the left. The path soon forms another "ridge" that offers a view on either side. In 0.2 mile, reach an overlook of the red clays and clear waters of Sandy Creek. This rewarding spot ends this segment. Adventurous hikers might want to explore the area before returning to Point K. Once you reach Point K, however, bear right to hike 0.3 mile to the Mississippi Redoubt site.

The left wing of the Mississippi Redoubt saw the first time in history that African American soldiers, all members of the First and Third Louisiana (U.S.) Native Guards, participated in a large-scale attack. Of all the earthworks at Port Hudson, this one was closest to the Mississippi River in 1863. Because the river has changed course several times, there is not even a view of it from the site–or from anywhere else on the property.

Your hike's next and final destination is Fort Desperate. To get there, backtrack to Point K, bearing to the right to reach Point J. Following your map, go left at Point J, then again to reach Point G. Go right at Point G to cross Foster Creek again, then bear right to hike 0.3 mile to Fort Desperate. As you hike, notice that the trees have changed from primarily pine near the Alabama–Arkansas Redoubt back to hardwoods–yellow poplar, oak, and hickory, among others.

In the next 0.1 mile, you'll cross two footbridges over sandy creek beds below. The level trail continues to meander, making for a very pleasant, green walk in the spring and summer. In spring, look for trillium and violets among the wildflowers. As the trail turns into yet another "ridge" between ravines, you'll have another winter view of Foster Creek to the right. The wide ridge gradually climbs a slight incline, and the trail swings left, then turns to the right. You'll soon reach a developed area, the site of Fort Desperate. This is not a fort in the traditional sense; it was instead a name given by the Confederate defenders to the area, which was often under fire during the siege. Under the command of Confederate Colonel Benjamin W. Johnson, fewer than 300 soldiers had built the surrounding earthworks *while under artillery fire.* The surrounding U-shaped earthwork allowed the Confederate soldiers to be within 150 feet of their attackers at any time, ensuring close targets for small-arms fire.

Fort Desperate is now a developed area with ramps and a three-sided building that includes a kiosk with information about the battles fought here. Also interesting are the photographs of the troops, both Union and Confederate, who fought here, as well as maps showing the logistics of the attacks. Interpretive signs are plentiful in this area. If you're more interested in hiking than history, you'll be tempted not to linger here. Try not to leave too quickly. Check out the signs and pictures in the kiosk, then follow the ramps along various sections of the ditchlike earthwork, full of exposed roots of the trees that were not there during Civil War times. It's a fascinating history lesson, one of the most interesting you'll find on this trail.

Two paths lead away from the site of Fort Desperate. A wheelchair-accessible path goes to the Fort Desperate parking lot. The other route is the trail you've been hiking. To follow this trail back to the museum, bear to the right every time the trail forks. After 0.6 mile, you'll find yourself back at the museum, at the end of your hike.

42

Baton Rouge–Area Hikes

In the past, Baton Rouge hikers had to drive an hour or more—usually to the hills of Mississippi—for a decent hiking experience. While the Tunica Hills of our neighboring state remain a popular draw for south Louisiana hikers, Baton Rougeans are seeing an increase in hiking opportunities closer to home. The Baton Rouge Recreation and Park Commission (BREC) maintains several trails, and the Louisiana Department of Wildlife and Fisheries recently opened the Waddill Outdoor Education Center, which features several short nature trails as well. Summarized below are the short trails in this region, most of them less than a mile in length.

South Baton Rouge

Bluebonnet Swamp Nature Center:
Total distance
(circuit plus one round-trip): 0.8 mile
Hiking Time: 30–45 minutes
Habitats: Cypress swamp
Maps: USGS 7½' St. Gabriel,
nature center map
Highland Road Park Observatory–
Semita Minor and Semita Major:
Total distance (two circuits): 0.8 mile
Hiking Time: 30–45 minutes
Habitats: Mixed bottomland hardwood
Maps: USGS 7½' St. Gabriel,
observatory map

In south Baton Rouge, BREC offers short, gentle hikes through the bottomland hardwood and cypress swamp habitats that once characterized Louisiana's floodplain regions. Bluebonnet Nature Center's 0.8-mile trail/boardwalk winds through a 65-acre swamp, while the two short trails at Highland Road Park explore mixed bottomland hardwood habitat. Both trails are educational in nature. While they are ideal for parents who are introducing their small children to the joys of hiking and the outdoors, they are also pleasant hikes for anyone needing a short break from the workaday world of Baton Rouge.

The Bluebonnet Swamp Nature Center is a good solution for the Baton Rouge-area hiker who wants to experience nature but doesn't have time for a lengthy road trip or a half-day hike. Located just minutes from I-10 and the Bluebonnet Branch of the East Baton Rouge Parish Library, the center offers an opportunity to slip out of busy Baton Rouge and settle into a seemingly pristine environment of swamp, where cypress, tupelo, wading birds, and other wetland trees and wildlife thrive. The engine sounds of

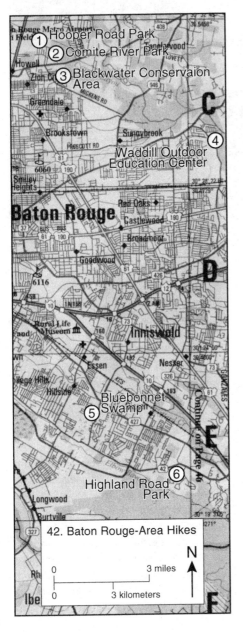

Continue on Page 46

42. Baton Rouge-Area Hikes

N

0   3 miles

0   3 kilometers

Bluebonnet and Perkins Roads may compete for your attention, but you'll probably forget about them once you step onto the boardwalk and take in the beauty of this otherwise suburban area of Louisiana's capital.

To get there, take I-10 to the Bluebonnet exit in Baton Rouge, then go south to the light at North Oak Hills Parkway. Turn right onto North Oak Hills, which dead-ends at the parking area, where signs point you to the nature center. The path from the parking lot is very scenic and offers an ample taste of what is to come on your hike. Pick up a trail map at the nature center before starting this maze of trails. Also at the nature center, you can view live specimens of swamp inhabitants and learn about swamp habitat.

The wide, gravel-paved trail begins behind the nature center, leading past various moisture-loving trees such as black willow, sugarberry, and water oak. The trail turns into boardwalk in the more swampy areas, and benches are provided throughout the walk.

The trails of Highland Road Park Observatory were brand new in 2003. Short and easy to hike, they serve as excellent educational tools for children. Like Bluebonnet Swamp, Highland Road Park is also a great nearby escape to the woods for Baton Rougeans.

The observatory is located at 13800 Highland Road Park in Baton Rouge. To get there, you can take I-10 to Siegen Lane (Exit 163). Go south on Siegen to Highland Road, then turn left. Look for the sign to the observatory on your right as you make the short drive down Highland Road. Parking is available before you reach the observatory. Be sure to pick up a map of the trails there before you begin hiking.

The quarter-mile, gravel-paved Semita Minor ("Short Path") begins next to a large live oak northeast of the observatory, next to

Highland Road Park Observatory

a picnic table and behind a campfire area with six benches. This is an interpretive trail, so you'll see various signs along the way to identify the trees and other features of this habitat. The trail has several mild climbs and descents before ending at the entrance road.

The Semita Major ("Long Path") trailhead is southeast of the observatory, at the far corner of the large field. Like the Semita Minor, this trail is interpretive, but it is a dirt trail rather than gravel-paved. It is also a loop; you'll reach the start of the loop less than 100 feet into your hike.

North Baton Rouge
Hooper Road Park
Comite River Park
Blackwater Conservation Area
Waddill Outdoor Education Center
Total distance (circuits): 16+ miles
Hiking Time: Hooper/Comite Trails: 8+

hours combined; Blackwater
Conservation Area: 30 minutes;
Waddill Outdoor Education Center:
30 minutes
Habitats: Upland hardwood forest,
mixed bottomland hardwood forest,
forest gaps, and edges
Maps: USGS 7½' Comite (all trails)

Located in north Baton Rouge, the 16-plus miles of rugged trails at Hooper Road Park and Comite River Park are best for experienced hikers. Because these are primarily bike trails, built in the 1990s and maintained by the Baton Rouge Area Mountain Bike Association, you'll need to keep your eyes and ears open for oncoming cyclists. If you don't mind the extra traffic, or if you can manage to hike these trails on the less-popular weekdays, you'll be rewarded with challenging woods walks and the opportunity to see all sorts of wildlife. Trails can get very muddy in wet weather. You can pick up maps at the trailheads. Maps are vital, as the curvy, looping nature of the bike trails makes it easy to get turned around. Blackwater Conservation Area and Waddill Outdoor Education Center both offer short, level trails that are good nature walks for families with small children.

Hooper Road Park is located at 6261 Guynell Drive, in the Sharon Hills subdivision. To get there, take I-110 to Harding Boulevard, via the Baton Rouge Airport exit. Harding becomes Hooper Road at the first red light; remain on Hooper until you reach the next red light. Here, turn left onto Cedar Glen and drive through the Sharon Hills subdivision until Cedar Glen dead-ends.

Turn right onto Guynell, driving for two blocks until you reach the entrance to Hooper Road Park. A parking lot is available; the trailhead will be on your left. The Blackwater Conservation Area is across the street from the park.

To reach Comite River Park, which is at 8900 Hooper Road, take the same route to Hooper Road Park. Instead of turning onto Cedar Glen, however, keep going down Hooper for approximately a mile, looking for a green gate in front of a gravel road. No official parking is available at the trailhead at this time. The Waddill Outdoor Education Center is located near Comite River Park at 4142 North Flannery Road.

43

Tickfaw State Park

Total distance (three circuits): 2.3 miles

Hiking time: 1 hour

Habitats: Mixed pine and hardwood forest, forest, cypress swamp

Maps: USGS 7½' Frost, park map

Tickfaw State Park, whose 1,200 acres encompass mixed bottomland hardwood forest, wetland, and upland habitats, was developed as Louisiana's first state park for nature education. Five hiking trails—four of which are wheelchair accessible—highlight small pockets of various forest types. If you're interested in discovering what features characterize some of Southeast Louisiana's natural habitats, and in witnessing how those habitats differ, Tickfaw's trails are an ideal starting point. A short nature trail behind the nature center passes through several different plant communities, and the Gum-Cypress Trail leads through swamp habitat. The Pine-Hardwood Trail winds through a pocket of upland habitat, and the Bottomland Hardwood Trail leads past—you guessed it—bottomland hardwoods. It also leads to the River Trail, which is the park's only walking path that is not wheelchair accessible. More adventurous hikers will want to hike the River Trail; while it is neither difficult nor long, it does afford some nice views of the Tickfaw River and provides opportunities to view birds and wildflowers while taking a pleasant walk on a dirt trail. Be aware that it includes several tricky stream crossings, and that you're likely to get your feet wet on this one. The River Trail ends at the canoe launch road, which is a surprisingly interesting walk through mixed hardwood forest back to the parking area.

To get to Tickfaw State Park, take I-12 to LA 43 at Springfield (Exit 32). Go south on LA 43 for 3.9 miles, then merge with LA 42 and travel one more mile to Springfield. At

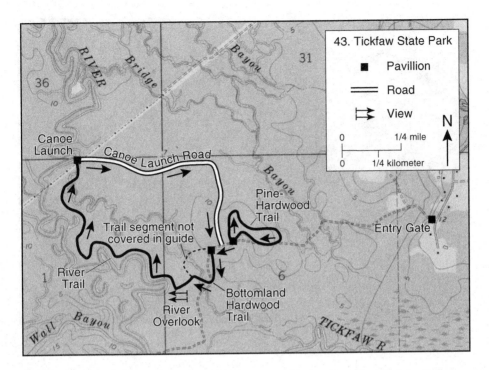

LA 1037 in Springfield, just after passing Springfield High School, turn west (right) and go 6 miles to Patterson Road, adjacent to Woodland Baptist Church. Going south (left) on Patterson Road, you will soon arrive at the park entrance. The Nature Trail is located behind the Nature Center, 0.3 mile from the entrance. Stop here for a trail guide, a park map, and a guide to the trees of the Pine-Hardwood Trail. A little farther down the road is the Gum-Cypress Swamp pavilion and trail. At the end of the road, one mile from the park entrance, is the parking area for the Pine-Hardwood and Bottomland Hardwood pavilions and trails. This guide focuses on these more isolated trails at the back of the park, so you want to park at the Pine-Hardwood pavilion. Although the Pine-Hardwood, Bottomland Hardwood, and River Trails do not exactly connect, they can be pieced together to form a 2.3-mile loop.

The limestone Pine-Hardwood Trail, a level walk beneath pines, beeches, magnolias, and various oaks, begins to the right of the back parking area. Begin by walking straight down the trail rather than bearing to the right. You might notice that the pines surrounding you are different from the pines on most of the other trails in Louisiana. Spruce pine is common in Tickfaw and the surrounding parish, and it's occasionally found alongside pineland streams throughout southeast Louisiana. Despite its abundance in this small pocket of the state, it's not commonly found elsewhere in Louisiana and does not occur naturally west of the Mississippi River.

You'll see small markers on some of the trees, to be used with the tree identification guide available at the nature center. The 0.3-mile loop ends just after you reach the ramp to the pavilion. From here, walk across the parking lot to the Bottomland Hardwood Trail to begin the next leg of your hike.

The bank of Tickfaw River

The Bottomland Hardwood Trail is a raised boardwalk through a habitat far different from the one you just left. Begin hiking straight ahead on the boardwalk, passing the pavilion to your right. You'll pass by beech and magnolia before reaching the swamp. Notice how drastically the setting changes. Although beech, magnolia, and pines are still present, they aren't as dominant as they are on the Pine-Hardwood trail. Instead, the most common trees are bald cypress and tupelo. Both of these trees can commonly be found at the lowest elevations of bottomland hardwood habitat. Bald cypress is known as the "wood eternal" for its soft but durable properties. During the heyday of logging, this relative of the California redwood was among the chief lumber trees of the Mississippi River floodplain. Today, practically all of Louisiana's virgin cypress swamps have been cut. This interesting tree has buttressed bases and peculiar root outgrowths called knees.

After 0.1 mile is a fork in the boardwalk. To the right, the Bottomland Hardwood Trail continues, ending back at the parking lot after 0.2 mile. To the left, steps lead down to the Tickfaw River and the beginning of the River Trail.

The River Trail is 1.3 miles long and is not wheelchair accessible. If you're not prepared to get your shoes muddy, you'll want to avoid hiking very far on this trail, unless it's been very dry in recent weeks. It parallels the winding Tickfaw River through a mixed forest type and crosses several sloughs—without the help of bridges, at the time of this writing. The trail eventually reaches the park's canoe launch. From this point, you can retrace your steps back to the Bottomland Hardwood Trail, or you can take the 0.4-mile canoe launch road back to the parking lot and the Pine-Hardwood trailhead.

At the time of this writing, the relatively new trail was not marked, though the last

0.1 mile before the canoe launch was marked by yellow and orange tape. If you become uncertain of the route, just follow the tape. There are also several signs along the trail, placed there by area Boy Scouts. Watch for snakes, particularly water moccasins, if hiking this trail in warm weather.

Approximately 0.3 mile down the River Trail is a slough to the right. This swampy area, with cypress and tupelo rising from it, will be visible for much of the hike. As the trail winds through the woods, another interesting sight is that of the tree roots along the riverbank, laid bare by the erosion around them. You'll see lots of oaks all around, including water oak, swamp chestnut oak, live oak, and post oak. A half mile down the trail, a small peninsula juts into the river. The trail, along with the river, will wind around this scenic little piece of land. The trail briefly diverges from the river path. Once it rejoins the river, it passes between two majestic southern magnolias. These large native trees, with their smooth, gray bark and large, leathery green leaves, have white, cup-shaped flowers that bloom from April all the way into November.

The trail along the river is just over a mile long, and that first mile is quite easy to follow. It ends with a River Trail sign on your right. (There is a sign before this one that says you've hiked a mile on the River Trail, but it's actually just at the three-quarter-mile mark!) The trail begins to work its way away from the river shortly after the second River Trail sign. This last segment gets confusing; while you're still following the river, you're no longer within sight of its banks. Watch for the makeshift orange-and-yellow trail markers. Although this segment is more challenging and harder to follow, you are entering perhaps the most scenic part of the hike.

Follow the tape markers to a small slough with cypress knees jutting from it. Here, take a sharp left and walk alongside the slough. You will encounter several slough crossings in close succession, the second one adjacent to a beautiful old cypress. This particular crossing can be very wet and muddy; in fact, I had to turn back on one occasion. About 0.1 mile from where the trail branched off from the river, reach a sign that reads: TO RIVER TRAIL.

The trail soon ends at the park's canoe launch. To complete the loop, turn right onto the canoe launch road and walk the remaining 0.4 mile to the parking lot and your car. This final walk is a pleasant one through mostly bottomland hardwood habitat, which changes to primarily pine and hardwood by the time you get to the parking area.

44

Bonnet Carré Spillway

Total distance (round-trip): 5 miles

Hiking time: 2 hours

Habitats: Bottomland hardwood forest, cypress swamp, forest gaps and edges

Maps: USGS 7½' LaPlace

Ever since Europeans first settled the Mississippi River floodplain in the early 1700s, artificial levees have been constructed to prevent the flooding of the world's widest river. Despite the best efforts of early engineers, these levees—the first of which was built by the French in 1717 to protect the site of New Orleans—were not always effective and gave way to horrific flooding. State governments assumed funding of levee construction in the 1830s, but the devastating floods continued; in fact, the levees failed no fewer than seven times between 1844 and 1874. The ravages of the Civil War proved another blow to an already imperfect levee system.

In 1879, the federal government improved the levee system somewhat by establishing the Mississippi River Commission. Flooding problems continued, however, as the swelling river periodically overtopped some levees and slashed crevasses (breaks) into others. Despite the improvements, including those of the Commission's Flood Control Act of 1917, the year 1927 saw a catastrophic flood that left more than 500 people dead, forced more than 700,000 from their homes, and carved 13 crevasses into the levee system. In response to this disaster, Congress's Flood Control Act of 1928 authorized the Mississippi River and Tributaries Project. This revolutionary project discarded the traditional levees-only policy and allowed the United States Army Corps of Engineers to plan floodways in conjunction with levees,

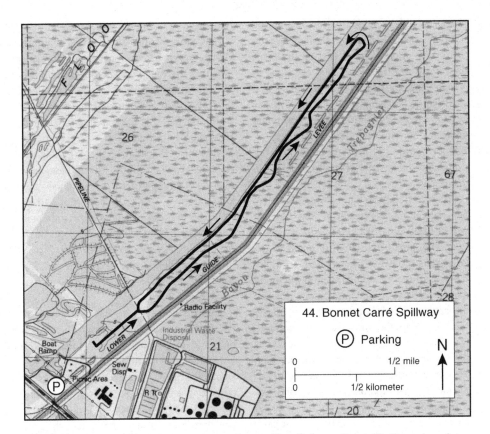

44. Bonnet Carré Spillway

P Parking

N

0   1/2 mile

0   1/2 kilometer

as well as a spillway to divert water from the Mississippi River into Lake Pontchartrain, north of New Orleans.

The chosen site for the spillway was at the 19th-century Bonnet Carré Crevasse, about 33 river miles north of New Orleans. This site had seen four major crevasses between 1849 and 1882—including a 7,000-foot-wide crevasse that flowed for more than 6 months in 1849. Despite the challenges of poor foundation conditions and the unpredictability of the great river itself, the Bonnet Carré Spillway was completed in 1931, following 3 years of research and construction. The $14.2 million project also included the 1932 completion of guide levees and the 1936 completion of a highway and railroad crossings.

The Bonnet Carré Spillway has been opened to divert flooding eight times since 1937, most recently in the spring of 1997. When not being used for that purpose, the spillway and surrounding levees provide hunting, fishing, biking, horseback riding, and hiking opportunities for city dwellers looking for a convenient getaway from the rush of New Orleans. Camping is allowed in the parish recreation pavilion area. To obtain a permit, contact the St. Charles Recreation Department at 985-783-5090.

At the time of this writing, the Bonnet Carré Spillway Trail was 2.5 miles long (one way), and plans were in place for a 2004 trail extension. Actually an old bike path, this trail, maintained by the Corps, area mountain bikers, and other volunteers, runs alongside the suction canal through mixed bottomland hardwood forest. The planned trail extension will lead farther up the canal bank to where the elevation drops ever so slightly and the mixed bottomland forest yields to a section of the vast cypress swamp that dominates the southeast Louisiana terrain. Contact the spillway office for updates on trail progress and opportunities to assist with trail building and maintenance.

The trail begins in the spillway recreation area, about 18 miles west of New Orleans and 5 miles east of LaPlace. To get there from I-10, take I-310 (Boutte) south to US 61 (Airline Highway). Go west on US 61 for 6 miles. You'll see the entrance to the recreation area on your right, just before crossing the spillway itself. You can also get to the trail by taking the River Road from either New Orleans or LaPlace. The trail begins at the fire ring toward the back of the camping area. Black willows thrive on the border between the campground clearing and the woods. Black willows often grow along banks of canals and ponds and can actually help to prevent erosion along these border areas. These trees, which have narrow, lancelike, finely toothed leaves, are also an important caterpillar host for the viceroy butterfly. The viceroy's orange and black wings are said to fool predators into thinking it is the bad-tasting monarch butterfly. Viceroys tend to inhabit moist, open areas and willow thickets, both of which you'll find here.

The beginning of the trail takes you past ragweed, horsetail, and other low plants. A cleared area at 0.1 mile is good for spring, summer, and fall wildflowers, and you can spot turtles, snakes, and alligators where the trail borders the canal. You might also see rabbit, raccoon, deer, or even beaver. The trail forks after reentering the woods; bear right, following the arrow. As you get deeper into the wooded area, look for more sugarberry, water oak, and sycamore. Watch for poison ivy, which is plentiful along the trail. Another unwelcome inhabitant is the mosquito; however, if you can stand these bloodsuckers in early summer, you'll find countless blackberries ripe for picking, all along the trail.

Like the Blackfork Trail at Cat Island National Wildlife Refuge, the land has been drastically changed—and will continue to be influenced—by the Mississippi River. Although the river only floods this area periodically, you'll see some interesting effects of the flooding. For example, at 0.2 mile, look to your left to see one of the massive pins that got loose when the spillway was opened in 1997.

The trail forks shortly afterward. Bear to the right, away from the canal. The woods here are very junglelike, even in winter. The ferns and vines are large, the trees relatively small. The trail arcs to the left at 0.3 mile and crosses an emergency-use ranger service road. You can clearly see the canal to your left; look for a heron gracefully stepping through the waters of the spillway, searching for a meal. You're also likely to see a fisherman or two, angling for a dinner of largemouth bass, crappie, bluegill, catfish, or freshwater drum.

The trail soon exits the woods to cross a pipeline. Before reentering the woods, the trail swings right, then left again to avoid a small slough. When the trail forks at 0.5 mile, bear right. As the trail leads away from the water, you will get a sense of being in the woods, particularly in summer when the narrow trail is shaded by sugarberries and lined with blackberries, wild grape, smilax, and catbrier. Hikers may find it surprising that such a narrow tract of land provides such an interesting, wooded trail.

Not only is the land narrow, but it's also

A New Orleanian enjoys the locally accessible Bonnet Carré Spillway Trail

quite flat; in fact, in the 6 miles from the river to Lake Pontchartrain, the elevation change is only 12 feet–from 12 feet above sea level at the river to actual sea level at the lake! Surprisingly, you will ascend several miniscule "hills" as you hike along the spillway. No, there isn't an interesting geological explanation for the small bumps and dips that make this trail so nice for cyclists. The "hills" are simply the result of the dirt that was hauled out to build the canal. Despite the contrived nature of the terrain, the Bonnet Carré Trail winds pleasantly over these gently rolling miniature hills. At 0.6 mile, you will cross a long ridge, though you might not recognize it as a ridge during a drought. If Louisiana has experienced its usual wet weather, you'll see that the land slopes down to a bald cypress-filled slough to the right. Even in dry weather, the numerous cypress knees, along with an increase in dwarf palmettos, reveal the typical wetness of this site.

The trail meets the ranger service road again at 0.7 mile. Bear right to walk through stands of thick, green, whiplike horsetail–another indication that you've descended into a wetter area. The trail swings right and crosses a culvert to exit the woods at 0.8 mile. Swing left, then cross a small metal bridge before bearing left again and heading back into the woods.

You're now walking along the bank of the canal, with the water about 8 to 10 feet below you. This is a great vantage point to spot reptiles, particularly turtles, alligators, and snakes. Alligators and red-eared sliders sun lazily on the logs in the canal. Although you'll certainly need to watch for water moccasins, most of the snake species in this vicinity are nonpoisonous: ribbon snakes, water snakes, and green snakes are all common here.

The trail soon splits. Bear to the right, then swing left shortly afterward, back toward the water. The trail parallels the water, though it winds and twists, successfully giving the illusion that this narrow strip of woods is wider than it is. Some of these twistings may seem pointless to the hiker; remember that this is also a bike trail, and that sharp curves make mountain biking more challenging and fun. After several twists and hairpin turns, the trail emerges onto the banks of the canal again at 1 mile. Once again, you are clearly on a Louisiana-style ridge; the terrain slopes downward to the right, flattening out to a palmetto-filled floor. To your left, the land drops down, blufflike, to the canal 15 or 20 feet below. Look for water oak and cottonwood, as well as blackberries and wild grape.

The trail exits the woods again at 1.5 miles to cross a Corps of Engineers range line. Although it is not their primary purpose, these cleared areas serve as excellent vantage points for viewing wading birds in the canal; in fact, this entire site is extremely popular with birders. White pelicans, brown pelicans, and double-crested cormorants, as well as various ducks, gulls, and terns frequent this area. Many are winter visitors only, though there are summer residents as well, such as the Mississippi kite. Red-shouldered hawks and red-tailed hawks can be seen overhead, and bald eagles have been spotted here numerous times. Perching birds are always abundant; look for eastern bluebirds, blue-gray gnatcatchers, Carolina wrens, Carolina chickadees, ruby-crowned kinglets, cedar waxwings, yellow-rumped warblers, swamp sparrows, and red-winged blackbirds, particularly in winter.

At 1.8 miles, you'll see more and more dwarf palmetto–and they'll be larger and less "dwarflike" than those that you saw previously. At 1.9 miles, you're back on the bluff with the canal downslope. When the trail forks at 2 miles, bear to the right, away from the canal, and into the woods. This area can get very wet, as evidenced by the wealth of cypress knees along the path. Bear right again at 2.1 miles. The trail continues to wind away from the water until it completes the loop. Once you have swung to the left to complete the loop, head back to the parking area. Whenever the trail forks on this pathway back, simply bear to the right, staying on the canal bank until you reach the trailhead.

45

Horse Branch Trail

Total distance (circuit): 1.2 miles

Hiking time: 45 minutes

Habitats: Longleaf pine savanna, small-stream forest, bogs, and seeps

Maps: USGS 7½' Martinville, Nature Conservancy map

Once upon a time, a seemingly endless forest of giant longleaf pine reached from Virginia's southern coastal plain to the eastern flatlands and rolling hills of the Carolinas, Georgia, and Florida, and from northeastern Alabama's mountain ridges to the coastal plains of Mississippi and eastern Louisiana. Some reached as far as the piney woods of southwest and central Louisiana and east Texas. Today, in the wake of logging operations and fire-suppression forestry practices, the great majority of that habitat is gone.

Why the onetime dominance of longleaf pines over more than 74 million acres of the Southeast? Fire. These 74 million acres saw frequent forest fires, and fire is the single most important factor in maintaining the longleaf habitat. This fire-driven habitat is considered among the richest habitats worldwide. The 100-plus animal species and estimated 900 plant species native to the longleaf pine community are specially adapted to periodic fires, and many cannot thrive under other conditions. Just days after a lightning-ignited fire, scarified, fire-dependent seeds germinate, new, green growth thrives in the open sunshine, and the scorched longleaf pines continue to grow.

In the early twentieth century, a combination of factors destroyed the longleaf habitat in many places and transformed these unique plant communities into literal graveyards of forgotten stumps. One factor was the idea that fire was harmful and needed to be suppressed. Another was the huge demand for lumber; as the United States' population increased, lumber became a major industry, particularly in Louisiana. In many cases, lumber companies replaced the hardy longleaf with loblolly and slash pines, which germinate much faster and could earn more immediate profits—despite their inferior quality to longleaf. Loss of long-leaf habitat has resulted in a federally threat-ened or endangered status for 26 plant species and 7 wildlife species, including the red-cockaded woodpecker, which lives in communities that build their nesting cavities in clumps of mature longleaf pine.

Today, efforts are being made to restore and preserve some of these ecologically im-portant forests. In St. Tammany Parish, The Nature Conservancy has acquired about 500 acres of the 1300-acre Lake Ramsay Preserve to maintain one of the few remain-ing pure stands of longleaf pine in eastern Louisiana (the other 800 acres are state-owned). Comaintained by the Conservancy and area volunteers, the preserve's Horse Branch Trail winds through the small-stream habitat of Horse Branch Creek for 0.5 mile before ending in the midst of a longleaf pine savanna—a unique seasonal wetland habitat characterized by open grassland and a scattering of longleaf. In addition to the pines, you'll see wetland plants on this trail, including the carnivorous pitcher plants. Unfortunately, you're not likely to see red-cockaded woodpeckers here. You may spot them—and will see their numerous nesting trees—nearby at Big Branch Marsh National Wildlife Refuge. (Hike 47).

The Lake Ramsay Preserve is located northwest of Covington. From I-12, take US 190 (Exit 63) north for approximately 5 miles, and then turn west, staying on US 190, at the intersection with LA 25. Drive 2 miles to Penn Mill Road, which is 0.5 mile west of Covington High School. Turn north onto Penn Mill Road and travel 2 miles to

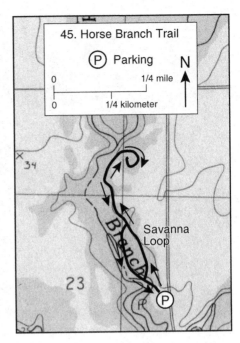

45. Horse Branch Trail

(P) Parking N

0   1/4 mile
0   1/4 kilometer

Savanna Loop

the Horse Branch Creek trailhead parking lot, which will be on your left. The trail is marked by brown posts topped with red paint, and informative signs are placed along it. Seasonal hunting is allowed in Lake Ramsay Wildlife Management Area. Although only the northern part of the trail is located in the management area, it's not a bad idea to wear hunter orange when hiking this trail during hunting season.

The Horse Branch Trail begins with an immediate fork just past the trailhead. Go to the right to begin the Savanna Loop. You aren't in the woods yet, but you will be soon. The predominant trees along this sec-tion of the trail aren't longleaf pines; instead, you'll see mostly hardwoods: magnolias, oaks, and hickories. In the understory, look for common sweetleaf, also known as horsesugar—a tree whose leaves look simi-lar to those of mountain laurel, though the two trees are not related. The Savanna Loop ends after 0.2 mile. Bear right, head-

Cypress roots along the Horse Branch Trail

ing downhill to cross a small bridge. You actually get to climb a few feet after crossing the bridge; after your "climb," the trail bears to the left, leading you alongside Horse Branch Creek. This scenic little creek is home to beautiful cypresses. Fingerlike cypress roots and knees are visible along the creek's eroded banks.

Reach an interpretive sign at 0.4 mile and bear right as the trail winds through a mixture of pines and hardwoods. If you're hiking in the winter when the leaves are down, you can see the beginning of the longleaf pine savanna to your right. On your left, the creek meanders alongside the roots and knees of cypresses. It is interesting to observe how radically the habitats change as you look from one direction to another.

The trail enters the pine savanna at 0.5 mile and loops through this interesting area. The grassy ground cover of the longleaf pine savanna consists of hundreds of plant species and is one of North America's most diverse habitats. The tall grasses provide seeds and browse for the many animal species that live within this ecosystem. Note the large pine cones among the tall grasses. These cones, while smaller than the giant cones of the American West, are the largest of any found in the East. Longleaf also has the longest needles of any eastern pine, ranging from 10 to 15 inches. On the eastern side of the loop, you can learn more from a sign that explains longleaf pine forest and the growth-form of this tree. Nearby, look for another interesting plant species growing among the grasses: pitcher plants. These carnivorous plants flower in mid- to late March, but the "pitchers" themselves are visible for most of the year.

After completing the loop through this remarkable area, hike 0.3 mile back to the junction where the Savanna Loop left off. Bear right, following the trail as it winds through a forest that includes water oak, swamp chestnut oak, yaupon, and American holly—much different from the longleaf pine savanna several hundred feet away! The trail dips several times before meeting the Horse Branch Creek once again, less than 0.1 mile after rejoining the Savanna Loop. Shortly afterward, cross a small bridge next to a giant magnolia. Once again, you'll climb uphill from the bridge, then take a pleasant walk through the remainder of the woods back to the trailhead.

46

Fontainebleau State Park

Total distance (two circuits): 6.7 miles

Hiking time: 4 hours

Habitats: Pine flatwoods, mixed pine and hardwood forest, fresh marsh

Maps: USGS 7½' Mandeville, park maps

One of Louisiana's oldest state parks, Fontainebleau rests on a land rich in history. From the Tchefuncte culture to the Acolapisa Native Americans, this land saw many inhabitants before yielding to European settlement in the 18th century. More than a century after Jean-Baptiste le Moyne, Sieur de Bienville's 1699 visit to the region, planter and politician Bernard de Marigny, Sieur de Mandeville began to acquire land along Pontchartrain's north shore. Here, he built and operated a sugar plantation, which he named Fontainebleau, after France's Chateau de Fontainebleau and its adjacent forest south of Paris. De Marigny, an entrepreneur with a knack for real estate development, also founded the town of Mandeville. Although the plantation changed hands several times over the next century, 1,000 acres were eventually purchased by Louisiana's State Park Commission in 1938.

Originally named Tchefuncte State Park, the park began operating in 1942. It is bordered on three sides by water, and approximately one-quarter of its 2,809 acres is fresh marsh. The trail system meanders from a typical pine and hardwood habitat to scenic Cane Bayou, and from a sizable marsh to moist areas adorned by colorful Louisiana irises. It ends with a breathtaking walk through an alley of centuries-old live oaks. The total hike, with retracing, is 6.7 miles. As you hike, notice that these woods are in different stages of maturity and regeneration. Sadly, heavy logging was necessary to control the disastrous effects of

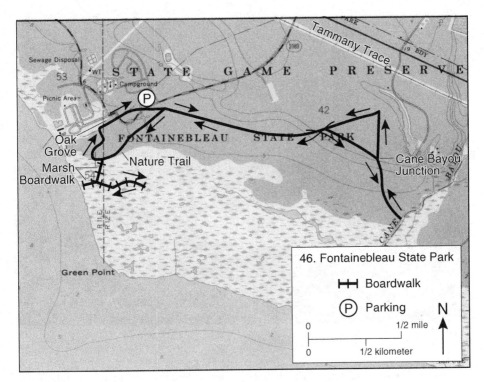

46. Fontainebleau State Park

├──┤ Boardwalk

Ⓟ Parking

N

0   1/2 mile

0   1/2 kilometer

the southern pine beetle. In addition, at the time of this writing, Hurricane Lili had recently felled numerous large trees, further changing the face of the trail.

To get there, take I-12 to LA 59 at Mandeville and drive south for 3.7 miles. Go west on US 190, driving 2.6 more miles to the park entrance on your right. Since this hike includes the park's interpretive nature trail, be sure to ask for both a trail map and the nature trail guide at the entrance.

Park at the trailhead, which is 0.7 mile past the ranger station on the left. The trail itself is not blazed, but its width makes it easy to follow. Begin on the gravel nature trail at the parking area, noticing the abundance of dwarf palmetto on the ground. After 0.1 mile, a footbridge marks the spot of an old railroad dummy line. From 1905 to 1938, this entire site was a working forest, and the Great Southern Lumber Company

used this line to facilitate lumber transport from deep within the woods.

The trail forks at two benches built by Americorps volunteers in 2002. Here, the gravel-paved nature trail continues to the right. Take the left fork, a dirt trail that leads ultimately to Cane Bayou. The trail winds a bit, then seems to split again after another 0.1 mile. The path to the right is not part of the official trail; it merely leads to the marshes, a sight you'll see later on when you hike the boardwalk. For now, stay on the main trail, enjoying the winter views of the marsh to your right.

Even without Lili's trail of damage, this area of Fontainebleau is typically one of heavy undergrowth and thicketlike clumps of small trees, bushes, and vines. A major benefit of hiking this trail in spring is the opportunity to see migrating wood warblers—some of which are seen in Louisiana for only

View of fresh marsh from boardwalk

several days each year. Look for pine warblers, wood thrushes, Carolina chickadees, and brown-headed nuthatches throughout the year.

The trail swings back and forth a bit before reaching another fork. A DO NOT ENTER sign marks the trail to the left. As you bear right, notice the wax myrtle, or southern bayberry, that lines this segment. The wax myrtle's fruits, which mature in autumn, are light green and covered with a bluish-white wax. In early days, colonists boiled the fruit and retained the waxy covering to make fragrant-burning candles. This attractive shrub loves the rich, muddy soils of the bayou country, and you'll see much more of it as you progress down this path.

At 1.4 miles, the trail becomes very straight. Both sides are overgrown with giant cane at times. This evergreen plant, along with the palmetto, blackberries, and various vines, gives the trail a junglelike feel,

even in January. When you reach the Cane Bayou junction at 1.8 miles, you'll find yourself in the presence of several grand magnolias and beeches—both common trees in Southeast Louisiana's low, moist regions. Take a right at the junction; the straight, wide, wax myrtle-lined segment that follows is the final leg of trail before reaching Cane Bayou. Be aware that this 0.3-mile segment can get quite muddy if the weather has been wet.

Cane Bayou is one of many bayous that meander slowly through Southeast Louisiana. This quietly remarkable scene is one that might typically come to mind when you imagine Louisiana: water-loving bald cypress and tupelo rising along the bayou's banks, and Spanish moss hanging gracefully from the branches. In the center of the open area next to the bayou is a lone red buckeye—the only buckeye species found throughout the state. Surrounding the area are wax myrtle, yaupon, some pine, live oak, water oak, and swamp chestnut oak. You'll want to stay here a while and take in the beauty of this modest but lovely site.

Once you've returned to the junction, go straight ahead, past large magnolias on your right. Less than 200 feet farther is a sign; you want to take a left here to complete the loop. This mostly straight section of trail runs through the mixed pine and hardwood habitat that has characterized so much of the trail thus far. Once you've rejoined the trail at the DO NOT ENTER sign, retrace your steps the mile back to the nature trail.

At the nature trail, go straight ahead to resume the gravel path. In spring, look for violets, violet wood sorrel, Carolina jessamine, and many other showy wildflowers. A long row of live oaks soon greets you, Spanish moss hanging gracefully from the gnarled branches. Interestingly, Spanish moss isn't really a moss; this epiphyte, or "air plant," is actually in the same family as the pineapple. Its threads are covered by gray scales that receive and hold moisture—basically doing the job that roots do for other plants.

The trail forks shortly after winding through the mossy oaks. Take the left fork, which leads to the lengthy boardwalk through the marsh. This is an enchanting area, particularly for birders. Wading birds, shorebirds, ducks, and common loons can be seen here at different times of year. Gaze across the expanse to see an airborne flock of white pelicans, or a group of blue-winged teals in the water below, fishing for a meal. Scopes at various observation points allow you to see even more: a large, brown swamp rabbit swimming slowly through the reeds, or a distant alligator "yawning" as it suns on a log. In winter, you might catch a rare glimpse of a snow goose, osprey, or bald eagle high overhead.

On returning to the trail junction, hike straight ahead to complete the nature trail. When you reach a footbridge, notice the April-blooming irises on either side of the bridge. Several hundred feet beyond, after passing an historic public restroom built by the Civilian Conservation Corps in the 1930s, the nature trail officially ends at a sizable live oak. This tree, like many others here, is covered with Spanish moss and resurrection fern—another epiphyte. The fern's common name refers to its ability to curl up and seem dead when low in moisture, then quickly open, turn green, and "resurrect" after rain.

To return to the trailhead, turn right to walk through a magnificent alley of giant live oaks. Cross the road, walking until you reach the ruins of an old sugar mill—a remnant of the days of de Marigny. Just beyond the ruins are the parking area and the trailhead. Taking this route, it's about a quarter of a mile from the oak alley back to the trailhead.

Not tired of hiking yet? Head over to the Northlake Nature Center, just a few hundred feet east of the park on US 190.

47

Big Branch Marsh National Wildlife Refuge

Total distance (two round trips): 6 miles

Hiking time: 3 hours

Habitats: Pine flatwoods, mixed pine and hardwood forest, longleaf pine forest, fresh marsh

Maps: USGS 7½' Lacombe, refuge map

Located on 15,000 acres of Lake Pontchartrain's north shore is an exciting diversity of natural habitats that attract a great wildlife, much of it unique to southeast Louisiana. Established in 1994, Big Branch Marsh National Wildlife Refuge's habitats range from sandy beaches to pine ridges, to marshes and stands of hardwoods. Two hiking trails offer a taste of what this fascinating area has to offer.

Boy Scout Road is not your typical hiking trail. An old roadbed accessible to foot, bike, and horse traffic only, the rutted gravel path is flat and mostly straight. This hike offers more than initially meets the eye, however. A level walk through pine forest and swamp gives way to the expansive Big Branch Marsh. The scenic terminus features huge live oaks clothed in Spanish moss and resurrection fern. Both the road and the boardwalk afford opportunities to view red-cockaded woodpeckers and see water lilies in bloom. Spring summons hundreds of wetland wildflowers in the ditches alongside Boy Scout Road, and both spring and fall see countless migrant flocks passing through. Winter affords pleasant weather and a relatively snake- and mosquito-free environment.

To get there, take I-12 to LA 434 in Lacombe and drive south 2.5 miles to LA 190. Approximately a mile down LA 434, stop at the Southeast Louisiana Refuges headquarters/visitor center for their excellent trail guide, a refuge map, and a bird list. At US 190, turn left and drive 2.3 miles to Transmitter Road. Turn right and drive 2

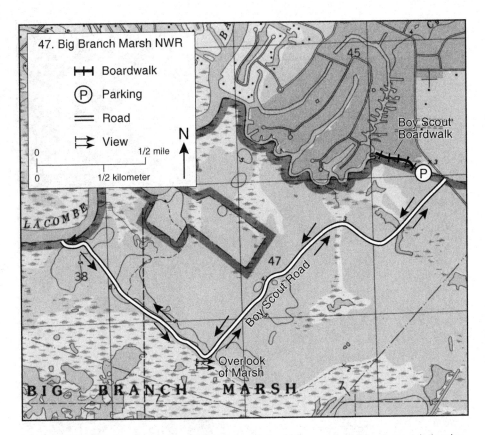

47. Big Branch Marsh NWR

⊢⊣ Boardwalk

Ⓟ Parking

= Road

↦ View

N

0 — 1/2 mile

0 — 1/2 kilometer

LACOMBE

38

47

Boy Scout Road

45

Boy Scout Boardwalk

Ⓟ

Overlook of Marsh

BIG BRANCH MARSH

more miles to Bayou Paquet Road, where you will again turn right. Following the signs for Boy Scout Boardwalk and Trail, turn left into the parking area after approximately one mile. The boardwalk is just ahead, and Boy Scout Road begins just beyond the yellow gate adjacent to the parking area. You'll first hike the 0.8-mile boardwalk through a mostly pine habitat, then you'll hike Boy Scout Road to Bayou Lacombe.

The boardwalk snakes through pine flatwoods to a branch of Bayou Lacombe. As you hike, you'll notice that several of the pines have wide, white bands painted on their trunks. These are part of an effort to restore red-cockaded woodpecker populations here. Years ago, when old-growth pines were plentiful, these small birds

thrived. Demands for lumber and development have all but eliminated the woodpecker's natural habitat, however. Now endangered, these birds favor longleaf pines between 60 and 300 years old, though they'll sometimes settle for loblolly and slash pines. To build its home, the woodpecker spends up to 3 years carving out a single cavity. Trees with heartwood disease—common in mature pines—are ideal for the woodpeckers, as the wood is softer and more malleable. The woodpeckers bore holes below the cavity as well, both for the sticky sap and to discourage predators.

This bird's social system is unique among woodpeckers; it is the only woodpecker that nests in family groups. Colonies generally include a breeding pair

White water lilies thrive along the Boy Scout Road and Boardwalk Trails.

and several "helpers"—often young males that stay with their parents to help raise future generations. Woodpecker colonies excavate clusters of up to 20 pines on as many as 60 acres. They prefer pure pine stands to hardwood or pine and hardwood forests, which tend to have a dense understory where predators can easily hide. Abandoned woodpecker cavities are prime real estate for various other creatures: reptiles, amphibians, bees, wasps, squirrels, and other small birds.

Stands of old longleaf and other pines, in concert with the efforts of refuge biologists, have made the refuge an attractive home for this endangered species. You'll see more white-banded pines along Boy Scout Road. If you have binoculars or can look closely enough, you can see the shiny surface of the bark where the sap has dripped. You might even spot one of the woodpeckers. The males are black and white with zebralike backs, have a large white cheek patch, and wear a black "cap" on their heads. The red cockade for which the bird is named is usually hidden, so don't look for it. As you hike, listen for the bird's raspy, reedy call.

The boardwalk ends at a scenic spot where you may see numerous wading birds. In spring, this swampy branch is full of blooming water lilies. From here, you'll need to retrace your steps back to the parking lot to begin the second, and longer, leg of your hike.

The first 0.1 mile of Boy Scout Road leads through the same pine flatwoods that you saw from the boardwalk. On either side of this road, however, are shallow ditches that serve as exciting miniature habitats of their own. In addition to frogs, tadpoles, and snakes, these small ditches are also home to beautiful water lilies, spider lilies, morning glories, and irises. Remember that standing water is also a haven for breeding mosquitoes; take the proper precautions if you plan to hike this area in the warmer months.

Soon, the woods begin to clear and the road passes through a swampy area, where hundreds of water lilies bloom in spring, and wading birds are plentiful. The road soon reenters the realm of pines. Many of these pines are longleaf, though the refuge has four species of pine growing here: longleaf, loblolly, slash, and spruce. Pines are very resistant to fire; in fact, some actually depend on fire to open their cones and release seeds, ensuring species regeneration. Any hardwood undergrowth gets destroyed, but the older pines remain and new ones slowly take root. Fast-growing grasses take over the forest floor.

The road curves slightly to the left after half a mile, and the woods soon clear out briefly, once more giving way to sloughs on either side. In spring, Carolina jessamine makes its appearance along Boy Scout Road, and you'll begin seeing it at 0.8 mile. These showy yellow flowers grow on vines, but they are so plentiful that they seem to grow out of the trees themselves.

The trail soon approaches Big Branch Marsh. To your left are more white-banded pines with shiny, sticky sap oozing down the trunks. Straight ahead is a marsh overlook. As you gaze over the marsh, notice the sharp transition between marsh and pine, caused by the slightest of elevation changes. As you continue along the trail, the forest transition is nearly as striking as the move from pines to marsh. You'll start to see more oaks, and the understory includes devil's walking stick, privet, and yaupon. If a slight elevation change marked the transition between pine and marsh, what caused this change from pine to a forest of live oaks? As you'll learn from an interpretive sign on the trail, this transition is due to the periodic overflowing of Bayou Lacombe. Over the years, sediments were deposited to create the fertile soil that these hardwoods love.

At 1.7 miles, the rutted road takes a wide curve to the right as the surrounding flora continues to change. Moss and resurrection fern adorn the dominant live oaks, and the ferns at your feet add to the area's striking lushness. The ruts in Boy Scout Road are often filled with water after a heavy rain, and you may notice tadpoles and frogs thriving in these makeshift puddles. At 2.2 miles is a clearing near Bayou Lacombe. The trail swings left, leading to the bayou's banks at 2.3 miles. This marks the end of the Boy Scout Road Trail. From here, retrace your steps to the trailhead for a total hike of 6 miles.

48

Bayou Sauvage
National Wildlife Refuge

Total distance
(one circuit plus one round-trip): 7 miles

Hiking time: 4 hours

Habitats: Fresh marsh, cypress swamp,
forest gaps, and edges

Maps: USGS 7½' Little Woods,
refuge brochure

Just a few minutes from New Orleans, 23,000-acre Bayou Sauvage National Wildlife Refuge (NWR)—the largest urban wildlife refuge in the United States—teems with life, from alligators cruising down the Maxent Canal to snow geese and common loons wintering in the extensive marshes. Here, wintering waterfowl populations can reach thirty-thousand, and a heron rookery guarantees a springtime abundance of graceful wading birds. Hundreds of herons and egrets can be seen year-round at Bayou Sauvage, which is considered one of Louisiana's best birding sites. The refuge offers two trails for hikers. The Bayou's Edge Trail is a 0.6-mile boardwalk that leads through a jungle of palmettos, mulberry, sweet gum, and oaks. The Maxent Levee, or Ridge Trail, is a raised path that follows the Maxent Canal.

To reach the shared trailhead, take I-10 or I-510 in New Orleans to US 90 east. Shortly after entering Bayou Sauvage NWR on US 90, turn left into the Ridge Trail parking lot. In addition to trail access, the parking area includes a water fountain, wheelchair-accessible restrooms, and a covered shelter with picnic tables—making it a good meeting place for group excursion. Brochures, maps, and a refuge activity schedule are available next to the water fountain.

The Bayou's Edge Trail begins to the right, or northeast, of the shelter. As you begin your hike along the boardwalk, you'll see palmetto, mulberry, and yaupon, as well as a few red cedars. In spring, spiderwort is

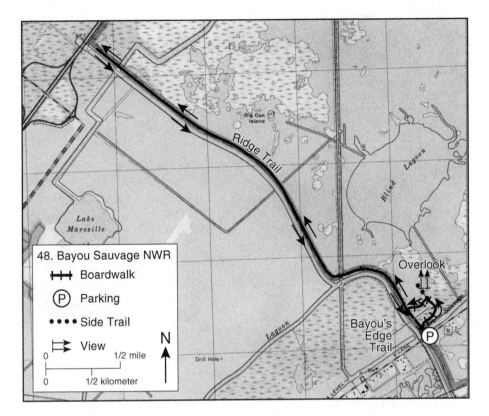

48. Bayou Sauvage NWR

├┼┤ Boardwalk

Ⓟ Parking

●●●● Side Trail

↦ View

N

0   1/2 mile

0   1/2 kilometer

among the most common wildflowers growing here. Larger trees include sweet gum, red maple, green ash, and various oaks and hickories. After just 300 feet, a side trail to the right leads to a canoe launch. If you're planning to canoe, be aware that numerous bald cypress stumps in the immediate area make this particular spot less than desirable for launching a boat.

A little after 0.1 mile, the trail passes a pair of "kissing trees" on the left. You'll see quite a few trees growing together in this area, their trunks crisscrossing each other and even merging at times. This is particularly common with the sugarberries, though it happens with other tree species, too. Shortly afterward, you'll reach a huge old live oak and a sharp left in the boardwalk. Just beyond is a sweetgum sign; beyond it

is a sugarberry with several cavities high in its trunk—each of them likely homes for any number of animals, such as raccoons and barred owls.

Look for honey locusts as you walk. This interesting tree is a member of the legume family and is easily identified by its odd trunk, which seems to have thorny balls of spines growing randomly along it, from bottom to top. Not surprisingly, this tree, which can grow quite large, is also known as thorny locust. It's common throughout much of Louisiana, as it thrives in the moist alluvial soils of river floodplains.

When the trail forks, go straight ahead toward an overlook. You'll soon pass the most photographed tree at Bayou Sauvage—an ancient live oak whose trunk seems to grow at an angle out of the ground. After stopping

Golden silk spider

Joe Madere

to admire this fascinating tree, go straight ahead past more palmetto and red maple to an overlook of Blind Lagoon. This area, which was once a gigantic bald cypress forest, provides a great opportunity to view wading birds and perhaps a few alligators. You're also likely to see an American coot, or *poule d'eau.* These dark gray, chickenlike, water-adapted birds are abundant throughout Bayou Sauvage from September to May.

Once you've retraced your steps to the original trail, bear right to continue the hike. Notice that you're entering a lower, wetter area, where the palmettos are much taller than previously. An abundant tree throughout this trail—and many other Louisiana trails—is the invasive tallow tree. Introduced to the United States from China in the 18th century by Benjamin Franklin, this tree bears white, waxy fruits that were used by the Chinese to make soap and candles. Also an excellent shade tree, it was widely

planted in the southern United States. Although it is a beautiful tree, with aspenlike leaves that turn brilliant red and yellow in autumn, the tallow tree is a highly invasive plant—a kind of giant weed that grows in thickets and alters the surrounding soil, making entire areas inhospitable to Louisiana's native plants. Various efforts, some more successful than others, have been made to remove this quickly spreading tree from Louisiana's natural habitats.

At 0.6 mile, look for aged bald cypresses in the distance to your right. Shortly afterward, the trail passes a large mulberry tree and exits the woods onto the gravel-topped Maxent Levee, or Ridge Trail. You can return to the parking lot by turning left and walking 400 feet.

To continue hiking, turn right to walk up to 6 miles (round trip) on the Ridge Trail. This levee runs between the Maxent Canal and Blind Lagoon, and it passes near historic Little Oak Island. The entire levee is a great vantage point for spotting alligators, wading birds, and more.

The slope to the south is a popular nesting spot for mottled ducks; in fact, the United States Fish and Wildlife Service keeps the grass low in order to make it even more attractive to these birds. Closely related to mallards, the mottled duck lines its grassy nest with contour feathers and down, and it conceals the entire nest in vegetation close to water. The male and female mottled ducks, unlike other species, are similar in appearance; both look a little like the female mallard. While most ducks nest farther north, mottled ducks nest along Louisiana's coast and can be seen in the state at just about any time of year, though they're a little less common in winter.

At about 0.7 mile down the levee, you begin to see an island ridge on your right. This is Pine Island Ridge; on the other side of it is Little Oak Island, where prehistoric Native American middens have been discovered but are not open to the public.

You can continue this levee walk until it stops at I-10, a couple of miles northwest. The view doesn't seem to change much. If you look closely, however, you'll notice the many changes that constantly occur here: alligators and turtles intermittently sunning from the canal or from Blind Lagoon; a flock of cattle egrets making its way—like you—down the levee; or even a mockingbird perched in a nearby tree. Deer, raccoons, and squirrels are plentiful in this area; you might well catch a glimpse of one as it moves beyond the trees on either side of you. Other birds to look for include purple gallinules, common yellowthroats, and pine warblers. During the migration seasons, look for mallards, blue-winged teals, American widgeons, indigo and painted buntings, orchard orioles, swamp sparrows, and northern parulas. You may even catch the extremely rare glimpse of a flock of brown pelicans, rising and falling gracefully as they glide just inches above the water in search of small fish.

Bayou Sauvage is one of those places you'll want to explore repeatedly. Although it offers plenty of hiking opportunities, you'll need to hit the canoe trails in order to get a full sense of this amazing place. If you're more comfortable using hiking sticks than canoe paddles, contact the refuge; on weekends, the staff provides guided canoe trips that allow you to view the marshes up close.

49

Barataria Preserve Trails

Total distance (round-trip): 1.8 miles

Hiking time: 1 hour

Habitats: Bottomland hardwood, cypress swamp, fresh marsh

Maps: USGS 7½' Bertrandville, USGS 7½' Cataouatche East, preserve map

The hikes at the Barataria unit of Jean Lafitte National Historical Park and Preserve will appeal to history buffs and nature lovers alike. Trails are short and level, and each offers countless opportunities to see alligators, egrets, turtles, gray squirrels, swamp rabbits, and many other wetland creatures. Be aware that these creatures include mosquitoes, jokingly referred to as Louisiana's state bird. Take the proper precautions to avoid these biting critters. The Barataria Preserve is an excellent place to hike in all but the hottest months. Late March through mid-April is the most popular time to visit, when the swamps are bejeweled with thousands of blooming great blue irises. Fall and spring are also good for viewing migratory birds.

Prehistoric Native Americans first settled these fertile wetlands more than 1,000 years ago. The Mississippi River, following a different course than it does today, sent fresh water surging down its various channels, including present-day Bayou des Familles. These bodies of water, along with Bayou Coquille, allowed these early settlers access to the nearby swamps, marshes, and other sources of food and raw materials.

As you hike the trails of the Barataria Preserve, however, you might wonder why, or at least *how* anyone would choose to settle a region so clearly hostile to human occupation. The Native Americans were subjected to the land's stifling heat and humidity, incessant deerflies and mosquitoes, and razor-sharp marsh grasses, not to mention the constant threat of destruction by

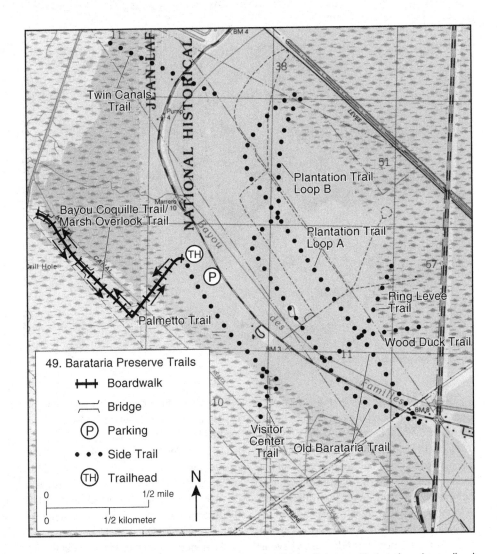

The following labels appear on the map:

- JEAN LAF
- Twin Canals Trail
- NATIONAL HISTORICAL
- Bayou Coquille Trail
- Marsh Overlook Trail
- Plantation Trail Loop B
- Plantation Trail Loop A
- Ring Levee Trail
- Palmetto Trail
- Wood Duck Trail
- Visitor Center Trail
- Old Barataria Trail

49. Barataria Preserve Trails

┣┼┫	Boardwalk
⥤⥥	Bridge
Ⓟ	Parking
• • •	Side Trail
ⓉⒽ	Trailhead

N

0 ——— 1/2 mile

0 ——— 1/2 kilometer

tropical storms and hurricanes. Also, much of the land here is swamp or marsh—too fragile to support most plant life, much less huts and villages.

Still, much of southeast Louisiana was coveted land for early Native Americans. With a long growing season, an endless supply of water, and hundreds of acres of rich soils, this region was heavily populated throughout the millennium prior to European discovery. Settling on the natural levees of the river and its tributaries south of present-

day New Orleans, Native Americans lived on dry, elevated land while enjoying easy access to the nutrient-rich waters surrounding them—a diverse environment that provided everything from freshwater mussels to brackish-water clams to saltwater oysters. Other nutrient sources included crabs, crawfish, fish, ducks, geese, mink, otter, and alligator. From these same resources, Native Americans obtained containers and implements (from shells), as well as pearls, feathers, and furs.

Egret in swamp at Barataria Preserve

The flowing channels of the Mississippi began to shrink when the great river started to favor the LaFourche course between 1,000 and 3,000 years ago. The once-strong Bayou des Familles, whose distributaries included Bayou Coquille, is now completely cut off from the great river. Although they are now quiet bodies of water, whose depth and flow depend on the power of wind, rain, and tide, these bayous were once powerful enough to form their own levees through sediment buildup and regular flooding. It was on these levees that we find evidence of Native American habitation. In fact, the Bayou Coquille Trail begins at a midden, or shell pile of accumulated Native American refuse from centuries past. Bayou Coquille is actually named for these shell piles; *coquille* is French for "shell."

From New Orleans, you can reach the trails by taking the West Bank Expressway (US 90) out of the city and turning south on LA 45 (Barataria Boulevard) in Marrero. Jean Lafitte National Historical Park and Preserve is about 8 miles from this junction; you'll start to see directional signs approximately three miles down Barataria. From the west, you can take I-10 to I-310 (Boutte), then to US 90. Going east on US 90, drive approximately 5 miles to Barataria Boulevard.

After stopping at the visitor center to pick up a trail map, continue down LA 45 to the Bayou Coquille trailhead and parking lot, which will be on your left. Note that the parking lot gate closes after 6 PM. Note also that this entire hike is wheelchair-accessible.

As you begin hiking the Bayou Coquille Trail, notice all the dwarf palmetto. Because it loves low, wet areas like this, dwarf palmetto is common in much of Louisiana. In spring, this area boasts numerous wildflowers. Be aware that these woods are crawling with poison ivy; it carpets the ground in some places, and its hairy vines snake up the trunks of trees. It is definitely in your best interest to stay on the trail!

The trail turns into asphalt shortly before reaching Bayou Coquille; it will alternate between asphalt and boardwalk for a half mile. At the bayou, you are standing on a natural levee that was built by Bayou des Familles and Bayou Coquille. It was on this natural levee—which the trail will follow for some time—that the Native Americans settled intermittently for 500 to 1,000 years. Shortly after you turn left at Bayou Coquille, the trail passes a visible midden site on your left, marked by a sign and partially topped by a gnarled live oak.

The dry natural levees throughout this region support numerous species, including live oak, black willow, water oak, sweet gum, sugarberry, wax myrtle, and dwarf palmetto. At 0.2 mile, the trail descends into the natural levee's backslope. Although the elevation change is minimal and barely noticeable, the ground and the trees it supports change drastically. Notice how much swampier the area becomes. Where you saw oak, elm, and willow before, you'll see swamp red maple, Nuttall oak, and Carolina ash. Dwarf palmettos are still common, but look how much taller they are than those growing along the "high and dry" levee. Some of these "dwarfs" are more than 7 feet tall! As you descend further, you'll see fewer palmettos and increasing numbers of bald cypress and tupelo—the signature of a true swamp.

Spaced along the trail are overlooks into the swamp—excellent vantage points for viewing all sorts of wetland wildlife, including egrets, turtles, and alligators. When sunning, alligators hold so still that you might mistake them for logs lying in the swamp. If you don't see an alligator when you first gaze out over the swamp, look again . . . there may well be an alligator right in front of you, disguised as a log. Pay attention to the many signs posted throughout the park warning visitors not to feed the alligators—regardless of how small, cute, or friendly they seem.

As the land gets wetter, the irises become more plentiful. Toward the end of March, this whole area is taken over by a profusion of marvelous blooms that generally last through mid-April. The blooming irises summon crowds of sightseers, and this little boardwalk gets busy in spring. The irises are worth the trip, however—even if you generally prefer quieter, more isolated trails.

At just under 0.6 mile is the Kenta Canal, where the trail takes a sharp left and becomes the Marsh Overlook Trail. This segment leads alongside a spoil bank, formed by dredge spoils dumped here when the canal was dug. The canal's initial purpose was for irrigation and drainage, but it was eventually widened so loggers could access the vast bald cypress forests. Oil companies later used the canal to transport supplies and lay pipelines.

The trail soon crosses a finger canal of Bayou Coquille. A second bridge, 0.3 mile farther along, crosses Kenta Canal and leads to an overlook of the surrounding marsh. Stark and brown in January and lush and green in the summer, the marsh is an extremely productive ecosystem. Because the soil is too unstable to support trees, the marsh landscape is dominated by grasses, particularly bulltongue and spike rush. Of the few trees that do grow here, most are actually rooted to the stumps of felled cypresses.

Retrace your steps to return to the trailhead. The Barataria Preserve offers approximately 10 miles of boardwalk and dirt trails. Although the Bayou Coquille and Marsh Overlook Trails are the most popular walks, you can also hike the nearby Palmetto Trail, and the quarter-mile trail behind the visitor center. Across the road from the visitor center are the park's dirt trails: the Wood Duck, Plantation, and Old Barataria Trails. North of the Bayou Coquille Trail is the Twin Canals Trail, a 0.6-mile walk along the Twin Canals. At the time of this writing, several of the trails were closed due to hurricane damage. Check at the preserve's visitor center for trail conditions.

If you are visiting New Orleans, you can also pick up trail information at the Jean Lafitte National Historical Park Visitor Center on Decatur Street in the French Quarter.

50

Lafitte Woods Preserve

Total distance (circuit): 2 miles

Hiking time: 45 minutes;
longer if you're a birder

Habitats: Oak and hackberry forest,
fresh marsh, salt marsh

Maps: USGS 7½' Grand Isle

Occasionally during the summers of the late 1970s and early 1980s, my family would vacation with friends at their camp on Grand Isle. At the time, I had no idea that this barrier island had such a rich history. Originally settled as a fishing village in the late 1700s, Grand Isle was settled by the "Gentleman Pirate" Jean Lafitte, who made it part of his base of looting operations. In 1841, Fort Livingston was constructed on nearby Grand Terre Island and was occupied by 300 Confederate soldiers during the Civil War. In later years, Grand Isle was a popular resort frequented by the elites, and is the setting for Kate Chopin's groundbreaking novella, *The Awakening*. A hurricane devastated the island in 1893, ending its glory days as Louisiana's coastal paradise.

Today, however, Grand Isle remains a popular weekend and vacation spot for Louisiana natives, and is popular with birdwatchers, history buffs, anglers, seafood lovers, and sun worshippers alike. Located between salt- and freshwater estuaries off the coast, Grand Isle is an excellent destination and habitat for migratory birds seeing land for the first time after crossing the Gulf. The island is also the site of The Nature Conservancy's Lafitte Woods Preserve, whose 13-acre Grilleta Tract features short trails and boardwalks that lead past thickets, beneath gnarled live oaks and sugarberries, alongside blooming wild lantana, and through patches of salt marsh. Even the most casual of birders could spend hours covering just a short section of these trails

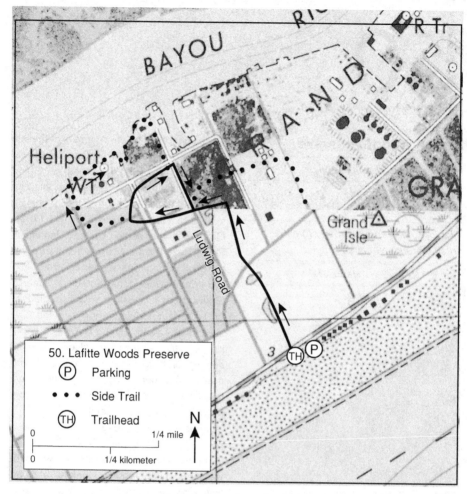

BAYOU

Heliport

WT

Ludwig Road

Grand △
Isle

GRA

R T

A N D

3 TH P

50. Lafitte Woods Preserve

P Parking

• • • Side Trail

TH Trailhead

N

0   1/4 mile

0   1/4 kilometer

during the migration seasons. Hikers aiming for a longer hike can begin with Lafitte Woods Preserve and end with a walk along the beach, or they can head several miles east to Grand Isle State Park. The state park's short loop trail was damaged by the storms of 2002; however, plans were in place at the time of this writing to rebuild, extend, and reopen the trail by the fall of 2003. If you're going to Grand Isle, check with the park on trail progress. This guide directs you on a walk through the Lafitte Woods Preserve.

Grand Isle is about two hours from New Orleans. To get there, take I-10 to the I-310 spur (Boutte) just west of New Orleans, and follow I-310 until it ends at US 90 (Airline Highway). Turn right and follow Airline Highway for about 20 miles to the LA 1 exit. Drive south on LA 1 for approximately 65 miles. Be alert to the speed limit signs as you pass through the small towns on the way. Also, the road will seem to fork when it meets LA 3090 to Fourchon Beach, just before you get to the coast. Be sure to remain on LA 1, bearing *left*.

Wild lantana blooming on an overgrown trail at Grand Isle

Drive 8.5 miles after bearing left at the LA 3090 junction, then cross the Caminada Bridge onto Grand Isle. Continue traveling for 3.5 more miles to the Lafitte Woods Preserve, which will be on your left. The entrance is marked by a Lafitte Woods Preserve sign, and a split-rail fence surrounds the parking area. The trail system itself begins just beyond the kiosk inside the fence. The preserve headquarters are five streets beyond the kiosk, at Landry House B&B on Hector Street.

To begin your hike, follow the unmarked trail into the woods, which consist heavily of overhanging live oaks and sugarberries. Birders and wildflower enthusiasts alike will be thrilled by the diversity that can be found in this small space. Casual hikers will also love the sheer beauty of the gnarled, rugged trees. The path forks shortly after 0.1 mile; bear left to reach the short Lafitte Boardwalk soon afterward. Look for pecan trees and giant cane growing to great heights in this lush area. Honeysuckle vines are rampant, and you'll see plump, ripe dewberries and blackberries in late spring and early summer. Other spring delights include colorful, pink-and-yellow lantana and violet wood sorrel.

At the end of the boardwalk, several narrow side trails lead away from the main trail. You want to stay on the main trail—unless, of course, you're in search of a quiet spot to sit for a while, looking and listening for birds. Each April, countless birders descend on Grand Isle for its Migratory Bird Celebration. If you're here in the spring, you might catch sight of the brilliantly painted yellow warbler. Listen for its song: a rapid whistle of *sweet sweet sweet, I'm so sweet.* These entirely yellow birds breed as far north as Canada, winter in Central and South America, and commonly light at Grand Isle on their migratory flights.

You will see more and more cane as you hike, some of it quite tall. Despite efforts to control this native plant, cane grows like wildfire and becomes tall and thick just months after being cut down—frustrating the preserve's dedicated trail maintainers! At 0.3 mile, the trail swings left. To the right is a small hump in the terrain; this is a great little birding observation spot. Well over 300 species of birds are spotted on Grand Isle each year—that's nearly half the species found in the United States! In winter, listen for the rapid chattering of a Wilson's warbler or the uneven buzzing song of a palm warbler—both of which summer in Canada and winter along the southern coast of the United States.

The trail winds for several hundred feet before it forks and makes a very small loop. Note that both trails reconvene after just a few feet. Exit the woods at 0.4 mile. Birders may want to continue the bird trail; however, to continue the Lafitte Woods hike, go to the left, toward the next kiosk. You'll pass a shop sign on the short walk down Medical Road, then swing right to find a picnic table and another trailhead. Cross the water, then swing to the left. You're now at a spot where the trail goes off to the left, onto a levee. In late spring, look for dewberries, blackberries, and sizable clumps of lantana. Walking along the levee, with the water on your right, you'll reach the Port Boardwalk at 0.7 mile. As you cross the 300-foot boardwalk, you might say a silent "thanks" to the hardworking Nature Conservancy volunteers and Baton Rouge-area retirees who constructed it.

Once you've completed the boardwalk, you can do some exploring of your own. Want to see seabirds, shorebirds, and wading birds? Head left for an exploratory trip to the bay, which is only about 0.2 mile ahead. While there is no actual trail along the shore, you'll find plenty of opportunities for birding, seeing wildflowers, and just enjoying the breezy Grand Isle climate.

To return to your car from the Port Boardwalk, turn right and walk down the wide, dirt extension of Ludwig Road. To your right are marsh grasses, including cattails, and to your left are some larger trees—chief among them the invasive Chinese tallow tree. Reach the kiosk at 0.9 mile, then take a right to complete the loop. This not-so-scenic, dirt-and-gravel road will take you 0.3 mile back to the kiosk on Medical Road. Turn left onto Medical Road, retracing your steps back into the oak and hackberry woods and turning right to pass the Lafitte Boardwalk and return to the parking area on LA 1. Back in your car, you can drive to the eastern end of the island, site of Grand Isle State Park. At the state park, you'll find salt marshes and a wealth of black mangrove and blooming wild lantana in spring. Before you leave Grand Isle, be sure to stop in at one of the restaurants along LA 1. If you love Louisiana seafood and relish the smell of fried shrimp and the taste of a spicy shrimp po-boy (my primary memory of Grand Isle from years past), you won't be disappointed!

Index